JEWISH
PHILOSOPHY

JEWISH PHILOSOPHY

An Historical Introduction

NORBERT M. SAMUELSON

continuum
LONDON • NEW YORK

Continuum
The Tower Building, 11 York Road, London, SE1 7NX
15 East 26th Street, New York, NY 10010

First published 2003 by Continuum

British Library Cataloguing-in-Publication Data
A catalogue record for this book is available from the British Library.

ISBN 0–8264-6140-9 (hardback)
    0–8264-6141-7 (paperback)

Library of Congress Cataloging-in-Publication Data
Samuelson, Norbert Max, 1936–
    Jewish philosophy: an historical introduction / Norbert M. Samuelson.
        p. cm.
    Includes bibliographical references and index.
    ISBN 0-8264-6140-9—ISBN 0-8264-6141-7 (pb.)
    1. Philosophy, Jewish—History—Textbooks. 2. Judaism—History—Textbooks.
    3. Maimonides, Moses, 1135–1204. 4. Rosenzweig, Franz, 1886–1929. I. Title.

B154.S26 2003
181'.06—dc21   2003043524

Typeset by BookEns Ltd, Royston, Herts.
Printed and bound in Great Britain by The Cromwell Press, Trowbridge, Wiltshire.

Contents

Tables, lists and figures

CHAPTER 1

Introduction

The purpose of the book

This book is intended to introduce students of all ages and backgrounds to the study of Jewish philosophy. The chapter structure presupposes that it will be used in one of two formats. The first is a university-level undergraduate course, in two semesters each approximately fifteen weeks long, the first semester dealing with Jewish philosophy in its origins in the Hebrew Scriptures up to the classical formation of Jewish philosophy by Moses Maimonides (1135–1204 CE),[1] and the second semester dealing with Jewish philosophy from Maimonides up to the middle of the twentieth century. The second format is a series of three mini-courses in adult education programs of approximately ten weeks in length each. The first course, on the origins of Jewish philosophy, deals with the textual foundations of Jewish philosophy in the Hebrew Scriptures and in early rabbinic literature, especially the Midrash,[2] when the leaders of the Jewish people developed the fundamental social and political structure of Jewish communal life up to the twentieth century. The second mini-course, on classical Jewish philosophy, deals with the classical formulations of Jewish philosophy in the so-called "Middle Ages," from at least the time of Saadia Gaon (882–942 CE) through at least the time of Hasdai Crescas (1340–1410 CE), when the rabbis determined the basic tenets of the faith structure of what everyone today would recognize as traditional Judaism. Finally, the third mini-course, on modern Jewish philosophy, deals with the philosophic writings of committed Jews in modern, western civilization, from at least Baruch Spinoza (1632–77 CE) through Franz Rosenzweig (1886–1929 CE), that have played a major role in the effort of thoughtful Jews to make sense out of their commitment to Jewish tradition and their equally strong commitment to live an honest life, both intellectually and spiritually: a life that takes seriously the lessons and challenges of modern culture, especially its philosophy and science.

Jewish philosophy as part of the study of Judaism

This book is intended primarily to be studied on its own as an introduction to Jewish philosophy, but it can also be used as part of a study program in either Judaism or philosophy. With respect to Judaism, this author presupposes that Jewish philosophy is a single but nonetheless central part of any understanding of Judaism. Judaism is the expression of the way the Jewish people have struggled both to survive and thrive as a people in the world. It involves history, customs, communal laws, liturgical practices, and beliefs, all of which have changed over the centuries. All of these elements of Jewish culture are dependent, so that one cannot adequately understand one without understanding the others. Hence, any adequate understanding of Jewish philosophy has to be located in a historical context of the collective life of the Jewish people, and, conversely, any adequate understanding of the collective history and culture of the Jewish people must include an understanding of Jewish philosophy.

Readers should be aware that what I claim here is controversial. There are some students of Judaism and religion who think that Judaism can be studied primarily as a set of beliefs, largely independent of any contextualization of those beliefs in Jewish history and culture. Conversely, there are some students of Judaism and religion who think that Judaism can be studied primarily as a system of religious and cultural practices, largely independent of any conceptual framework for them. This book presupposes that both extreme positions are false, and that to study Judaism in either way is to study not Judaism but a distortion of what this religion has been in the past and continues to be in the present.

Jewish philosophy as part of the study of philosophy

With respect to philosophy, this author presupposes that Jewish philosophy is a single but nonetheless central part of understanding western philosophy. Philosophy itself is an expression of a culture which, as such, ought to be studied within the context of that culture. However, culture is not static. It constantly changes both because of its own internal dynamics but also because most cultures most of the time are influenced by and have influence on other cultures. Hence, philosophy consists of different philosophies by different philosophers whose thought, to be adequately understood, needs to be situated in its intellectual, political, and cultural context. In the case of western civilization, the earliest beginnings of philosophy are expressions of the interaction of a number of different cultures in the Mediterranean world, including Egypt, Mesopotamia, and Greece. The interaction of these three culturally distinct locations gave rise to western civilization's earliest sciences, which we commonly identify as "ancient philosophy," including the schools of the Pythagoreans, the atomists, the Platonists, and the Aristotelians.

These early cultural interactions lead directly to at least three major religions—rabbinic Judaism, Christianity, and Islam. The interaction of these three religions in combination with the continued study of the ancient sciences promoted changes in the religions and the sciences themselves that resulted in what we commonly identify as medieval philosophy.[3] Because the study of science and philosophy at this stage of western civilization is viewed as a religious activity, it is appropriate to speak of Jewish or Muslim or Christian philosophy rather than just philosophy. However, it is a mistake to think that any one of these three can be studied independently of the others. On the contrary, as we shall see, the three religious civilizations are so intimately tied together in both time and space that the study of any one in isolation from the other two is a distortion, not only of the history of philosophy but also of the philosophy itself. Medieval Christian philosophy, for example, is not simply the product of the interaction of Christianity with ancient philosophy, where the ancient science remains relatively unchanged as science until the beginnings of modernity. Rather, the science of medieval Christendom is a new and developing science that the Christians learned from contact with Islam and Judaism, whose science, while rooted in ancient philosophy, is something that was then new, a distinctive product of the continued work in science by Muslims and Jews and not merely an unchanged, preserved copy of what they had inherited from antiquity; to a significant extent the Muslim and Jewish philosophies themselves reflect the contemporary interactions of committed Jews and Muslims, both drawing from their inherited revealed as well as philosophical texts.

This situation of multicultural and multireligious interaction does not simplify once we enter the modern period. Philosophy and science continue to be conceptually inseparable from the influence of the past. Islam's influence continues politically but not so much intellectually at this time, but Jewish and Christian cultures continue to influence each other and change because of that influence. Moreover, world trade as well as advancement in the study of intellectual history increase the influence of past non-Abrahamic religions,[4] long considered superseded, especially the pagan cultures of ancient Greece and Rome as well as the non-monotheistic religions of Asia, particularly Buddhism.

In brief, western philosophy is Christian, Muslim, or Jewish; these three develop historically from interaction with each other as well as with other religious cultures; and philosophy can only be studied adequately in its historical context. Hence, the study of the history of Jewish philosophy is an essential part of the study of western philosophy in general.

The importance of history

Readers should be aware that what I claim here about philosophy is no less controversial than what I affirmed above about Judaism. There are some students of philosophy who think that philosophy is reasoning about questions so abstract, objective, and universal that historical context is irrelevant. They tend to see the study of philosophy as having more in common with the study of mathematics and the modern physical sciences than with the diversity of subjects included in the humanities, especially literature. For example, whether we live in a steady-state universe (as most physicists believed at the start of the twentieth century) or in an ever-expanding universe whose origin is at a single point of space and time (as most physicists believe at the beginning of the twenty-first century) has nothing to do with human intellectual history or culture. What kind of universe this is is a question of fact, and human beings can discover the truth of what the fact is by the use of universally recognized mathematical techniques that are applied to observations that anyone can make today, irrespective of where they live or where they come from. In other words, the question of the origin of the universe is a factual question, determinable with reasonable certainty by modern scientific techniques that are simply that, scientific techniques. Science is science; there is no such thing as Jewish, Muslim, or Christian science, at least, not if it is good science. Similarly, there is no such thing as Jewish philosophy unless it is bad philosophy; there is only philosophy.

We, on the contrary, judge this view of philosophy to be a distortion not only of the history of philosophy but of contemporary philosophy itself, viz., that all philosophy at all times is a product of the specific interaction of individuals in their cultures with both the past cultures out of which they developed and the present cultures in which they are in interaction. Hence, to ignore the history and sociology of ideas and to focus only on the logic of the ideas themselves is to distort the ideas. Philosophy studied as the history and sociology of philosophy is better philosophy than philosophy studied simply as philosophy. Hence, there is no such thing as philosophy. There are only philosophies, of which Jewish philosophy is one kind. Furthermore, because of their history, the study of Jewish philosophy ought to be an essential requirement for all students of western philosophy, be they Christian (as most used to be) or post-Christian (as most are today).

Distinctions and qualifications

Jewish philosophy and Jewish thought

Let me point out to the reader that Jewish philosophy (*filosofia yehudit* in Hebrew) and Jewish thought (*machshevet yisrael* in Hebrew; literally, the thought of [the nation or people of] Israel) are not the same thing. In fact, in schools of higher education in the modern state of Israel these two terms name different academic departments. At one level the distinction between the two is clear. Jewish philosophy includes people such as Maimonides and Spinoza, viz., Jewish thinkers who thought about questions like all other philosophers. Hence, Maimonides is a Jewish philosopher because he thought about Judaism in the light of issues raised by Aristotle, and in this respect, as a philosopher, Maimonides is no different from the Christian Thomas Aquinas and the Muslim Ibn Rushd. Similarly, Spinoza is a philosopher because he thought about questions of philosophy in the same way as Christians such as René Descartes and Gottfried Wilhelm Leibniz. However, at a deeper level the distinction is not all that clear, primarily because it is not all that clear just what philosophy is.

What we call "philosophy" today is not what philosophy was called in the past. The term itself is Greek and means "the love of" (*philo-*) "wisdom" (*sophia*). Until the nineteenth century at the earliest, a philosopher was simply that, viz., someone who loved the pursuit of wisdom. As such the term included all that we today call "science." The term "science" comes from the Latin term *scientia*, which simply means "knowledge." Note that knowledge and wisdom are not the same thing, and much of what we today call science is simply knowledge (viz., propositions about all kinds of things that we can claim to be true with relatively high probability) and not wisdom (viz., what a being needs to know to have good judgment in a moral sense as much as a cognitive sense; what makes one "happy," not in the sense of pleasure but in the sense of what gives ultimate meaning and fulfillment to one's life). However, as we use the terms "philosophy" and "science" today, neither has much to do with anything that can be called "wisdom" in the sense of "happiness" as moral perfection. Philosophy today, at least in the Anglo-American world, seems to be the study of questions about which no clear science has yet been established. As such, it is epistemically an extension of science. The concern in both is to know, and the separation between them is a variable of how much probability can properly be credited to the claims made.

As scientific claims differ from philosophical ones primarily in their epistemic authority (viz., scientific claims have a higher degree of probability), so philosophical claims differ from mere thought. Statements that are "thought," especially "Jewish thought," and even more especially "Jewish religious thought," are merely opinions. Hence, when studying (for example) Jewish thought, what you study are the judgments being made rather than the reasons why the judgments are made. Texts on Jewish thought tend to read like opinion polls precisely because that is all they are—unsubstantiated opinions for which evidence is largely irrelevant. Philosophy therefore stands in the middle of an epistemic continuum between mere opinion ("thought") and relatively high probability claims ("science").

Similarly, what distinguishes "Jewish philosophy" from "Jewish thought" is that the former, more than the latter, is based on a kind of logical reasoning, rooted in claims drawn from experience, that purports to make the authority for its claims more than mere opinions. Hence, in studying Jewish philosophy we are not concerned solely with the conclusions of the philosophers but also with the reasons for their conclusions. Furthermore, in studying Jewish philosophy, the ways these philosophers reach their conclusions are often more important than the conclusions themselves. The study of philosophy is a study of ways of thinking no less and possibly more than it is a study of what was thought. That is true of philosophy in general and of Jewish philosophy in particular. The ways of thinking have a history and a location no less than do the thoughts thought.

Accuracy and generality

Readers should be aware that in order to clarify what Jewish philosophy is I have made differences sharper than they actually are. The line between Jewish philosophy and Jewish thought is not a hard one. The two constitute a continuum, and where the line is drawn is somewhat arbitrary. For example, in this text we will read Midrash as philosophy. There are some Jewish scholars who would deny that Midrash contains philosophy and say that it is only about Jewish thought. Similarly, in this text I will give considerable space to discussing rabbis such as Maimonides and Spinoza, who wrote philosophical works like *The Guide of the Perplexed* and *The Ethics*, rather than other gifted rabbis such as Rashi, Isaac Luria, and Abraham Heschel, whose writings have a less direct relationship to western philosophy. For the same reason, Maimonides' *Guide of the Perplexed* gets more attention than his *Mishneh Torah*, and Spinoza's *Ethics* more than his *Theological–Political Treatise*.

What this book offers is a very general map of Jewish philosophy. Because it is both a map and general, it is not altogether accurate. However, I believe it is as accurate as it can be for it still to do what it does, viz., provide in a single, affordable book an orientation for a student to begin to study Jewish philosophy.

I have made judgments of emphasis with which other scholars may (probably will) disagree. I, like all other scholars, try to avoid such criticism as much as possible, but not at the cost of not writing what I hope is a good introduction. In addition to this book students ought to read the original texts summarized, and works in Jewish philosophy other than the ones I emphasize, as well as other commentaries on these texts besides the ones that I have provided. Because costs of publication require me to restrict radically the number of books I would like to mention, the suggestions for further reading are not as extensive as I would like them to be. I have limited myself to primary texts in English translation, general and more extensive studies of Jewish philosophy that provide a more extensive bibliography, further readings for general Jewish history, and commentaries on the philosophical works emphasized that present a different interpretation from the one I present here. Students are strongly encouraged to read the books listed under "Suggestions for Further Study," as well as to take other university-level courses in Jewish philosophy, western philosophy, the history of science, Jewish religious thought, Jewish religious practice, and Jewish history (especially intellectual history).

Language study

Students should be aware that most Jewish philosophy was written in languages other than English and that students who study a text in its original language have a great advantage over those whose understanding is dependent on the work of a translator. The single most valuable language to study for reading Jewish philosophy is Hebrew, but other languages are useful as well, especially Arabic, German, and French.

Bible references

References to the Hebrew Scriptures (what many Christians continue to call "The Old Testament") are the masoretic version used by the rabbis. All Jewish publications of the Hebrew Scriptures use this version, whose division of the texts into chapters and verses differs from versions used in Christian publications. A representative example of a Jewish publication is *The JPS Hebrew–English Tanakh* (Philadelphia: The Jewish Publication Society, 1999). All English translations are my own from the Hebrew masoretic version.

Notes

1 "CE" means "The Common Era," as opposed to "BCE," which means "Before the Common Era." Both BCE and CE enable scholars, most often scholars of Judaica, to use in their dating the familiar numbers of BC and AD respectively without the Christian association of these designations, viz, "Before Christ" for "BC" and "Anno Domini" (in the year of the Lord) for "AD." An alternative would be to use the Jewish calendar, but most readers of these texts would not recognize the dates (e.g., that the 13th of the month of Tammuz in 5761 is July 4, 2001). This way of dating (in terms of BCE and CE) is itself an example (albeit a minor one) of "the effort of thoughtful Jews to make sense out of their commitment to Jewish tradition" and "to take seriously the lessons and challenges of modern culture."

2 Early rabbinic literature that is primarily in its literary structure a commentary on a text or texts of the Hebrew Scriptures. More will be said about this term in Chapter 9.

3 Note that philosophy is indistinguishable from science, because the

separation of science from philosophy does not happen until the modern period.

4 "Abrahamic religions" means the various expressions of Judaism, Christianity, and Islam. "Non-Abrahamic religions" are all other religions.

Suggestions for further study

Burrell, David B. *Knowing the Unknowable God*. Notre Dame, IN: Notre Dame University Press, 1986.

Flew, Antony. *An Introduction to Western Philosophy*. Indianapolis: Bobbs-Merrill, 1971.

Frank, Daniel H. "What is Jewish philosophy?" in Daniel H. Frank and Oliver Leaman (eds.), *History of Jewish Philosophy*. Vol. II of *Routledge History of World Philosophies*. London: Routledge, 1997, pp. 1–12.

Hamlyn, D. W. *A History of Western Philosophy*. New York: Viking, 1987.

Husik, Isaac. *A History of Mediaeval Jewish Philosophy*. New York: Atheneum, 1976 (first published 1916).

Russell, Bertrand. *A History of Western Philosophy*. New York: Simon and Schuster, 1945.

Wolfson, Harry Austryn. *Philo: Foundations of Religious Philosophy in Judaism, Christianity and Islam*. Cambridge, MA: Harvard University Press, 1982.

Wolfson, Harry Austryn. *The Philosophy of the Church Fathers*. Cambridge, MA: Harvard University Press, 1964.

Key questions

1. What is the purpose of this book?
2. What is philosophy? How is it different from science?
3. What is Jewish philosophy? How is it different from Jewish thought?
4. Why is it important that the study of western philosophy include Jewish philosophy? What are different ways to answer this question?
5. Why is it important that the study of Judaism include Jewish philosophy? What are different ways to answer this question?
6. Why is it important that the Abrahamic religions be studied in relation to each other?

I. THE ORIGINS

The Hebrew Scriptures

CHAPTER 2

Biblical history:
the story of the Hebrew Scriptures

Methodological qualifications

On the Hebrew Scriptures being "Jewish" and "philosophical"

We begin the story of Jewish philosophy with the Hebrew Scriptures. In truth, this compilation of ancient Hebrew writings is not a work of philosophy. Nor is it really Jewish if we mean by this term "rabbinic Judaism." Still, we begin with the Hebrew Scriptures for two reasons. First, rabbinic Judaism always has been and continues to be today, at least in literary form but probably in content as well, a detailed commentary on what these texts mean and how their meaning can be extended to apply to contemporary situations. Hence, while the Bible itself may not be "Jewish," its study is a primary Jewish activity. This description applies no less to Jewish philosophy than to any other form of Jewish literature. Until the modern period the Hebrew Scriptures were understood to be the word of God and that word contained within it the key to solving all central philosophical questions. As a result, the words of these Scriptures functioned no less than lived life as the data for philosophical analysis.

Second, implicit within the words of the biblical text is a world and life-view that is itself philosophical, because it includes claims about all the central topics of philosophical inquiry. Those include the following: How did the universe begin and how will it end? What kinds of things exist and what purpose do they serve in the universe? What are human beings and why do they exist? What is the Hebrew people, how did it begin, what is its place in the universe, and how will it end? What is good, what is bad, and how can human beings know the difference?

The Hebrew Scriptures taken as a whole provide answers to these questions that are more or less (how much more and how much less is something that scholars debate) coherent. The answers are part of a story of the history of the nation of Israel from the origin of the universe up to the establishment of its second political state in the sixth century BCE. Rabbinic Judaism begins with rabbis deciding which books should be included in these Scriptures and what these books mean. Just when the rabbis began to do this is a matter of scholarly debate. Jewish tradition maintains that the process began as early as the sixth century BCE, but most scholars of biblical history think it was much later, no earlier than the second century BCE, when the Judean state was subject to the Seleucidan Greek Empire, and no later than the second century CE, when Judah the Nasi compiled the Mishnah.

On knowing the historical setting of the Hebrew Scriptures

Readers are not expected at this stage to know anything about the historic references in the last paragraph. The establishment of the second Israelite nation will conclude the story of biblical history that will be presented in this chapter. Just who edited and wrote the Hebrew Scriptures will be discussed in the next chapter, and the story of Judah the Nasi and the Mishnah, including just what a "Nasi" is, will be told at the beginning of Chapter 8, where we will provide the historical background for discussing the Midrash and other early rabbinic literature. For now our concern is only to provide a historical context for looking at the philosophy implicit in the Hebrew Scriptures. However, to summarize that history is no simple task since there is widespread disagreement over just what it is. The Hebrew Scriptures say one thing, how the early rabbis subsequently interpreted the Bible's history is another thing, and how contemporary scholars use the data of the Hebrew Scriptures and archeology to reconstruct that history is yet a third thing. Furthermore, whichever story we choose to emphasize—biblical, rabbinic, or academic—there is no single line of normative or clear interpretation. What the biblical text itself says is in general not very clear about most matters when it is looked at with great care. The rabbis offer many interpretations of what the text says which are not always (when taken together) coherent, and contemporary scholars of biblical history are far from reaching a consensus about what in fact happened in the history of the first state of Israel. To straighten out all these differences goes far beyond the intent of this book. What I will do here in this chapter is to present a single line of interpretation of early Jewish history that basically accepts the accounts given in the Hebrew Scriptures themselves, attempting to read the text as free of presuppositions from subsequent readings as possible without rejecting scholarly insights (both rabbinic and academic) whenever they seem useful. The result should be a coherent account of the history that is good enough to serve our purpose of situating biblical philosophy in a temporal–spatial context even though that account is far from accurate (if for no other reason than because it is a coherent account).

Locating the story in space

Our story begins in a territory of the so-called "Near East" bordered by the Mediterranean Sea to the northwest, the Persian Gulf to the southeast, the Tigris and Euphrates rivers to the east, and the Nile River to the west. Picture this map as a rectangle in which the mountain ranges of modern Turkey are in the upper left-hand corner, northeastern North Africa and the mouth of the Nile River are in the lower left-hand corner, the Arabian peninsula (stretching beyond the map to the Arabian Sea) is the southern border, and the Caspian Sea is in the upper right-hand corner.

Mesopotamia and its astronomy

The valleys of the Tigris and Euphrates rivers in the north form a fertile territory that we shall call, as a shorthand, "Mesopotamia." It rises from the rivers' mouth at the Persian Gulf to the mountains of modern Turkey. In Mesopotamia there emerged a series of distinct world empires. These include Sargon of Akkad (2360–2180 BCE), Ur (2060–1950 BCE), the Hittites (1450–1200 BCE),[1] Assyria (the ninth to the sixth centuries BCE), the Medes and Babylonia (the early sixth century BCE), and, finally for our present purposes, the Persian Empire that was ruled by Cyrus from 556 to 530 BCE.

It is during the period of the Babylonian Empire that Babylon's priests developed detailed charts of actual movements of celestial objects over extremely long periods of time. The Babylonian priests, like their Hebrew counterparts, had a practical purpose for studying astronomy, viz., to be able to predict with accuracy when religious festivals were to begin. In the course of their engagement in this liturgical function, the Babylonian priests developed sophisticated records of empirical astronomy, the counterpart of which were not to be surpassed until fairly recent times, well after the invention of the telescope.

Egypt and its mathematics

The valley formed in the southern extreme of our mental map rises from its mouth at the Mediterranean Sea into the mountains of northeastern Africa. In this valley as well there arose a series of different imperial dynasties, each of which was called "Egypt." For our purposes it is important to single out the so-called "Old Kingdom" (2615–2175 BCE), during which the pyramids were built utilizing major developments in arithmetic and applied geometry.

The base numbers were 3, 4, and 5. (The number one was considered a principle of unity and two a principle of plurality [viz., duality]. Both were expressed through the grammar of nouns rather than through numerical modifications.)[2] Corresponding to these base numbers were the base geometric shapes, viz., lines, out of which were constructed all more complicated physical structures, each with its own corresponding arithmetic values. The simplest two-dimensional shape was the right triangle whose sides adjacent to the 90° angle were 3 and 4 and whose remaining side, opposite to the right angle, was 5. Strings were divided into 12 equal distant parts and then stretched out on the ground by spatial units of 3, 4, and 5 to form right triangles. A second triangle could be laid out in this way alongside the first to form a rectangle, and a series of rectangles could be laid out next to each other to form a rectangular plane of any size needed for the construction of a building.[3]

At a later time than we are considering here, the Greeks would conquer both Mesopotamia and Egypt, and, as an accidental consequence of doing so, Greek scholars would absorb and unify the astronomy and geometry of the Near East, and thus stimulate major developments in all kinds of new sciences that would be unified into what we commonly call "ancient Greek philosophy." That philosophy, which (as we will see) has more (or, at least as much) to do with the Greek and Roman empires (especially in Syria and Egypt) than Greece proper, would have a major impact on those rabbis who would produce the midrashic literature that we will study next in this historically framed introduction to Jewish philosophy. However, we are too far ahead of our story. For now, what we want to do is draw another mental map of the world in which the history of the biblical Israel takes place.

The land of Israel

Between these two primary areas of fertility and civilization—Egypt and Mesopotamia—stretches a narrow fertile strip at whose geometric center lies a territory called "Canaan," which after its conquest by the Hebrew tribes would be called "Israel," and which after Israel's destruction by the Romans would be called "Palestine" (because of the one-time dominance in the territory of the Philistines), but which again, since 1947 CE, has been called "Israel." This fertile strip runs from the Taurus (in Turkey) and Zagros (in Iran) mountains of the north to the desert-wilderness of the south, bordered by the Mediterranean Sea to the west and a mountain range to the east beyond which is the Arabian desert. The narrow area of fertility stretches in the north along the mountains in the west and the desert in the east through the town of Meggido in the center of Israel. At Meggido there is a mountain pass beyond which the fertile ridge stretches out with the sea in the west and the mountains in the east past the Judean hills, which are the last foothills of this mountain range that begins to the north of Persia.

It is the mountain pass at Meggido that gives Israel its importance in world history. The empires of Mesopotamia continually tried to expand to conquer the empires of Egypt and vice versa. For the invading armies to meet each other they had to pass through the connecting fertile strip that narrowed at Meggido. The nation that controlled this pass controlled the Middle East.[4] In general, Egypt was invaded by Mesopotamia; each time a Mesopotamian army came through it asked Israel to let it pass and each time Egypt asked Israel to join it in resisting the invaders. Israel, as a Third World nation, had to decide which superpower would win the conflict, because if it sided with the loser it would be destroyed. Each time Israel sided with Egypt, and each time Mesopotamia won and Israel was destroyed. In brief, from the perspective of world history, that is the sum total of the history of the first Jewish national state.

Why did Israel consistently choose the wrong side? From the perspective of secular history there are many possible answers. First, Israel's origins, at least culturally, were in Egypt, so the Israelites tended to favor the Egyptians over their enemies for much the same reasons today that Americans tend to favor the British in their conflicts even when many of America's citizens come from Britain's enemy (viz., Germany in the case of the First World War) and even when the enemy is a continental neighbor (viz., Argentina in the case of the Falklands War). Second, Egypt was the older civilization and therefore the more established empire. Hence, Egypt represented both a prestige and stability to the relatively poor Israelites (especially Israel's rulers) that could not be matched by countries like Assyria (who invaded in 722 BCE, less than 150 years after it was established) and Babylonia (who invaded in 587 BCE, fairly recently established as the successor to Assyria). Third, Egypt was Israel's immediate neighbor, which the Mesopotamians were not. However, none of these are the reasons that the Hebrew Scriptures themselves give, and the story of their reasons for Israel's continuous defeats is both a main theme of the texts of the Hebrew Scriptures and the basis for the questions that subsequently will dominate Jewish philosophy.

The biblical story

From Abraham to Moses

At some time between the twenty-first and the nineteenth centuries BCE, "God" (*Elohim*) appears to Abraham in the imperial city of Ur in Mesopotamia and tells him to leave with all of his family. God, not yet identified by a proper name, does not tell him where they are going, but Abraham, being the first faithful servant of this deity, follows him. Abraham arrives in Canaan during the Middle Bronze Age when Amorites and other distinct peoples settled throughout Mesopotamia and Canaan. Three generations later, Abraham's great-grandson, Joseph, settled in Egypt where he attained great political power as the second in authority to the Pharaoh who ruled Egypt. He brought his father, Jacob (Abraham's grandson), to Egypt, together with his eleven brothers and all of their families, to settle and prosper in Egypt as well. It was at this time, between 1678 and 1570 BCE, that Egypt was ruled by the Hyksos. However, when the Hyksos were overthrown and a new indigenous Egyptian dynasty was reestablished, the descendants of Abraham joined other exiles and combined with other Semite tribal units at the borders between the Sinai desert and Canaan.

Many biblical scholars locate this exodus between 1275 and 1250 BCE. Most of them do not believe that it occurred in the way that the Hebrew Scriptures say because they cannot find supporting evidence for the events that the Bible reports in any independent records. (A few scholars doubt that the events reported occurred at all.) According to the biblical texts, the Hebrews spent an entire generation in the Sinai desert where Moses, with God's directions and the advice of his Midianite father-in-law, Jethro, formed the people into a nation. The nation consisted of families ruled by elders who were members of twelve largely independent tribes, each descended from a different son of Jacob (whose name becomes Israel), that were loosely formed into a confederate nation. Together, under the leadership of Moses' successor as military leader, Joshua, the nation conquered most of the land of Canaan and settled into it as farmers. In each tribe there were altars administered by members of the tribe of Levi, which was made up of descendants of Joseph's brother Levi.[5]

From Moses to David

While the tribe of Levi was the seat of political power, it had neither military power nor wealth. With respect to wealth, the land was divided equally between all of the other tribal families. At the same time, Joseph received a double portion that was divided between his two sons, Ephraim and Manasseh, so that the tribal division remained twelve, viz., the original twelve tribes minus Levi and Joseph plus Joseph's two sons.[6]

In the case of the military needs, on the occasions that joint tribal action was required, the council of tribal elders met and appointed a temporary head, called a judge. This method was effective against most enemies; it was not effective against the Philistines, whose military technology reflects the beginning of the Iron Age. To counter the attacks of the Philistines the tribes gave up their claims to autonomy and appointed a king, viz., Saul from the small tribe of Benjamin, who ruled from 1020 to 1000 BCE. Saul, however, was an ineffective ruler, first because (as the Hebrew Scriptures claim) he did not obey the directions of God communicated to him through the judge and prophet Samuel, and, second because, being from a small tribe (Benjamin), he had limited authority with the other tribes and he lacked the military experience to bring Israel into the Iron Age. He and his descendants died in battle, and the new king became David of the tribe of Judah.

From David to Ezra

David was a man of experience with modern means of warfare, because, before becoming king, he and his followers served as mercenaries in the Philistine army.[7] Furthermore, he was supported by the tribe of Judah, one of the two major powers in Israel's tribal hierarchy, the other being Ephraim. David ruled from 1000 to 961 BCE. During his lifetime he defeated the Philistines, eliminating Israel's only serious external threat, and defeated all of the tribal revolts against his authority, unifying Israel for the first time into a single nation.

The rule of David was the political and military high point of Israel's history. The fruits of David's success were reaped by his son Solomon. Solomon ruled a powerful and united monarchy of Israel from 961 to 922 BCE. During his reign he developed the city of Jerusalem within the tribal territory of Judah into a national capital with a massive construction campaign whose crown achievement was the first Temple. The Temple was impressive as architecture and as a statement of national success, but it was also expensive. In truth, it was a capital that only a first-class Mesopotamian or Egyptian empire could afford and Davidic Israel, while powerful by Third World standards, was no empire. The costs set the stage for the first major national tragedy of decline immediately after Solomon's death, for Israel's construction program in Judah was paid for by the entire nation and the rest of the nation resented it.

In 922 BCE, the ten northern tribes formed a confederacy that successfully revolted against the rule of Solomon's son Rehoboam. The southern kingdom centered on Jerusalem became known as "Judah" and was ruled continuously by members of the house of David. The northern kingdom became known as "Israel." It had no central temple and city. Rather, two of many local shrines tended to dominate as locations for national deliberations, one in Shiloh and the other in Bethel.

This new Israel was even less unified monarchically than it was cultically. Jeroboam I became the first king, but failed to establish a dynasty. In fact, only two of the six kings who were to rule Israel during its brief history were successfully succeeded by their sons.[8]

Instrumental in the political and military decline of Israel was the institution of prophecy. As stipulated in the Torah, the state of Israel was intended to be a theocracy where the people were ruled directly by God. In fact it was governed in its daily life by a genetically generated bureaucracy of priests. These priests were associated with different sanctuaries throughout the nation. They administered the daily and special festive sacrifices that dominated the social life of the nation, and they also played a key role in political decision-making at the city, tribal, and national levels. In addition, there was a need for military leaders, judges, but this institution at first was charismatic (i.e., made up of individuals chosen for leadership on the basis of their personal talent and not on the basis of biological lineage). Out of the charismatic military leadership emerged a stable, hereditary monarchy that from the very beginning dominated the priesthood. As the monarchies (of both Israel and Judah) became politically stronger, the political voice of the hereditary priesthood grew weaker. In its place arose a (so-to-speak) charismatic priesthood of individuals known as "prophets."

The prophets were people possessed by God through whom God spoke to the people. From at least the time of King David (with the prophet Nathan) these prophets began to deliver addresses ("words") from God that were political, and the primary political message tended to be critical of the monarchy. This was especially true in the northern kingdom, and undoubtedly this institution was a major contributor to the nation's political instability and decline.[9] However, this last statement is not the judgment of the Hebrew Scriptures. Rather, they see the primary reason for the decline of the two Israelite states as the failure of both the people and its leaders to follow the prophetically reported words of God.

The northern kingdom of Israel became increasingly involved in idolatry, for which God punished it with destruction at the hand of the northern empire of Assyria. Assyria conquered Israel in 722 BCE, and deported its people to the north where they faded into social and political oblivion, only to survive in Jewish and Christian legend as the "ten lost tribes."

The southern kingdom of Judah was also destroyed for disobedience to God by means of conquest. However, in its case the story is more complex. During the reign of Josiah, priests in the Jerusalem temple claimed to discover an original copy of the covenant (*brit*) between God and the people of Israel that Moses brought down from Mount Sinai. According to that document, a plurality of sanctuaries was permissible only up to the time that God ordered the construction of his Temple in Jerusalem. From then on all worship was to be centralized in Jerusalem and administered by the Jerusalem priesthood. As far as we know, this discovery—known as the "Deuteronomic reforms" because its cultic precepts seem to match the text of the Book of Deuteronomy—provides us with the first written texts in what will subsequently be codified as the Torah and the Hebrew Scriptures.

Judah for the most part seemed to be obedient to God by centralizing worship in Jerusalem. It was also relatively (as compared to the northern kingdom) even if not consistently steadfast in not practicing idolatry, i.e., in not worshipping any deity but the God of the Jewish nation. Rather, as expressed especially by the Judean prophet Jeremiah, its major sin was a moral one. While it obeyed the cultic regulations of the Torah, it did not obey the ethical ones—to do justice to all and to show mercy to the politically and economically disadvantaged. For these moral reasons, as much as for its cultic failures, Judah too was destroyed.

In 587 BCE, the newly established empire of Babylonia conquered Judah, destroyed its Temple, and sent most of its people (or at least its leadership classes) into exile in the imperial city of Babylon. There Judah's spiritual and intellectual leadership struggled to make sense out of its tragedy. The two major voices of the period that survive are Ezekiel and a second Isaiah. Their explanation, following in the footsteps of Jeremiah, is that a world empire (here Babylonia) was the instrument by which God punished Israel for its failure to obey his will as it was revealed in the Torah, which at this stage is not so much a written document as an understanding of the original intent in the national covenant formed between God and Israel through Moses at Sinai. However, whereas Jeremiah's emphasis was, for the most part, particularistically centered on issues of social justice within the nation, the messages of Ezekiel and Isaiah were more global. Both prophets of this first exile believed that Israel had a mission to the world, but they did not necessarily agree on what that mission was.

For Isaiah it is universal. God, now known by the proper name of the Tetragrammaton,[10] is the creator and ruler of the universe. Everything in it is subject to his domain, yet no one other than Israel knows who he is by his proper name. It is Israel's mission to teach the world who the true God is, which, in practice, means to convert the entire world to worship of Israel's God. It is Israel's failure to do what it must do to fulfill its mission that caused God to punish Israel.

The deity of Ezekiel is no less the creator God of the world than is Isaiah's. Ezekiel also believed that Israel had a mission to the world, but his understanding of the mission was in many respects diametrically opposed to Isaiah's. For Ezekiel, Israel was intended to be a holy nation in the midst of profane (i.e., ordinary) nations. A "holy" thing is something that belongs especially to God. As such it is to remain pure and separate from everything else. The Sabbath is God's holy day; the land of Israel is his holy land; Hebrew is his holy language; and the people themselves are his holy people. As such Israel's mission is particularistic, and the reason why its people were punished was that they mixed too much with other peoples—adopting into their own lives foreign customs, practices, and speech, i.e., assimilating into the profane world.

Between 546 and 530 BCE the Persian Cyrus overthrew the empires of the Medes and the Babylonians and established the Persian Empire. In 538 BCE he granted permission to the Judean exiles to return to Judah, specifically within the vicinity of the city of Jerusalem, and to reinstate their nation. By 515 BCE the second Temple was complete and the second Jewish state began. In the middle of the fifth century a new wave of immigration from Babylonia settled in Jerusalem. Under the leadership of the new Persian governor over Judah, Nehemiah, and the new High Priest, Ezra, Judah became a nation whose policies followed more from the teachings of Ezekiel than Isaiah. Walls were built around the city, which were closed on the Sabbath and non-citizens were excluded; citizens were to be Israelites who were married to Israelites and the children of Israelites. The people were to be a holy people who lived in a holy city on the holy day. Judean life turned completely inward. There was no foreign policy other than to have no foreign policy. (That was left to the Persians and their garrison in the area.) Instead, Israel focused as a collective solely on the worship of God. The people of Israel literally ate collective meals in family units as an entire nation three times a day and four times on Sabbath, together with their ruling priests and their ruling God.

In addition to growing and eating food with God, they also listened to God's word. Once every year the people came together in the Temple to hear the High Priest read them what the "Torah" said. By then the Torah—what God said to Moses at Sinai—was a written document. Just what that means is the subject of the next chapter.

Notes

1 Hammurabi ruled Babylon in Mesopotamia from 1792 to 1750 BCE.
2 For example, in biblical Hebrew one foot is a *regel*, two hands are *raglayim*, and any number of feet more than two are *regalim*. How many more requires the designation of modifying number assignments.
3 In time, no later than the sixth century BCE, this bit of geometric engineering was formalized as the Pythagorean theorem, viz., the sum of the squares of each adjacent side of a right triangle is equal to the square of the hypotenuse. Pythagoras of Samos, after whom this geometric law is named, lived between 580 and 500 BCE, but historians of mathematics believe that the theorem itself is much older.
4 The victory of the Christian European British and the French against the Muslim Turks at this pass during the First World War made the Middle East a colony of Britain and France and effectively brought to an end the 1000- to

1500-year-old military struggle between the national forces of Islam and Christianity. This perspective on the First World War does much to explain the seemingly unsolvable persistence of the post-World War Two conflict between Israeli Jews and the Palestinian Arabs, for it is a conflict as much about ideology and faith (i.e., religion) as it is about land and power (i.e., nationalism).

5 Among these descendants were Moses, his brother Aaron, and his sister Miriam. Aaron functioned as the first priest, from whom all the other priests of Israel are descendants.

6 Whatever is the real reason, no matter what shifts occur in actual political power among tribes, the tribal structure continues to be twelve. In this connection it is interesting to note that 12 is the sum of the base numbers in Egyptian arithmetic—3, 4, and 5. Furthermore, the tribes descend from twelve sons who in turn descend through a line of three fathers (Abraham, Isaac, and Jacob) and four mothers (Abraham's wife Sarah, Isaac's wife Rebekah, and Jacob's two wives Leah and Rachel). In this context it is also interesting to note that the product of 3 and 4 is 12.

7 Israel entered Canaan at the end of the Bronze Age, i.e., the period of human history when tools (and weapons) were made out of bronze. However, the Philistines (or so some scholars speculate) entered Canaan in the eleventh century BCE at the beginning of the Iron Age. Presumably one reason for the Philistines' military superiority over Saul's Israel was that the formers' army had weapons of iron while the latter's weapons were only bronze. It was David, armed with the lessons he learned in Philistine military service, who, so the theory goes, brought Israel into the Iron Age and enabled Israel to defeat all of its neighbors, including the Philistines.

8 The dynasty of Omri lasted into a third generation, from 875 to 842 BCE. His other notable accomplishment was to make the city of Samaria the nation's permanent capital.

9 The most famous prophets of this period are Elijah and Elisha (who lived during the reigns of Omri and his son Ahab in Israel, 875–842 BCE), Amos and Hosea (who lived during the reign of Jeroboam II in Israel, 785–745 BCE), and Isaiah and Micah (who lived during the reign of Hezekiah in Judah, 715–687 BCE).

10 Four Hebrew consonants (yod, he, vav, he) whose pronunciation is a secret that each High Priest passed on to his successor. We cannot be sure how it was pronounced and rabbinic law forbids its pronunciation. We will say more about this when we discuss the biblical conception of God in Chapter 4.

Suggestions for further study

Anderson, G. W. *The History and Religion of Israel*. London: Oxford University Press, 1966.

Bright, John. *A History of Israel*. Philadelphia: Westminster Press, 1981.

Eissfeldt, O. *The Old Testament, An Introduction*. English translation by Peter R. Ackroyd. New York: Harper and Row, 1965.

Kaufmann, Yehezkiel. *The Religion of Israel: From Its Beginnings to the Babylonian Exile*. Translated into English by Moshe Greenberg. Chicago: University of Chicago Press, 1960.

Pritchard, James B. *The Ancient Near East: An Anthology of Texts and Pictures*. Princeton: Princeton University Press, 1958.

Seltzer, Robert M. *Jewish People, Jewish Thought: The Jewish Experience in History*. New York: Macmillan, 1980. Part 1, "The Ancient Near Eastern Period," pp. 7–162.

West, James King. *Introduction to the Old Testament*. New York: Macmillan, 1981.

Wright, G. Ernst. *The Old Testament against Its Environment*. London: SCM Press, 1950.

Key events of biblical history

21st–19th cent BCE	The Middle Bronze Age in Canaan; the time of the Hebrew patriarchs
1678–1570 BCE	Canaan and Egypt ruled by Hyksos; the time of Joseph in Egypt
1275–1250 BCE	Israelite exodus from Egypt
1250–1200 BCE	Israel conquers Canaan. Nation ruled by tribal confederacy, priests, and judges
1020–1000 BCE	Saul of Benjamin named king of united Israel
1000–961 BCE	David, second king of united Israel
961–922 BCE	Solomon, third king of united Israel
922 BCE	Civil war; division of the Hebrew nation into northern kingdom of Israel and southern kingdom of Judah
722 BCE	Fall of Israel and population deportation (the 10 lost tribes)
640–609 BCE	Josiah King of Judah; period of Deuteronomic cultic reforms
587 BCE	Fall of Judah; destruction of Jerusalem and deportation of Judeans to the city of Babylon
538 BCE	Cyrus of Persia grants permission for Judean exiles to return to Jerusalem
515 BCE	Completion of second Temple in Jerusalem

CHAPTER 3

What is the Bible and how was it created?

What is the Bible?

The Hebrew Scriptures, as it exists today, is the Bible that is used by Jews throughout the world. Most of the books are written in Hebrew although some (Daniel and Esther) are sufficiently late to have been written in Aramaic.[1] The punctuation of the text follows the Masoretic text, which is the accepted tradition, going back to at least the seventh century CE, of determining the vowels, phrase and sentence demarcations, and chapter divisions of each book.[2] The collection of books themselves is divided into three parts. The first is the Torah proper. It consists of five books—Genesis (*bereshit*), Exodus (*shemot*), Leviticus (*vayikra*), Numbers (*bamidbar*), and Deuteronomy (*devarim*). Genesis is almost entirely a narrative that runs from the creation of the world through Jacob and his family relocating in Egypt at the time of Joseph. Exodus continues the narrative with the story of Moses and the exodus from Egypt up to the "theophany" at Sinai when God appears and reveals his law for Israel. The statement of these laws runs through the second part of Exodus, all of Leviticus, and the beginning of Numbers. This statement of the intended constitution of the political state of Israel is clearly the central content of the Pentateuch with the preceding and succeeding narrative functioning primarily as a contextual setting for the law code. Numbers continues the narrative with Israel's life for forty years in the wilderness of Sinai and a series of endless revolts against Moses and God. Deuteronomy begins at the end of the desert wanderings. With the exception of Moses and Joshua, all of the original generation to leave Egypt had died, which means no one in the nation except these two leaders was present when the law code was revealed. The content of Deuteronomy consists of Moses' repetition of the law to prepare the people for the conquest of the land of Canaan and the establishment of their new nation. Deuteronomy concludes with the death of Moses and the words

And there has not arisen a prophet since in Israel like Moses, whom the Lord knew face to face, in all the signs and the wonders, which the Lord sent him to do in the land of Egypt, to Pharaoh, and to all his servants, and to all his land, and in all the mighty hand, and in all the great terror, which Moses wrought in the sight of Israel. (Deut 34:10–12)

Rabbinic Judaism would interpret this sentence to mean that there never has been and never will be a prophet who is Moses' equal, so that the Pentateuch or Five Books of Moses or Torah proper—which becomes identified in its entirety with the law that God revealed to him on Sinai—has no equal as divine revelation in any other holy text of any people, be it revealed to Israel or to any other people.

The second part of the Hebrew Scriptures, called the "Prophets," consists of two subdivisions. The first, called the "Former Prophets," consists of books that continue the narrative of the nation Israel through the original conquest on to the reigns of all the kings of Judah and Israel in the first state of Israel. The Book of Joshua is the story of the conquest. Judges is the story of the national history prior to the establishment of the monarchy. The first Book of Samuel begins with the life of the last judge, the prophet Samuel, and tells how he agrees, against his own good judgment, to allow Israel to establish a monarchy. The book concludes with the reign of the first king, Saul, and focuses on his relations with the young David. The second Book of Samuel is the narrative of the reign of David as king. The first Book of Kings begins with the death of David, the succession of his son Solomon, the civil war that followed Solomon's death, and the history of the two kingdoms through the reign of Ahab in Israel and his conflict with the prophet Elijah. The second Book of Kings continues with the fall of the house of Ahab, including more stories about Elijah and his successor Elisha, on through the last kings of Israel and Judah, up to the beginning of the Babylonian exile.

The second subdivision of the second part of the Hebrew Scriptures is called the "Latter Prophets." It consists of collections of speeches by prophets who all speak in the name of God. The first three—Isaiah, Jeremiah, and Ezekiel—have the longest collections and therefore they are known as the "major prophets." The remaining twelve, whose books are much shorter, are called "minor prophets." The exception to this rule is the Book of Jonah, which is most likely a story composed at some time during the second state of Israel. Jonah is a prophet who is forced against his will to call for the people of the city of Nineveh, the capital of Assyria, to repent, which, to Jonah's great disappointment, they do. However, the

story does not purport to be an account of a historical event and the
prophet is not a historical character, as are the remaining eleven
prophets—Hosea (in early eighth-century Israel), Joel (probably post-
exilic), Amos (in early eighth-century Israel), Obadiah (living shortly after
the Exile began), Micah (in late eighth-century Judah), Nahum (who
writes an ode on the fall of Nineveh at the end of the seventh century),
Habbakuk (probably at the end of the seventh century), Zephaniah
(probably at the end of the seventh century), Haggai (post-Exile, towards
the end of the sixth century), Zechariah (post-Exile, towards the end of the
sixth century) and Malachi (post-exile, probably in the fifth century BCE).

The third and final part of the Hebrew Scriptures is called "Writings."
It consists of a variety of very different kinds of writings most of which
were written after the Torah and the two sections of the Prophets.
Included in this collection are Psalms (which consists of 150 poems, many
of which were used as part of the liturgy of the sacrifices in the first
Temple), Proverbs (which is a collection of aphorisms about a personified
wisdom), Job (a drama about a non-Jew's search for an explanation of his
apparently unjust suffering who in the end is permitted to confront God
directly), Daniel (a story of faith and heroism by Jews in sixth-century BCE
Babylon serving God and risking martyrdom in that service), Ezra (an
account of the life and political reforms of this High Priest of the early
second state of Israel), Nehemiah (a continuation of the narrative begun in
Ezra through the life service of this governor of the early second state of
Israel), the first Book of Chronicles (which summarizes the history of the
first state through the reign of David), and the second Book of Chronicles
(which summarizes the history of the first state from the reign of Solomon
through to the beginning of the Babylonian exile). Much of the two Books
of Chronicles matches the content of the two Books of Kings, but there
are significant differences, some of which can be attributed to the
apparent fact that the emphasis in Kings is more on Israel than Judah and
the emphasis in Chronicles is more on Judah than Israel.

Also included in this third part of the Hebrew Scriptures are five scrolls
that will have special liturgical roles in rabbinic Judaism. There are the
Song of Songs (a collection of youthful poems that speak of a love triangle
involving a shepherd, a peasant girl who loves him, and a king who loves
the girl), Ruth (the story of a Moabite woman who marries a Judean who
give birth to a lineage that includes King David), Lamentations (a dirge on
the first destruction of the Jerusalem Temple), Ecclesiastes (mature
reflections on the meaning and value of life), and Esther (a story about the

salvation of the Jewish people from anti-Judaism in Persia through the manipulation of court power by Mordecai and his cousin, Esther, who becomes the queen). The Song of Songs is recited on Passover, Ruth on Shavuot, Lamentations on Tisha Be-Av, Ecclesiastes on Sukkot, and Esther on Purim.[3]

Let us now ask who wrote these books. None of them identifies an author internally and we have no clear time and place for the final canonization of these different texts into the Hebrew Scriptures. Rabbinic tradition will tell us that God wrote the Pentateuch that he revealed to Moses at Sinai. Belief in this claim is the single most critical, dogmatic claim in rabbinic Judaism. This same tradition also tells us that Joshua wrote the Book of Joshua, the books of the prophets are by the prophets named, King David wrote the Psalms, Jeremiah wrote the two Books of Kings, and Solomon wrote the Song of Songs (in his youth), Proverbs (in his maturity), and Ecclesiastes (in his old age). Academic scholars of the Bible, however, make radically different claims about the Bible's origins.

Who wrote the Bible?

Historical background

Late in the nineteenth century, the Christian German Bible scholar, Julius Wellhausen, put forth a thesis, known as the "Documentary Hypothesis," that the Five Books of Moses (i.e., the Torah) are a composite work of no single authorship, put together from previously existing materials that themselves are composite works of no single author. In making this claim he identified four basic layers—(1) a source called "J" that consists primarily of narratives in which God is called by the proper name of YHVH; (2) a parallel source called "E" that consists primarily of narratives in which God is called by the general term "El" or "Elohim"; (3) a source called "D" that constitutes primarily the Book of Deuteronomy, viz., the text of what prima facie is Moses' discourses to the new generation of Israelites after forty years in Sinai, immediately before Moses' death and the initiation of Israel's conquest of the land of Canaan; and (4) a source called "P" that is made up of priestly laws dispersed through the entire Pentateuch.

The hypothesis has undergone considerable modification since Wellhausen first proposed it, and there is considerable disagreement among academic scholars of the Bible over the details. However, there tends to be a consensus about the most general features of the hypothesis, which is, contrary to the traditional claims of rabbinic scholars, that the Hebrew Scriptures is a many-layered work which conceals within its words rewritings, omissions, and additions through the course of history, from when it began some time in Israel's early origins as oral traditions about the nation's laws and origins until it became the more or less unified text that we recognize today as sacred Scriptures. What follows is one telling of this story of the history of the text from a contemporary Bible scholar.[4]

As we read in the last chapter, the Israelites emerged as the dominant people in the geographic region of the contemporary state of Israel around 1200 BCE. Politically they were ruled by interrelated but distinct groups of priests and military leaders. Out of the military leaders ("judges") emerged a united monarchy, and, during the reign of David, the city of Jerusalem became the political capital. At these times there were different groups of priests who administered different sanctuaries throughout the Israelite state. Among the priesthood three groups in particular are to be distinguished— (1) "Aaronide" priests, i.e., a clan of priests who trace their descent back to Aaron; (2) "Mushite" priests, i.e., a clan of priests who trace their descent back to Moses; and (3) other clans of priests of less distinguished pedigree who functioned throughout the land in a diversity of locations. Our interest, for now, is solely with the Aaronide and Mushite clans.

When David became king and established Jerusalem as his capital, he brought to the city two governing priests—Zadok and Abiathar. Zadok was an Aaronide, whose clan, until then, functioned out of the southern city of Hebron, located within David's familial tribe of Judah. Abiathar was a Mushite, whose clan, until then, functioned out of the northern city of Shiloh. By bringing both to the capital, David responded to the political reality of the power rivalries between the different tribes under the newly created monarchy. This compromise lasted only one generation. Solomon felt sufficiently strong that he could turn the power over exclusively to his Judean priesthood. Hence, while Zadok remained, Abiathar was expelled, thereby disenfranchising the northern tribes and its dominant Mushite priesthood.

Following the civil war of 922 BCE, the northern kingdom of Israel achieved whatever slight stability it had in the continuity of its Mushite priesthood centered in Shiloh. In the far more stable south, all kings were members of the Davidic dynasty, all governing priests were Aaronides, and all of them governed together from the city of Jerusalem.

The northern kingdom of Israel survived for two hundred years, while Judah continued to exist for more than 335 years. Notable for our purposes during this period are the reigns of two kings—Hezekiah (715–687 BCE) and his grandson Josiah (641–609 BCE). It was Hezekiah who centralized all worship in the Temple of Jerusalem. However, the unification lasted only for his reign. His son, Manasseh, reestablished the local sanctuaries, governed by clans of local (non-Aaronide and non-Mushite) priests. Hezekiah's theocratic centralization was reinstituted by his great-grandson, Josiah.

Josiah was only three years old when he became king. Clearly, at that age he could not himself govern, so the real power lay in the hands of his guardians. It is reasonable to speculate that those guardians came from the Aaronide priesthood of Jerusalem. It is in this context that we should interpret the statements in the Bible (2 Kgs 22:8 and 2 Chr 34:14–15) that in the year 622 BCE Josiah (then 22 years old) was informed by the scribe Shaphan that the priest Hilkiah found a "scroll of the Torah" in the Jerusalem Temple. It was this scroll that provided both the legitimization of and blueprint for the cultic reforms of Josiah's reign. The "discovery" of this scroll of Torah is for our purposes one of the two most critical events in biblical history.

In the year 587 BCE, Nebuchadnezzar of Babylonia burnt down the city of Jerusalem with its palaces and Temple. He exiled a significant portion of Judah's population to Babylonia and set up a governor, Gedaliah, to rule the subject nation. Gedaliah was murdered, which brought reprisals from Babylonia, with the result that the remaining Judean leadership fled for refuge to Egypt. Among those who joined the exiles in Egypt was the prophet Jeremiah. Notable among the refugees in Babylonia were the prophets Isaiah and Ezekiel.

The Exile lasted for about 50 years. In 538 BCE Persia authorized the reestablishment of a Jewish state in Judah, and a second Temple was completed just 23 years later, in 515 BCE. However, it was a Temple that lacked the ark, cherubim, Urim and Thummim, of the first Temple, and the new state lacked prophets and (most notably) kings. While there were allusions to a Davidic descendant at the beginning of the state, references to him (Zerubbabel) disappear by the time that Ezra was appointed the city state's civil governor, with authority over its exclusively Aaronide priesthood, and Nehemiah was named the city state's military governor. Ezra introduced a series of political and cultic reforms that included cultic centralization with an exclusively Aaronide (Zadokite) priesthood.

Ezra was not only a priest. He was also a "scribe," and, as a scribe, he was associated with a "Torah" (Neh 8:13). The Book of Ezra refers to cultic regulations "written in the Torah of Moses, the man of God" (Ezra 3:2), and Nehemiah says that Ezra, the "priest" and "scribe," read its words to all of the people in the seventh month of his rule (Neh 8). The reading of this Torah of Moses is our second critical event.

So far we have not said anything that is not explicitly stated in the biblical text. As yet what we have said is only the background for the Documentary Hypothesis. It is not the hypothesis itself, which describes a certain way to understand the historical events described above.

The Documentary Hypothesis

Our story begins with two separate narratives of the entire history of the first Jewish polity that are presently situated both in the Torah proper (the Pentateuch) and in what rabbinic Judaism calls the "early prophets" (viz., Joshua, Judges, 1 and 2 Samuel, and 1 and 2 Kings).

One is called the "J" source, because the predominant reference to God is by the Tetragrammaton. This source was an oral tradition known to the Aaronide priesthood centered in Hebron. It reflects the understanding of the nation's history from the perspective of the southern territory. Its notable features are that it presents a relatively anthropomorphic conception of a merciful deity, and that it either de-emphasizes the importance of the tribal founders (i.e., the sons of Jacob) or presents them in a negative light, with the lone exception of Judah. The other is called the "E" source, because the predominant reference to God is by the general terms *"El"* and *"Elohim."* This source was an oral tradition known to the Mushite priesthood centered in Shiloh. It reflects the understanding of the nation's history from the perspective of the northern territory. Its notable features are that it presents a relatively transcendent conception of a deity of justice, locates Jacob at Peni-El in places where J locates him at Hebron, and gives all of Jacob's sons considerably more attention than does J.

J and E were composed sometime after the civil war (in 922 BCE) and before Israel's demise at the hands of the Assyrians (in 722 BCE). We do not know when they reached the form in which we find them in the Hebrew Scriptures. We do know (at least according to the hypothesis), however, who unified them. It was the priests of Shiloh.

The author of the "D" source also came from the class of Shiloh priests. As noted above, D is primarily the main part of our present book of Deuteronomy as well as the books of the "early Prophets" in the Hebrew Scriptures. Its signature feature is that it calls for the centralization of all cultic activities in Jerusalem. The composer (of original material) and editor (who adapted earlier materials to fit his creative plan) of D is identified by some scholars as either the prophet Jeremiah and/or his scribe Baruch Ben Neriyah. (The Babylonian Talmud, in Baba Batra 15a, identifies Jeremiah as the author of 1 and 2 Kings, as it identifies Moses as the author of the Pentateuch, and Joshua as the author of Joshua.)

D is not our first written text. Predating it was at least the so-called "Covenant Code"—Exod 21:1–27; 22:1–30; 23:1–33, whose source is also attributed to the Shiloh priesthood who wrote E. However, the Covenant Code is only a priestly law code. It is not a sacred narrative, and therefore significantly different from what we would recognize as a "Torah from Moses." It is D that is our first "Torah" so understood. Note further that D is not intended to include the Covenant Code, but to replace it. As such, D is a politically radical document that, while appearing to be conservative (i.e., to conserve what had always been the nation's laws), is in fact a revolutionary displacement of the existing order.[5]

D is our first written Torah and, if the Documentary Hypothesis is correct, it is what W. M. L. De Wette in 1805 called a "pious fraud."[6] At least on the interpretation considered here, the D document was composed by a single individual (or, a small group of individuals) with the conscious intent of passing his/their creation off to a general public as an authentic copy of the original constitution between God and the nation of Israel centuries before. That makes it clearly a fraud, viz., something that intentionally claims to be what it is known by its author(s) not to be. Whether or not the lie was "pious" or not depends on the intention of the liars. That, for now at least, remains an open question. In any case, it is sufficient to note that, if it is a fraud, it is not the last one in this story of the composition of the Bible. As D was written in the guise of a conservative work whose real intention was revolutionary, so other frauds were composed that do to D what D did to his/its predecessors (at least to the Covenant Code).

We mentioned before that Jeremiah, together with Baruch, wrote two versions of D. A first (Dtr[1]) was composed during the reign of Josiah, which is to say, no later than 609 BCE. In this original version the narrative of our first Torah concludes with the glorification of this monarch's reign.

As such, the tale it tells has a happy ending. It begins with greatness (with Moses and the theophany at Sinai) and ends with greatness (with Josiah and his cultic restoration). However, the story does not have a happy ending. A still fairly young Josiah (35 years old) was killed in battle, his successors decentralized the cult (again), and the nation was destroyed by Babylonia in 587 BCE. The happy ending turned out not to be true, so our author reconstructed his narrative with a new, truer, account (Dtr²).

What was written as a, so-to-speak, "comedy" (i.e., not a funny book, but a book that has a happy ending) was transformed into a "tragedy" (i.e., a book that has an unhappy ending). The nation returned to its former sinful ways, and that in turn led to its destruction. Hence, D established a tragic view of history as its model for the nation's self-understanding.

It is not a picture without hope, for there is hope of restoration. But the restoration itself is not part of the narrative. If there is hope, as there seems to be, that hope lies beyond the world that the narrative presents. Within the world of the story, life ends in death, not in rebirth. As such D pioneers the way the Jewish people will continue to understand their world and their lives. It is not a picture of the world as they would want it to be. Whatever the intention of the author of the Hebrew Scriptures, it was not to create a fantasy. Rather, it is a model for understanding the world as it is. Whatever the quality of fraud in its authorship, it does not intend to present a view of reality that is not true. In this sense it is not a fraud, and perhaps that is what it means to call the lie "pious."

At some time after the destruction of the northern kingdom (722 BCE), during the reign of Hezekiah (715–687 BCE), an Aaronide priest(s) composed and edited his/their own distinctive sacred history of Israel, comparable in form to Jeremiah's, that focused its happy ending on the reign of Hezekiah rather than on the reign of Josiah. The name scholars have given to this fourth source is "P."[7] If this thesis is correct, then it is P that incorporates more ancient legal material such as the Holiness Code. On this reading, Jeremiah's D was written to supplant P as well as J and E.[8] The combined JE favored Moses over Aaron. P was composed by an Aaronide priest whose intent was to rewrite history in a way that would favor his ancestry and, consequently, his clan. Hence, what P did to JE—rewrite sacred history and law, effecting a revolution in conception and politics under the guise of preserving both—D does to P. However, what D does to P and P does to JE, the final redactor of the Pentateuch (called "R") does to D.[9] This final redactor is Ezra.

How are we to read the Bible?

We will attempt as much as possible to take a neutral stance between the presuppositions of traditional rabbinic Judaism and modern academic biblical scholarship in interpreting the philosophical content of the Hebrew Scriptures. My own personal belief is that they are texts that were divinely inspired. Just what this expression means will be explained in the course of this book, especially in connection with medieval (Chapter 17) and modern (Chapter 28) Jewish philosophy. In brief, it says that the Bible should not be understood literally as a text that God dictated to his prophets, but it also cannot adequately be understood as a human creation. There are important differences between claiming that God revealed the Scriptures, claiming that he inspired them, and claiming that human beings created them, but that will not affect our description of what the Hebrew Scriptures say. What does matter, however, is when they were written, for, more than the role that God plays in the authorship, the location of the writings in a specific time and place does change what we think the texts say.

We will also try to remain neutral on the claim of rabbinic Judaism that each book of the Bible is a unity and the claim of the academic scholars that most books of the Bible are compilations of layers of earlier existing texts. Even if we accept what the source critical academic scholars say about the Bible, what matters to us is the meaning of the final edition of each text in the Hebrew Scriptures and not the independent meaning of the parts that the editors assembled for their creation. It is the final compilation that matters because that is the work that influenced subsequent Jewish philosophy. Hence, for our purposes, there is no reason to decide who is right about the composition of the Hebrew Scriptures, traditional rabbis or contemporary academics.

I will assume in what follows that what the text literally says is what it means. That, as we shall see, is a radical assumption, since no one, at least since the rise of rabbinic Judaism, believes that what the words of the text say literally are what they really mean.

We will also assume, in agreement with the rabbis, that of all the works in the Hebrew Scriptures, the Torah (Pentateuch) is the most important and that the most important book in the Torah is Leviticus, which lays out the full constitution of the first theocratic Jewish state. As such, the editors of the Hebrew Scriptures were priests whose primarily intellec-tual–spiritual sources in editing their masterpiece were the prophets

Jeremiah, Ezekiel, and Isaiah, and of these prophets the single most important intellectual and spiritual influence was Ezekiel. That means that what the Hebrew Scriptures are is an all-encompassing philosophy— one that deals with the meaning of the world and life in general, that focuses on the meaning and value of humanity in general in the world, that focuses on the meaning and value of the people of Israel within humanity. It further assumes that the universe and everything in it has moral value and purpose and that at the center of the determination of that purpose and those values is the sacrificial cult of the Jerusalem Temple. This line of interpretation further assumes that the problematic that led to the composition of the Torah and the historical books of the Bible was the destruction of the first Temple, possibly during the reign of Ezra as the High Priest of Judah, and that the problematic that led to the codification by the rabbis of all of the books of the Hebrew Scriptures into the Hebrew Scriptures was the destruction of the second Temple, something that we will examine in the second section of Part I.[10]

Notes

1 Aramaic became the "lingua franca" of the entire fertile crescent in the seventh century BCE, and one of the official languages of the Persian Empire. Jews began to speak it during the Babylonian exile. I use the term "Jews" here for the first time. The source of its usage is as "Judeans," viz., the citizens of Judah (the southern kingdom of the first state of the people Israel) and Judea (the citizens of the second state of the people Israel).

2 This is an important factor in determining the meaning of any text in the Hebrew Scriptures. The text itself is a collection of consonants separated into word units, but there are no vowels and no punctuation. Different vowel assignments to the same consonants can produce different words, and different assignments of punctuation like commas and periods can produce even more radical differences in determinations of what the words mean.

3 The one notable omission here is the Book of Maccabees, which deals with the events related to Hanukkah. For reasons that we will discuss in the unit on rabbinic Judaism, the Book of Maccabees is not included in the Jewish canon, although it is part of the Christian canon of the "Old Testament."

4 The story I will summarize is the one presented by Richard Elliott Friedman in *Who Wrote the Bible?* (San Francisco: Harper Collins, 1989). Friedman is a professor of biblical studies at the University of California, San Diego, and a student of Harvard University's Frank Moore Cross. Cross' version of the Documentary Hypothesis constitutes a kind of "orthodoxy" in this ever-evolving field of scholarship, and Friedman is one of his more prominent

disciples. What recommends his *Who Wrote the Bible?* to us as a focus text, besides the credentials of its author within the field, is its comprehensiveness and clarity.

5 Actually this statement is more radical than anything that Friedman himself explicitly says. Friedman's intent is to play down the radicalness of the reforming nature of each emerging written document in order to avoid the charge of their being "pious frauds." Other Bible scholars are less discreet. For example, Bernard M. Levinson, near the conclusion of his study of the laws of Deuteronomy, says that "Deuteronomy's polemic, although it does not name its object, rewrites literary history. By circumscribing Sinai and silencing the Covenant Code, the redactors of Deuteronomy sought to clear a textual space for Moab as the authentic—and exclusive—supplement to the original revelation (Deut 28:69)" (*Deuteronomy and the Hermeneutics of Legal Innovation*, New York/Oxford: Oxford University Press, 1997, p. 153).

6 See Richard Elliott Friedman, *Who Wrote the Bible?* San Francisco: HarperCollins, 1989, p. 102.

7 An earlier accepted scholarly view was that P was later than D and in fact P is the work of the final redactor (R).

8 Jeremiah 8:8 reads, "How do you say, 'We are wise, and Yahweh's Torah is with us'? In fact, here, it was made for a lie, the lying pen of scribes." On Friedman's reading (p. 209), the scribes are the authors of P and their "Torah" is the P source.

9 Friedman calls this "The Great Irony" (p. 217).

10 In Part I (Origins), Early Rabbinic Literature, Chapter 8 (Rabbinic History).

Suggestions for further study

Driver, S. R. *An Introduction to the Literature of the Old Testament*. New York: Meridian Books, 1956.

Friedman, Richard Elliott. *Who Wrote the Bible?* San Francisco: HarperCollins, 1989.

Levinson, Bernard M. *Deuteronomy and the Hermeneutics of Legal Innovation*. New York/Oxford: Oxford University Press, 1997.

Pfeiffer, R. F. *Introduction to the Old Testament*. New York: Harper and Brothers, 1941.

Segal, Moses Hirsh. *The Pentateuch: Its Composition and Its Authorship and Other Biblical Studies*. Jerusalem: Magnes Press, 1967.

Key questions

1. What are the different books in the Hebrew Scriptures and what (in very general terms) is the content of each?

2. According to rabbinic tradition who wrote Ecclesiastes? The two Books of Kings? The Pentateuch? Proverbs? Psalms? The Song of Songs?

3. According to modern academic biblical scholarship who wrote the Pentateuch?

CHAPTER 4

The God of the Bible

The description of God in Deuteronomy

The clearest, most explicit description in all of the Hebrew Scriptures of who God is is given by Moses at the end of his life to the new generation of Israelites who were born in the wilderness. It occurs in Deuteronomy. Before he dies Moses delivers three speeches[1] to the entire nation. The people have reached the end of their forty-year journey to the promised land. Encamped in the wilderness, just outside of the Jordan valley,[2] set to begin their invasion, Moses retells the people the divine law that is intended to become the constitution of their new nation. The provisions of the law themselves are the body of the second speech. It is surrounded by two other lectures that are rhetorical discourses intended to motivate the people to be obedient. The concluding third speech asserts the rewards promised for obedience and the punishments that will follow from disobedience. It is, if you will, the practical reasons for obedience. The preamble, viz., the first speech, summarizes the narrative history presented in the first four books of the Pentateuch with the intention of providing moral reasons for obedience. In brief, the first speech says that the new, wilderness-hewn Israel ought to obey the statutes that their parents covenanted with God because God, who created everything, including their ancestral people, also gave them the opportunity to become an independent nation under God. At the conclusion of this summation of the Toraitic narrative Moses says the following:

> Now, O Israel, take heed to do the statutes and ordinances which I will teach you so that you may continue to live after you enter and take possession of the land which YHVH, the god (*Elohim*) of your ancestors, gives you. Do not add anything to what I command you, and do not diminish from observing (any and all of) the commandments of YHVH your god which I command you.[3]

> Take care not to forget the covenant of YHVH, your god, which he cut with you, by making for yourselves a graven image in any likeness against which

YHVH your god commanded. For YHVH your god is a consuming fire (*esh ochlah*), a jealous deity (*El kana*).[4]

When you give birth to children and grandchildren and grow stale upon the (promised) land, you will become corrupt and make a graven image in the likeness of anything. (In so doing) you will do what is evil in the eyes of YHVH your god, which will anger him. I call to testify against you this day the sky and the earth, for you will quickly surely perish from upon the land that you cross over the Jordan there to possess. The days upon it will not be long, for you will surely be destroyed. And YHVH will scatter you among the (other) peoples, and you will persevere few in number among the nations where YHVH leads you.[5]

When you seek YHVH your god from there, you will find (him) when you seek him with all your mind (*l*ᵉ*vavcha*) and with all your life (*nafshecha*). In your distress when all these events find you, at the end of days, you will return to YHVH your god and you will take heed of his voice.[6]

For YHVH your god is a merciful deity (*El rakhum*); he will not fail you and he will not destroy you; he will not forget the covenant with your fathers that he swore to them. For please ask about the ancient days which were before you, from the day on which god (*Elohim*) created a human upon the earth. (Ask everyone) from one end of the sky to the other, has there (ever) been (any event) like this great event or has (anything) like it (ever) been heard? Have (ever) a people heard the voice (*kol*) of god speaking from the midst of the fire, as you have heard, and lived? Or has (ever) god attempted to go and take for himself a nation from the midst of a nation by trials, signs, wonders and war, with a strong hand, an extended arm and great terrors, according to all which YHVH your god did for you in Egypt before your (very) eyes? You were shown (all this in order) to know that YHVH is your god; there is no other. From the sky he made you hear his voice (in order) to instruct you, and upon the earth he showed you his great fire and you heard his words from the midst of the fire. Because he loved your fathers he chose its[7] seed after it and brought you forth from Egypt in his presence[8] with great power to dispossess nations greater and mightier than you from before you (in order) to bring you to give to you their land as an inheritance as of this day.[9]

Know today and set it in your mind that YHVH is the god in the sky above and upon the earth below; there is no other. Keep his statutes and his commandments which I command you today, which will be good for you and your children after you, in order to lengthen (your) days upon the land which YHVH your god gives to you (for) all days.[10]

The character of God

For our purpose here, which is to unpack the literal sense of what the Hebrew Scriptures say about who God is, this text is of paramount importance. First, it is the most complete single description of God given in all of the Torah. Second, it is in itself by intention a summary of everything the Torah has said about God. And third, it is the voice of the individual whom the Hebrew Scriptures claim to be the foremost of prophets, Moses,[11] reflecting, literally at the end of his life, on all that he has learned in his extraordinary life about God, the world, the people Israel, and the relations between them.

Note first that God has a proper name, YHVH,[12] which is used, as it is with any individual, to uniquely identify him. Second, he has a proper description, i.e., a general statement which, although all the terms in it are general (which is why I use a small g in translating *Elohim* as "god" and a small d in translating *El* as "deity"), applies uniquely to him, viz., that he is the god (*Elohim*) of Israel's ancestors, from the patriarchs (Abraham, Isaac, and Jacob) to the present people's immediate parents who followed Moses from Egypt into the wilderness where Moses' audience was born. YHVH is no more unique as a god than any parent, simply by being a parent, is unique. The Hebrew Scriptures often explicitly say that other nations also have gods and that Israel itself, even after it becomes a nation, much to its own peril, will adopt other gods besides YHVH.

Just what a god is is known primarily by what he/she does and with whom he/she is related. In general, gods stand in relation to political entities with whom they form alliances of mutual interest. The states serve or worship[13] the deity, in exchange for which the deity provides for or takes care of the state. Worship generally consists in providing desired sacrifices and specified voiced praises, but it can also include obeying civil and moral laws. Just what is the specific content of any worship between a state and its deity depends on the specific provisions of the covenant formed between them. Similarly, the services provided by the deity to the state also depend on the nature of the covenant agreement.

In general, the deities provide states with perseverance, which generally means national success in finding adequate provisions, especially food, to survive, success in procreation, and success in war against those who threaten the nations' existence. I say that generally gods are legally bound to nations, but it is also possible for individuals who are members of different nations to worship a foreign god and for that god to provide for them as well.

YHVH himself is such a deity. He is contractually tied to the nation Israel through a covenant codified in the wilderness upon Mount Sinai shortly after the people first left Egypt. His initial intention was to keep the terms of the covenant flexible. What he wanted was a direct form of theocracy. He would rule them in such a way that when there were things he wanted from his people, he would simply tell them. But this provision was not acceptable to the people themselves.[14] After the first time he addressed the nation as a whole directly, the people asked Moses to plead with their deity not to speak directly to them again. They urged their god, through the intercession of Moses, to settle instead for what I would call a representative theocracy. Instead of the god speaking to the people as a whole, he will designate from them representatives with whom he will speak. The first representative is Moses, and possibly his siblings, Aaron and Miriam,[15] as well. Their god is to address them and they will relate to the nation what he says. For their god this was a compromise. It was a diminishing of his power and authority, and he recognized it as such. But he accepted it.

In general, throughout the Hebrew Scriptures, the god wants relationship with Israel and Israel does not want relationship with him. The god continually conjoles them with rewards and punishments to move them to love him, and they continually recoil in fear against the power that they recognize behind his courtship. The people continually plead with him for separation, which he reluctantly grants, in full recognition that by withdrawing the people will suffer. The first withdrawal is this pentateuchal substitution of direct for representative theocracy. Later, once the promised land is conquered, the people will ask for a further separation.

In Canaan those who become the divine representatives are the judges. God picks them without constitutional restriction and he tells them what he wants of the people, again without constitutional restriction. Eventually, the people urged the judge Samuel to plead with the god to allow them to have a king. Both the god and Samuel recognized that this request is a further rebellion against Israel's god. To be ruled by a king, whose succession is established by law rather than divine fiat, limits the god's power over Israel precisely because the choice of representative is formally established. The god granted their desire, and from the death of the judge Samuel and the beginning of the reign of King Saul, the god withdrew and refrained from speaking to the nation. In effect, he left the nation on its own to determine its own destiny.

With rare exceptions,[16] the god leaves the kings alone to rule the nation, generally with disastrous consequences for the nation's well-being. In their stead he is restricted to communication with the nation through multiple individuals designated as prophets and sons of prophets, but these individuals have no formal, legitimate authority within Israel's nation states.

In the passage quoted above, we see Moses pointing to this future history of the Jewish state in relationship to its parent deity. After Moses, Israel will experience collective high points of well-being under the governance of the judge Samuel and the monarchs David and Solomon. But the monarchy will continuously decline, and the nation with it, until in the end, in 2 Kings, we read of a monotonous succession of weak and bloody royal dynasties, where the sole voices of collective hope are politically powerful prophets who are civilly illegitimate and therefore politically rebellious voices of social disorder, who foresee and even contribute to the doom of the first Jewish polity, notably Elijah and his successor, Elisha.

All of this succeeding narrative suggests another sense in which the god of Israel named YHVH can be uniquely identified. He is a jealous god. "Jealousy" is a character trait. Other gods are more generous with their peoples. They are content to be one among many, but the deity named YHVH is not. If Israel so much as associates with any other god, then YHVH exhibits another of his character traits, anger,[17] and when god is angry he exhibits his terror[18] through the forces of nature[19] that he created, the sky and the earth.[20]

Israel's god's other major character trait, which offsets his jealousy, is "mercy", through which he exhibits his unequaled power to prosper his people for obedience. Through mercy he demonstrates his goodness,[21] holiness,[22] kindness,[23] and, most important of all, his love.[24]

In general, the god's polarity of primary personality traits, jealousy and mercy, are the means by which the god governs the world and everything in it, especially the nation Israel. This picture of the god is primarily political and oral. The god does many things. He is the cause of both life and death[25] who slays Israel's enemies[26] and even smites Israel itself.[27] He closes as well as opens wombs,[28] hardens hearts to cause harm[29] as well as blesses[30] and delivers[31] others to cause them benefit. He fights wars against some[32] and redeems others.[33] All of these actions express the god's major constant action in history as the deity of providence.[34]

The act by which this divine ruler governs his domain is speech. The god of Israel is a god of action[35] and work.[36] But the action he performs primarily is speech. Again, the model is political. He the ruler speaks, and his messengers[37]—earth and sky, wind,[38] and sound[39]—carry out what he requires. But for the most part his primary messengers for administering his governance upon the earth are human, especially his prophets, the so-called "men of god"[40] who act upon the god's "word".[41]

Because the primary identity of YHVH is with the oral, viz., word and speech, there is in general throughout the Hebrew Scriptures an abhorrence of visual association with the deity and a paucity of descriptions of anything that is visible. This is true in general, but the restriction is not rigorous. The god has a finger,[42] a hand,[43] an arm,[44] a mouth,[45] and a face.[46]

The description of God in the Book of Ezekiel

The most graphic visual description of the god's appearance to a prophet is provided in the opening chapter of the Book of Ezekiel. However, properly speaking, what is described is not the deity. Ezekiel sees a storm cloud approach which takes the shape of a rectangular complex creature hovering above wheels and below the appearance of a human form seated upon a throne, which Ezekiel identifies as "the appearance of the likeness of the glory of YHVH,"[47] but not as the appearance of the god. This likeness is associated with a divine sound (kol) through which he hears his prophetic commission. But the sound or voice is not the god and the voice itself is not the visual creature that Ezekiel so elaborately describes.

In general, to the extent that the god is associated with the visible, he is associated with fiery substances,[48] as in the case of Ezekiel's vision. The same is true of the pillar of cloud that leads Moses' fledgling nation through the wilderness and descends upon the tabernacle whenever the god is present within it.[49] The god inhales the fire from sacrifices, presumably as his means of sustenance, and generally causes things made from the earth both to live and to die when he exhales upon them, gently in the former case and with force in the latter.

It is not unreasonable to postulate that the other physical attributions of bodily parts to the god are also in some sense, as in the graphic description provided by Ezekiel, an appearance and a likeness, i.e., an external form or shape, of what substantially is composed of fire. But this is more than the texts of the Hebrew Scriptures actually say. Again, in general, the Hebrew Scriptures have a distinctive aversion for sight. The visual references employed seem less to be descriptions of who the god is than peripheral, poetic ways to assert what the god does. Furthermore, the confusion of physical manifestations of the deity with god himself is considered idolatrous, viz., a primary form of disobedience. Israel seems to want to see the god, but the god only wants to be heard.

The description of God in the Hebrew Scriptures

In summary, the god of Israel presented in the Hebrew Scriptures is the deity who creates the world, governs it through delegates, primarily human, to whom he reveals himself, most often through the spoken word, and who makes known his will to them as well as responds to their will in prayer—at least to Abraham,[50] Ishmael,[51] Isaac,[52] Jacob,[53] Moses,[54] Joshua,[55] Gideon,[56] Manoah,[57] Samson,[58] Hannah,[59] Samuel,[60] David,[61] Solomon,[62] Elijah,[63] Elisha,[64] and Hezekiah.[65] He is recognized through his relationship with his people and his distinctive personality that is expressed through the effective actions of his spoken word. His presence is physical, although its form is primarily perceived as sound. The universe that he created is entirely physical, composed of distinct regions of space—earth, water, and sky—formed through the action of elemental wind or air and elemental fire. It is with the latter two elements that he is associated. The objects that mark his visual presence—pillars, clouds, mountains, etc.— are generally composed of fire. But these expressions of divine location within the visible world are generally secondary in relationship to the oral expressions—wind or spirit, voice or sound—which most clearly identify who or what he is.

When the Hebrew Scriptures are taken as a whole, as they were classically by the followers of the religions of both Judaism and Christianity, and when they are read as literally as possible, this is the view of God that emerges. However, most representatives of the Christian religions and no classical rabbis have ever read the Scriptures this literally. The issue for them is not what the Scriptures mean literally; it is what they mean truly as they were intended to be understood by the deity that all believed, at least until the modern period, revealed them. Rarely was the texts' true meaning seen to be their literal meaning. How the early rabbis interpreted what the Scriptures say about God will be discussed in

Chapter 10. But let us continue now to summarize the philosophy implicit in the Scriptures. We turn next to the conception of Torah.

Notes

1 Deut 1–4, 5–26, and 27–30.
2 Deut 1:1–2.
3 Deut 4:1–2.
4 Deut 4:23–24.
5 Deut 4:25–27.
6 Deut 4:29–30.
7 Viz., the fathers.
8 B^efanav: literally, in his face.
9 Deut 4:31–38.
10 Deut 4:39–40.
11 Cf. Deut 34:10–12.
12 I.e., the Tetragrammaton. Cf. Exod 6:2–8; 9:16; 33:12, 17; 34:5; 2 Sam 6:2. He is also named ehyeh in Exod 3:14.
13 In Hebrew the verb is the same, viz., 'avad.
14 Cf. Exod 20:15–18; Deut 5:5.
15 Cf. Exod 15:20; Lev 10:12–15; 11:1–47; 13:1–59; 14:33–15:33; 17:1–16; Num 2:1–32; 4:1–20; 12:5–8; 14:26–38; 18:1–24; 19:1–22; 20:23–26; 26:1–2.
16 Viz., speaking to Saul in 1 Sam 10:9; to David through an ephod in 1 Sam 30:7–8; to Solomon in 1 Kgs 3:5–15, 9:1–9, and 11:11–13; and to Jehu in 1 Kgs 16:1–4 and 2 Kgs 10:30.
17 Cf. Judg 2:14, 20; 3:8; 10:7; 2 Sam 6:7; 24:1; 1 Kgs 11:9.
18 Cf. Gen 35:5; Exod 23:27.
19 Cf. 1 Sam 7:10; 12:17–18; 2 Sam 21:1.
20 Cf. Gen 1:1–31; 6:9–8:6; 2 Kgs 19:15.
21 Cf. Exod 33:19.
22 Cf. Lev 19:2; 20:26; 1 Sam 2:2; 2 Kgs 19:22.
23 Cf. 1 Sam 20:14.
24 Cf. Exod 15:13; Deut 7:7–8.
25 Cf. 1 Sam 2:6.
26 Cf. Josh 10:11.
27 Cf. Exod 32:35.
28 Cf. 1 Sam 1:5–6, 26–27; 2:1, 21.
29 Cf. Exod 14:8, 17–18; Josh 11:20.
30 Cf. Gen 26:12, 29.
31 Cf. 1 Sam 11:13; 14:23; 26:23.
32 Cf. Exod 15:3; 1 Sam 17:46–47.
33 Cf. Gen 29:31.

34 Cf. Exod 1:20; 2:24–25; 13:18; Judg 14:4, 19; 15:14; 16:20; 1 Sam 2:6–10:25.
35 Cf. Deut 32:39–42.
36 Cf. Exod 34:10.
37 Cf. Gen 18:1–22; 21:17–19; 31:13–16; 2 Kgs 19:35.
38 Cf. Judg 11:29; 13:25; 14:6; 1 Sam 10:6, 10; 11:6; 19:20, 23; 1 Kgs 18:12.
39 Cf. Deut 4:12, 30, 36; 5:20, 22.
40 Cf. 1 Sam 2:27–36; 9:6–10; 1 Kgs 12:22; 13:4–32; 2 Kgs 1:12–13; 4:25, 27, 40; 5:8, 15; 6:15; 7:17–19; 8:2, 4, 7–8.
41 Cf. 1 Sam 3:21; 9:27; 15:10–11; 2 Sam 7:4; 12:9; 1 Kgs 6:11–13; 13:5–32; 17:2–16; 18:1; 2 Kgs 1:17; 3:12; 4:44; 7:16; 9:26, 36; 10:10, 17; 20:4, 16, 19.
42 Cf. Exod 8:15; 31:18; Deut 9:10.
43 Cf. Exod 15:6, 12, 17; Deut 7:19; 11:2; Judg 2:15; 1 Sam 5:6, 9, 11; 6:5, 9; 1 Kgs 8:15; 2 Kgs 3:15.
44 Cf. Deut 7:19; 11:2.
45 Cf. 1 Kgs 8:15.
46 Cf. Gen 32:30; Exod 33:11, 14–16, 20, 23; Lev 20:4–5; Num 14:14; Deut 5:4; 34:10.
47 Ezek 1:28; also cf. Exod 16:10; 24:16–17; 33:18, 22; 40:34–35; Num 14:21; Deut 5:21; 1 Sam 4:21–22; 6:5.
48 Cf. Gen 15:17; 19:24; Exod 13:21–22; 19:19; 24:17; 33:9; 34:5; 40:34–38; Num 9:15–22; 16:35; 28:2; Deut 4:24, 33, 36; 5:5, 19–24; Josh 13:14; 2 Kgs 1:12, 14; 2:11.
49 Cf. Exod 13:21–22; 40:34–38.
50 Cf. Gen 20:17.
51 Cf. Gen 21:16–20.
52 Cf. Gen 25:21.
53 Cf. Gen 32:10–13.
54 Cf. Num 12:13–15.
55 Cf. Josh 7:6–15.
56 Cf. Judg 6:36–40.
57 Cf. Judg 13:9.
58 Cf. Judg 15:18.
59 Cf. 1 Sam 1:10–20.
60 Cf. 1 Sam 7:5, 7–9; 8:4–9, 21–22; 12:16–25.
61 1 Sam 23:2–4, 9–23.
62 1 Kgs 8:22–54.
63 1 Kgs 17:20–22.
64 2 Kgs 6:17–18, 22.
65 2 Kgs 19:15–20; 20:2–6.

Suggestions for further study

Allbright, William Foxwell. *Yahweh and the Gods of Canaan: A Historical Analysis of Two Contrasting Faiths*. Garden City, NY: Doubleday and Co., 1968.

Baab, Otto J. *The Theology of the Old Testament*. New York and Nashville: Abingdon Press, 1949.

Carmy, Shalom and Shatz, David. "The Bible as a source for philosophical reflection," in Daniel H. Frank and Oliver Leaman (eds.), *History of Jewish Philosophy*. Vol. II of *Routledge History of World Philosophies*. London: Routledge, 1997, pp. 13–37.

Levinson, Jon D. *Creation and the Persistence of Evil: The Jewish Drama of Divine Omnipotence*. San Francisco: Harper and Row, 1988.

Lichtenstein, Murray H. "Biblical poetry" in Barry W. Holtz (ed.), *Back to the Sources: Reading the Classic Jewish Texts*. New York: Summit Books, 1984, pp. 105–27.

Samuelson, Norbert. *The First Seven Days: A Philosophical Commentary on the Creation of Genesis*. Atlanta: Scholars Press, 1993.

Sarna, Nahum M. and Potok, Chaim (eds.) *The JPS Torah Commentary*. Philadelphia: Jewish Publication Society of America, 1989–96. *Genesis* and *Exodus* commentary by Nahum M. Sarna, *Leviticus* commentary by Baruch A. Levine, *Numbers* commentary by Jacob Milgrom, and *Deuteronomy* commentary by Jeffrey H. Tigay.

Key questions

1. How does the prophet Ezekiel describe his vision of God?
2. How does the prophet Moses describe God?
3. What is unique about the biblical deity? How is Israel's deity both like and unlike other deities?
4. How is God like and unlike an earthly ruler? How is God like and unlike a human being?
5. What are the personality traits or characteristics of the biblical deity?
6. What actions does the biblical deity regularly perform in governing the world?
7. What is the covenant relationship between God and Israel and how does it change?
8. What is the attitude of the authors of the Hebrew Scriptures toward speech and vision?

CHAPTER 5

The biblical conception of Torah

Torah as covenant

When the deity (*El* or *Elohim*), whose personal name is the Lord,[1] brings the Israelites (the descendants of Abraham and Sarah, through Isaac and Rebekah, through Jacob/Israel and his wives Leah and Rachel, through his twelve sons) out of Egyptian slavery into the wilderness of Sinai, he forms them into a nation by means of a covenant (*brit*). What precisely a covenant is is something that scholars still debate. It is like a business contract between two people in that it stipulates terms of responsibility for both parties and the success of the relationship depends on the parties fulfilling their obligations. However, a covenant is qualitatively more serious than a mere contract. If either party of the contract decides that the relationship is no longer in their interest, they may break the contract. The contract itself may stipulate penalties for termination, but otherwise termination is permissible at any time. A covenant may not so easily be broken. Just how difficult it is to break is a matter of debate. In the centuries that followed the end of biblical Judaism, some people (notably Christians) were to argue that if one party (namely, Israel) failed to fulfill its obligations under the covenant, then the other party (namely, God) may sever that relationship and create a new covenant with another people. In contrast, other people (especially Jews) argued that a covenant is eternal and cannot be severed. In this sense, the Jews understand the national covenant between God and Israel to be a covenant very much in the way that the Roman Catholic Church (but not most Protestant churches) understand marriage to be a covenant, i.e., non-dissolvable.

There is textual support for both interpretations in the Hebrew Scriptures. Some passages in the writings of the prophets suggest that God previously had a covenant with the earlier occupants of the land of Canaan, and that God established his new covenant with the people of Israel and gave them the land formerly given to others, because the others failed to fulfill their obligations under his covenant. On this model, the covenant is rather like a lease on the land, and the Lord is more a deity of the land of Canaan than he is a deity of the people Israel. God rents his land to nations, and if they fail to keep the terms of their lease, he terminates the contract and signs a new lease with another people. That many of the pre-Exile prophets suggest that Israel will be totally destroyed for their disobedience supports this view that a covenant is like a contract. However, other texts, often by the same prophets, suggest that God will never totally destroy his people; he will always preserve at least a remnant with whom he will renew his commitment. On this view the covenant is forever and the deity, the Lord, is more a deity of the people Israel than he is a deity of the land.

You might think that because the deity of Israel is the God of the entire universe that the latter interpretation, that God's commitment to his covenant with Israel is eternal, is more coherent. Remember that our interest is not in what the purported different textual components of the Hebrew Scriptures say. Rather it is in what the edited whole itself says, and we have located the compilation of these texts some time after the end of the first Exile under the authorship of priests of the second Jewish state whose philosophic–religious orientation is deeply influenced by the pre-exilic and exilic prophets—especially the exilic prophet and fellow priest, Ezekiel. On this reading the account of the creation of the universe with which the Pentateuch begins sets the framework in which the covenant itself is to be understood. Let us then first look at the covenantal character of the creation story before we look in more detail at the covenant between God and the people Israel in the wilderness of Sinai.

Creation as covenant

If we read the words of the Hebrew Scriptures as literally as possible then something like the following narrative emerges of the origin of the universe. Independent of the order that God imposes on the stuff of the universe, the universe has a central spherical core of solid, earthly material that is surrounded by a ring of liquid, watery material, that is surrounded by a divine wind (*ruach Elohim*), which, in some interpretations, may be understood to be an outer ring that is composed of a gaseous material that is a combination of an airy stuff (the "wind") and a fiery stuff (the "divine").

This material of the universe is ruled by God who, as an ideal governor, merely says what he wills and his faithful servants execute instantly what he says. In brief, what he says/commands is the following: First, the universe as a whole shall be separated into two distinct regions—one of light (called "day") and one of darkness (called "night"). Second, the encompassing divine wind shall separate the waters into two regions. The globe of the earth is to be located within the region of water below the wind. This region is called "earth," and the region of wind and water above the earth is called "sky" (*shamayim*). What God did in his second act of creation is to command the divine wind in much the same way that he commanded the universe as a whole in his first act of creation, viz., to make a separation. The first separation is between day and night; the second separation is between earth and sky. These separations, precisely because they are "separations," are called by him "good," as if separate and good were functional synonyms.

In all, the deity of the Hebrew Scriptures creates seven separations through seven assertions or imperatives. The result is an earth sphere whose surface is occupied by vegetation-eating living things that are ruled by one earth-located living thing, the human; and a celestial ring of fiery living things called "stars" who are governed by two fiery things, the sun and the moon. God's final command is for there to be a Sabbath day, which is to be separate from all the other days with which God began his act of creation.

What purpose does this divine ordering serve? In the case of the sky the answer is clear. It exists primarily to house the stars whose motions determine when times for sacrifices occur. The distinction between day and night is to determine the time of the daily sacrifices; the distinction between the Sabbath day and the other days is to determine the time of the special weekly sacrifices; the periodic movement of the moon determines the special sacrifices of the month; the periodic movement of the sun divides the year into seasons which, in combination with the lunar-monthly cycle, determine the time of the special sacrifices for Pesach (or Passover, when the spring season initiates summer), Shavuot (or the feast of Weeks, fifty days after the beginning of Pesach), and Sukkot (or the feast of Booths, when the fall season initiates winter). In other words, the primary purpose for the existence of the heavens is to serve the sacrificial cult of the Temple in Jerusalem.

For what purpose then does the earth survive? Based on what we have said so far, the earth exists to house the vegetation that feeds the animals. The animals in turn are divided into distinct species defined by their fitness for sacrifice in the Temple. In other words, animals are understood within the philosophy of the Bible to be first and foremost food—for each other, for humans, and, most importantly, for God. On this interpretation at least, the meaning of the universe is determined by its function in service to God, and that function is defined by the way everything in the universe relates to the proper function of the Jerusalem Temple cult. For this purpose various separations are made. We have already noted in creation some of them—sky from earth, animals from vegetables and minerals, and humans from those animals who fly in the sky (birds), swim in the water (fish), creep upon the earth (insects), and walk upon the earth (animals).

As the account of the Book of Genesis continues, additional separations are made by God. The descendants of Noah are chosen for survival from the other descendants of the first human (Adam). God's first covenant (beyond the initial commandments at creation) is formed with them (Gen 9:1–17). It repeats the one commandment given at creation to all life forms, viz., to be fruitful and multiply, i.e., to procreate (vss. 1 and 7). In addition, however, humans—as distinct from all other animals—are to be feared by all other animals (vs. 2), shall kill their prey before eating them (vss. 3–4), and shall not commit acts of murder (vss. 5–6).[2]

God's second covenant is with Abraham (Gen 17:1–14), in which a single commandment is added to the obligations of all of humanity—the commandment to circumcise every male child. Who are his descendants? Abraham's children are Ishmael and Isaac. Ishmael's children are listed in Gen 25:13–15. Of the names given, only Nebaioth is recognizable as the ancestral name of the Nabateans. (Rabbinic tradition identifies Ishmael's succession through the Egyptians.) Isaac's children are Esau and Jacob. Esau's children are listed in Gen 36. They include Israel's neighbors in occupied Canaan. Of them the most notable in the text are the Edomites and the Amalekites. (Rabbinic tradition identifies Esau's succession through the Romans.)

In general, species are distinguished in biblical philosophy not by physical characteristics, as they are in the contemporary life sciences, but by the terms of their relationship to God. Non-life forms are related to God as a creator to a creation, but, because they are not alive, they have no commandments. Life forms in general have one—to procreate. In addition, human beings have another—to kill prey before eating them, and the descendants of Abraham have another—to circumcise male children. These commandments are cumulative. God's covenant with humans includes the covenant with animals; God's covenant with the descendants of Abraham includes the duties of humans; and God's covenant with the descendants of Israel includes the duties to Abraham's descendants. Those obligations are stipulated in the law that Moses brings down from Sinai. It is the statement of this law that is the central purpose of all of the Hebrew Scriptures, from creation through what will come to be known as redemption.

The statement of the law—three versions

There are within the Pentateuch three distinct statements of the laws of the covenant between God and Israel. The first occurs after the initial "theophany" at Sinai (Exod 19). Moses goes down from the mountain and tells the people what God said. His assertion begins with what subsequent traditions (Jewish and Christian) identify as the Ten Commandments (Exod 20:2–14). Whatever it is they say (and it is not entirely clear if we read the text literally, independent of rabbinic interpretation, just what it says), what follows is a more detailed stipulation than these commandments contain of just what are the covenant's provisions (in Exod Chs. 21–31).

The second occurs after the story of the "golden calf." While Moses is on the mountain receiving the first set of laws, the children of Israel get Aaron, the priest and Moses' brother, to collect the gold taken out of Egypt and fashion it into the shape of a calf, which they address with the words "This is your God (*Elohekha*), O Israel, who brought you up out of the land of Egypt" (Exod 32:4). Throughout the forty days that Moses is on the mountain with God, Israel brings it a variety of sacrifices and "the people sat down to eat and drink, and they arose (most) happy" (Exod 32:6). God wants to destroy the people and start over again with Moses (Exod 32:9–10), but Moses dissuades God from his plan (Exod 32:11–14). However, when Moses returns from the mountain and sees what Israel has been doing, he becomes angry and breaks the tablets on which the covenant is inscribed (Exod 32:19).[3] God punishes the people, the people repent, and Moses returns to receive a second stipulation of the covenant. This statement begins with a proclamation by God of his own nature (Exod 34:5–7, which subsequent rabbinic tradition will interpret to be God's "thirteen attributes") and a formal renewal of the covenant.[4] The statement of the laws themselves begins in Exod 35 with the laws of the Sabbath and continues through the end of the chapter (Ch. 40) on through the entirety of the Book of Leviticus.

The third statement of the legal conditions of the covenant is given in the Book of Deuteronomy (Chs. 4 through 26). The book begins with Israel preparing for its invasion of Canaan just east of the Jordan River across from Jericho. Moses repeats the terms of the covenant described in Exodus and Leviticus, warns the people that as obedience to the agreement will bring Israel great material reward and success in its collective, national life, failure to live up to the terms of the covenant will bring it great national and individual disaster. The end of Deuteronomy is a statement of the editors' view of divine providence (specifically Chs. 27–30) in the mouth of Moses. The book concludes (Chs. 31–34) with Moses' transfer of political authority to Joshua and the priesthood, and a description of Moses' death.

Scholars, both rabbinic and contemporary academic, debate just how far these three versions of the law are the same and are different. Some difference would not be critical. The first law need not be entirely the same as the second, since the golden calf experience could lead God to refine some of the initial statements. And the third need not be precisely the same as the second, since the second is Moses' immediate report of what God said on Sinai and the third is Moses' repetition in somewhat summary form of Moses' second reading of the law. It would not be surprising, staying strictly within a literal interpretation of the text, to say that the law changes. In fact, the narrative ends with a good example of how the law can change.

The dynamics of the law—the daughters of Zelophehad

When Moses was joined by his Midianite father-in-law, early in the exodus from Egypt, Jethro proposed that Moses should not himself sit in judgment over every dispute and every legal question that would arise between Israelites, their families, and their tribes. Rather, Jethro proposed, there should be appointed a chain of judges to sit in judgment and govern domains of thousands, then hundreds, then fifties, and then tens (Exod 18). This text in itself suggests that the Torah is not a fixed text. Rather, it is a set of guidelines intended to be determined creatively in concrete situations by "valiant men who fear God, honest men who hate (personal) profit" (Exod 18:21).

In support of this thesis that the law consisted initially of guidelines rather than strictly determined, concrete provisions, it should be remembered that God's intention at first was that he would communicate directly with the people to let them know in the concrete situation of times and places what it is he wants of them.[5] However, direct communication with God was more than the people themselves could tolerate. Hence, they implored Moses to go to God to get permission from him for the ruling prophet to represent them in their relations with God. The people themselves (and this is a theme that runs consistently through the narrative of the entire Hebrew Scriptures) wanted as little contact with God as possible. Moses successfully intercedes on the behalf of the people. It is understood that God will not directly address the people; rather he will appoint prophets through whom communication will occur. However, why need there be communication at all if the law itself is clear and determinate? Obviously it is not. New situations will constantly require new laws that are not overtly and clearly stipulated in even the detailed provisions of the Books of Leviticus and Numbers. Hence, there is a need for prophets to instantiate, in their direct communion with God, new specific legislation. This situation seems clearly to fit the case of the daughters of Zelophehad (Num 27:1–11).

The setting is at the end of the narrative of Israel's forty-year wandering in the wilderness of Sinai. Israel was at the borders of Canaan and was making plans for how the land was to be divided among the tribes and families after the conquest. The rule was that an equal portion would be given to every family and every family was to be ruled by the eldest surviving son of the previous family elder. Zelophehad had no surviving sons but had five daughters who were important enough, even though they are women, to be mentioned by name—Mahlah, Noah, Hoglah, Milcah, and Tirzah (Num 27:1). Zelophehad was the son of Hepher who was the son of Gilead who was the son of Machir who was the son of Manasseh who was the son of Joseph. He was a loyal follower of Moses throughout the wilderness experience, and therefore, so the daughters argued, his house deserved a share of the land even if there were no sons. Moses listened to their argument, "brought their cause before the Lord," and received a communication that "the words of the daughters of Zelophehad were correct" (Num 27:5–7), and awarded them as an inheritance the portion of the land that their father would have received if he had lived long enough to be part of the conquest. In other words, faced with a new situation, the judge/prophet communicates directly with the deity and, under his guidance, innovates a new law.

The innovation does not end here. It could be said that this case is nothing more than an exception to the general law; it neither negates it nor modifies it. However, shortly after Moses had given the daughters of Zelophehad what they wanted, the male leaders of the family of Gilead appeared before Moses to appeal against his decision (Num Ch. 36). What would happen, they argued, if the daughters were to marry men from a different tribe? Their inheritance, which was now in the tribe of Manasseh, would pass on through their husbands to a different tribe, so that the tribe of Manasseh would be robbed of its proper tribal inheritance. This is clearly a consequence of Moses' decision that neither Moses nor (presumably) God had considered. Again, Moses agreed with the petitioners and rendered a new ruling that modifies what he had ruled for the daughters. In effect, he said that if daughters inherit land from their fathers because the fathers have no male descendants, the daughters are entitled to the land as long as they do not marry or, if they marry, they marry members of their own tribe. Otherwise the land goes to the tribe. It is with this radical reinterpretation of the law that the narrative of the Book of Leviticus ends. Hence the Scriptures themselves tell us that, within a single generation of its reception, the law had to be amended despite the fact that it was received by a prophet, the like of whom "has not risen ... in Israel" for he was a man "whom the Lord knew face to face" (Deut 34:10).

Notes

1   I.e., YHVH. Rabbinic tradition requires that these words, whose proper pronunciation is God's proper name, should not be written, let along spoken. They are written for use exclusively in prayer and, once written, the paper on which they are written cannot be destroyed, for its destruction would constitute a profanation of God's name. When they are written the speaker says instead *Adonai*, which literally mean, "my lord" as in "lord and master." Even *Adonai* has become so intimately associated with God's proper name that traditional Jews in contexts other than prayer will say *ado-shem* instead which is formally meaningless. (It combines *ado* from *Adonai* with the Hebrew word for name [*shem*].) Out of respect to this tradition, every place our texts say the Tetragrammaton, we will write "the Lord."

2   Rabbinic Judaism interprets this passage to be more about social and political justice than about a seemingly slight distinction between humans and other members of the animal species. According to rabbinic interpretation, these seven verses will become seven commandments that set the standard by which the moral virtue of all humanity is to be judged. On this interpretation God forms a covenant with humanity in general in which humanity is obligated (1)

to establish just courts, (2) not to blaspheme, (3) not to practice idolatry, (4) not to commit incest, (5) not to commit murder, (6) not to steal, and (7) not to eat an animal that is still alive. On my interpretation of the literal meaning of the biblical text, the only one of these commandments that is a general human obligation is the seventh. Otherwise humans are morally no different from any other animals, viz., judged exclusively by their success in reproducing their kind.

3   What precisely makes the construction and worship of the golden calf sinful is not as clear as it would seem at first glance.

4   I believe that Exod 34 constitutes a preamble to the statement of the law, and that the two statements of the so-called "Ten Commandments," viz., Exod 20:1–14 and Deut 5:6–18, are also to be understood as preambles to the constitution rather than as part of the constitution itself.

5   Readers should be aware that the interpretation of the biblical text I am now presenting is controversial. It is based on my own reading of Exod 19. God told Moses to tell the people that "if you now listen to my voice and keep my covenant, then you will be for me more precious than all (other) people ... " (vs. 5) and the people responded "everything that YHVH says we will do" and Moses delivered the response of the people to God (vs. 8). God's first speech-act is the Ten Commandments. The experience terrified the people who said to Moses, "You speak for us and we will obey, but do not let God speak (directly) to us lest we die" (Exod 20:16). There are other verses in this passage that qualify this seemingly clear reading (e.g., Exod 19:23–25), but it would be inappropriate in this context to discuss these texts in detail.

Suggestions for further study

Alter, Robert. *The Art of Biblical Narrative*. New York: Basic Books, 1981.

Barr, James. *The Semantics of Biblical Language*. New York: Oxford University Press, 1961.

Fishbane, Michael. *Text and Texture: Close Readings of Selected Biblical Texts*. New York: Schocken, 1979.

Greenstein, Edward L. "Biblical law," in Barry W. Holtz (ed.), *Back to the Sources: Reading the Classic Jewish Texts*. New York: Summit Books, 1984, pp. 83–103.

Halbertal, Moshe and Margalit, Avishai. *Idolatry*. English translation by Naomi Goldblum. Cambridge, MA, and London: Harvard University Press, 1992.

Hertz, Joseph H. *The Pentateuch and Haftorah*. London: Soncino Press, 1969.

Kramer, Samuel Noah (ed.). *Mythologies of the Ancient World*. Garden City, NY: Doubleday and Co., 1961.

Levinson, Jon D. *Sinai and Zion: An Entry into the Jewish Bible*. San Francisco: Harper and Row, 1987.

Key questions

1. What is a "covenant"? How is it different from a "contract"? What are some consequences of this distinction?
2. How according to the Hebrew Scriptures did God create the universe? Why did he create it? How does God "act"? How many actions are involved? Why are they "good"?
3. How many special covenants does God form? What are their provisions?
4. What are the three statements of the laws that define the covenant between God and Israel?
5. Who are the daughters of Zelophehad? What is their complaint to Moses? How may this story influence the way we read the Torah's own account of the Torah?
6. Give two examples of Moses successfully interceding with God on behalf of the Israelites?
7. According to the Torah, how was the institution of prophecy established?

CHAPTER 6

The conception of Israel as the Chosen People

From the perspective of modern history, no Jewish doctrine is more controversial than the concept of the chosen people. This is not yet the time to enter into that discussion other than to say that no subsequent rabbinic doctrine is more rooted in the literal meaning of the Hebrew Scriptures than is this one. The term "chosenness" itself does not appear in the Bible, but it is quite clear that in some sense the nation is chosen, which is indicated by the four times that God calls it his "precious thing" (*segulah*).[1] The question remains, however, just what do the Hebrew Scriptures mean, especially the Pentateuch, by so characterizing the nation. The answer is tied to the conception of Torah as covenant discussed in the previous chapter.

Chosenness as covenant and promise

The covenant of Noah

Ten generations after God created the universe[2] he destroyed humanity with a flood and began history all over again with the descendants of Noah. Noah is the first person whom God chooses. God destroyed humanity because it was "wicked" (*ra'*), and he singled out Noah to be saved. Noah "found favor in the eyes of God" (Gen 6:8), because, in comparison to the other people of his generation, he was "perfectly righteous" (Gen 6:9). However, this is only by comparison.[3]

God brought on the flood because humanity's evil had corrupted God's created earth, which caused God to "repent" creating humanity (Gen 6:7). However, after the flood God again repented what he had done. He said to himself,

> I will not ever again curse the ground because of the human, because the inclination (*yetser*) of the human heart is evil (*ra'*) from youth, so I will never again smite all (other) life as I have done. Throughout all the days of the earth seedtime and harvest, cold and heat, summer and winter, and day and night shall not cease (*yishbotu*, whose root is the same as *shabbat*). (Gen 8:21)

God decided that there was no point in ever destroying the earth again on account of the evil deeds of humanity, because to do evil seems to be inherent in human nature, even in the nature of his chosen one, Noah. God realized that Noah's descendants would be no better than Noah's ancestors. God promised Noah that he would never repeat the flood, but he does not make this promise for Noah's sake; rather, he does it for the sake of his obedient servant, the earth who suffered through no fault of its own.[4]

It is in this context that God made a covenant with Noah (Gen 9:1–17). God blessed Noah and his sons and commanded them (1) to be fruitful, multiply, and fill the earth (like all the other animals on the earth), and (2) to eat anything they pleased, but only after the blood of the animal has been removed. The reason the text gives for this limitation is that the blood of the animal is its life, and (by implication) the life belongs to God. Hence, Noah and his descendants (3) were forbidden to "shed the blood of" (i.e., murder) any other human being. Here the reason given is, alluding back to Gen 1:27, that the human was made "in the image of God." God then promised never again to bring a flood, and he placed the rainbow in the sky to appear whenever God brings rain, as a "token" (*ot*) of the covenant as well as a reminder of his promise never again to flood the entire earth.

The significant features of this story for our purpose are that someone and his descendants are chosen by God for God's own reasons that need not relate to the merit of the person and persons chosen; that the terms of the covenant are in effect as long as there continues to be a universe; that the covenant carries with it obligations to obey specified commandments from God; and that obedience and disobedience to those obligations carry with them rewards and punishments even though the perpetuation of the covenant is unconditional.

The covenant of Abraham

The next covenant that God forms with a human descendant of Noah is with Abraham. After bringing him and his family from their home in Ur of the Chaldees to live as "strangers" (Gen 15:13), i.e., foreigners or alien residents, in the territory of the Canaanites, God makes a covenant with him in which no reasons and no precepts are stated. All that is said about it is that after four hundred years (Gen 15:13) or four generations (Gen 15:16), Abraham's descendants will return to take possession of this land as their own.[5]

After the birth of Ishmael, when Abraham was 99 years old, the Lord again appeared to him and set the descendant's obligations under the covenant (Gen 17). God promised to make Abraham the father of a multitude of nations (vs. 2), that the covenant between God and Abraham's descendants would be an "everlasting covenant" (*brit 'olam*) (vs. 7), and that his descendants will establish a nation of their own in Canaan (vs. 8). However, only one distinct duty is stipulated (vss. 11–14)—circumcision of every male child[6] at the age of eight days. The punishment for failure to fulfill this commandment was that the "soul" (i.e., life) of every uncircumcised boy "shall be cut off from his people" because he had violated the covenant (vs. 14). However, the covenant is nullified only with the disobedient individual, and not with the people collectively.[7]

The covenant of Moses

The term "covenant" is used several more times in Genesis to describe compacts between Isaac or Jacob with neighboring nations, but the term "covenant" does not occur again with reference to God until the time of the giving of the Torah to Israel through Moses at Sinai. We have already discussed in the previous chapter the general nature of this covenant. In return for obedience God will give the land of the Canaanites to the people of Israel and the nation will prosper as long as Israel fulfills its obligation to obey God's will for the land. Israel no more deserves this merit from God than Noah and/or Abraham and/or Isaac and/or Jacob. In fact, we the readers know the end of the story. From the beginning God loves the people and wants to be with them as a lover wants to be with his beloved, but God's love is repulsive to the nation, which continually struggles to distance itself as much as possible from God.

What the narrative explains is not why God loves Israel, but why Israel is punished by God and why that punishment does not end the relationship. Israel is to be destroyed because it fails to fulfill its obligations under its covenant with God, but God, because of his great love for it, will always preserve a remnant out of which will grow a new opportunity for fidelity. For no apparent reason, no matter what Israel does, God continues to think of this people as something precious.

Chosenness as preciousness

As the children of Israel prepared for the coming theophany at Mount Sinai, God told Moses to tell the people the following:

> If you will surely obey/listen to my voice and keep my covenant, you will be for me a precious thing over and above all the (other) peoples, because all of the earth belongs to me. (Exod 19:5)

When Moses repeated this phrase to the next generation after the theophany, its use is slightly different. He told Israel that after it conquered the land it should totally destroy everything connected with its former inhabitants, the people and their culture, especially every vestige of their ways of worship, and Israel should not "cut a covenant with them and not show them (any) mercy" (Deut 7:2). There is a clear suggestion in the text that Israel is being commanded to do something horrible, because the text goes to great length (given the compactness of biblical statements) to justify the commandment. Israel is told to so act

> because you belong to the Lord your God as a holy (*kadosh*) people; the Lord your God chose you to be his precious people (*'am segulah*) over all the peoples who are upon the surface of the earth. (Deut 7:6)

God repeated these same words again later, in Deut 14:2, when he ordered Israel in more detail not to follow any of the ritual or cultural forms of the life led by the to-be-displaced inhabitants of the land. Then, at the conclusion of this oration to the people, Moses announced that God said that the people are obligated to obey everything that God says because the Lord ordered Israel to become his "precious people" (Deut 26:18). The reward for this obedience would be that Israel would be exalted above all the other nations of the earth in praise, reputation, and glory (Deut 26:19). However, what remains unsaid, at least in this speech, are the dire consequences of the failure to do what God says. These are given in Moses' next (and final) speech to the people where he states the rewards for obedience in just fourteen verses of general blessings (Deut 28:1–14), but elaborates in considerable detail the punishments for disobedience (Deut 28:15–68).

Why are the rewards so brief and vague while the punishments are so elaborate and specific? An obvious answer is that this speech was written by people who had in fact experienced first-hand what it was like to have their nation defeated and destroyed in warfare. Given this setting for the biblical narrative, the concept of Israel as God's chosen, as a "precious people" (*'am segulah*), is given not so much to justify a hoped-for triumphalism on Israel's part but to come to terms with the nation's humiliation at the hand of the Assyrians and the Babylonians. It was intended to explain collective subjugation and not nationalist imperialism. If anyone is triumphant in this story, it can only be God; it certainly is not Israel.

It is in this context that we should read Ps 135:4. This final use of the expression "precious" with reference to Israel is in a poem about the exclusive praiseworthiness of God. The psalm concludes with the words

> O house of Israel/Aaron/Levi, bless the Lord; O those who fear the Lord praise the Lord. Blessed is the Lord from Zion, who dwells in Jerusalem. Praise *Yah*. (Ps 135:19–21)

Israel is here represented by its priesthood. Its sole obligation is to perform the rituals in the Jerusalem Temple that praise God. There is no praise due to Israel other than its unique obligation to praise God daily. Moreover, the praise hides a hope for the end of days. God is certainly praised here for who he is and what he has done already. Yet the psalm also expresses in a cohortative voice a hope for the future, for an end of history, when Israel will finally live up to God's expectations for it and become a holy nation of priests who worship and serve its one God of the universe.

Notes

1   In Exod 19:5, and Deut 7:6; 14:2; 26:18. Also see Ps 135:4.
2   Gen 5 lists the generations of humanity from Adam to Noah as Adam, Seth, Enosh, Kenan, Mahalalel, Jared, Enoch, Methuselah, Lamech, and Noah.
3   The fact that Noah could get drunk in the presence of his children suggests that he is far from perfect (cf. Gen 9).
4   The suggestion seems to be that even God, through error, can act unjustly.
5   The promise given here, in Gen 15, is the textual basis for those contemporary Jews who claim a divine right for Jewish possession of all of the land "from the river of Egypt to the River Euphrates" (vs. 18), which includes the territories of "the Kenite, the Kenizzite, the Kadmonite, the Hittite, the Perizzite, the Rephaim, the Amorite, the Canaanite, the Girgashite, and the

Jebusite" (vvs. 19–21). The text is used this way by a very small minority of contemporary Jews in the modern state of Israel. Most secular Jews, who are at present the majority, reject the legitimacy of this kind of use of biblical texts, and most religious Jews interpret this statement to be a prophecy about the messianic age. At no time in Israel's history, including the time of King David, were the territories under Israelite sovereignty so expansive.

6   Included here is every male "that is born in your house or purchased with money" (vs. 13).

7   Cf. Exod 4:24–26. Moses, on the way from Sinai to Egypt, with his Midianite wife Zipporah and their newly born son Gershom, is met by God who seeks to kill "him." Zipporah circumcises her son and casts the foreskin at "his" feet. She then says the words, "For you are a bridegroom of blood for me" and then adds "a bridegroom of blood for the circumcision." No one is sure just what this three-sentence story means. Who is being circumcised, Moses or his son? If it is the son, presumably Moses had reasons for this failure that we are not told. Perhaps, being raised as an Egyptian, he did not know about the obligation. Perhaps, because his wife was a Midianite, he thought his son was also a Midianite, not an Israelite, and therefore not subject to circumcision. In any case, as God promised Abraham, failure to practice circumcision carries with it a death penalty. It is not clear, however, just who is supposed to die— the father (Moses) who failed to do the circumcision, or the son (Gershom) who was not circumcised.

Suggestions for further study

Novak, David. *The Election of Israel: The Idea of the Chosen People*. Cambridge: Cambridge University Press, 1995.

Key questions

1. Why does God choose certain people and not others? Your answer should reflect what the words of the Hebrew Scriptures say about Noah, Abraham, and Moses.
2. What are the obligations of both God and humanity under the Noahite covenant? Under the covenant with Abraham? Under the Torah?
3. Is the God of the Hebrew Scriptures perfect? Your answer should reflect what the texts say about God repenting.
4. Why will God never again destroy humanity with a flood? What does this tell us about human nature? About divine nature?
5. What are the consequences of failure to fulfill God's obligations under the terms of any of his covenants?

The categories of the Mosaic covenant

Exodus 21–30, 36–38

Civil Legislation (Exod 21–23)

Personal injury (Exod 21:1–32)
  Rights of Hebrew servants (Exod 21:2–11)
  Murder (Exod 21:12–14)
  Kidnapping (Exod 21:15–17)
  Personal injuries (Exod 21:18–32)
Property damages (Exod 21:33–22:14)
  Caused by neglect (Exod 21:33–36)
  Caused by accident (Exod 22:4–5)
  Theft (Exod 21:37–22:3)
  Through safe keeping (Exod 22:6–14)
Political offenses (Exod 22:15–23:9)
  Seduction (Exod 22:15–16)
  Witchcraft (Exod 22:17)
  Sodomy (Exod 22:18)
  Polytheism (Exod 22:19)
  Oppression of the weak (Exod 22:20–23)
  Loans and pledges (Exod 22:24–26)
  Respect for God and rulers (Exod 22:27)
     Offering first fruits (Exod 22:28–29)
     Forbidden meat (Exod 22:30)
  Truth in justice (Exod 23:1–3)
  Love of enemy (Exod 23:4–5)
  Impartiality in justice (Exod 23:6–9)
Liturgical offenses (Exod 23:10–18)
  Sabbath day and Sabbatical year (Exod 23:10–12)
  Pilgrim Festivals (Exod 23:14–18)

The Sanctuary (Exod 25–27, 36–38)

Sanctuary's utensils and purpose (Exod 25:1–9)
Construction of (Exod 25:10–27:21; 36–38)
  Ark (Exod 25:10–16; 37:1–9)
  Mercy-seat and cherubim (Exod 25:17–22)
  Table (Exod 25:23–29; 37:10–16)
  Candlestick (Exod 25:31–39; 37:17–24)
  Curtains (Exod 26:1–6; 36:8–19)

Tent coverings (Exod 26:7–14)
Boards (Exod 26:15–30; 36:20–34)
Veil (Exod 26:31–33; 36:35–38)
Altar (Exod 27:1–8; 38:1–8)
Court (Exod 27:9–19; 38:9–20)
Oil for lamp (Exod 27:20–21)

The Priests (Exod 28–29; 38–39)

Vestments (Exod 28)
Ephod (Exod 28:6–12; 39:2–7)
Breastplate (Exod 28:13–30; 39:8–21)
Robe (Exod 28:31–35; 39:22–26)
Other garments (Exod 28:36–43; 39:27–31)
Consecration and daily sacrifices (Exod 29)
Altar of shekel, laver, anointing oil, and incense (Exod 30:1–38; 37:25–27)

The Sabbath (Exod 31:13–17)

Book of Leviticus

Ritual Laws (Lev 1–10, 21–22, 24)

The Sanctuary's utensils (Lev 24)
Sacrifices (Lev 1–7, 22)
Burnt offerings of herd, flock, and fowl (Lev 1)
Meal offerings of fine and cooked flour, leaven, and first fruits (Lev 2)
Peace offerings of herd and flock (Lev 3)
Sin offerings by high priest, community, ruler, citizens, and others (Lev 4–5:13)
Guilt offerings (Lev 5:14–26)
Directions for priests sacrificing the different kinds of sacrifices (Lev 6–7, 21–22)
Regulations concerning the inauguration of the sanctuary rituals (Lev 8–10)

Liturgical Laws (Lev 16, 23, 25)

The Holy Days (Lev 16, 23)
Feast of Passover (Lev 23:5–14)
Feast of Weeks (Lev 23:15–21)
Rosh Hashanah (Lev 23:24–25)
Day of Atonement (Lev 16; Lev 23:26–32)
Feast of Tabernacles (Lev 23:33–43)
Sabbatical year and the year of Jubilee (Lev 25)

Laws of Purity (Lev 11–18)

Dietary laws (Lev 11)
Purification after childbirth (Lev 12)
Laws of leprosy (Lev 13–14)
Laws of bodily issues (Lev 15)
Laws of animal slaughter (Lev 17)
Sexual laws: marriage and unchastity (Lev 18)

Holiness Laws (Lev 19–20)

Ritual (Lev 19:5–8)
Moral (Lev 19:9–18)
  Social justice (Lev 19:9–10)
  Interpersonal relations (Lev 19:11–16)
  Love of neighbor (Lev 19:17–18)
Forbidden marriages, Molech worship, and necromancy (Lev 20)

Divine Reward and Punishment, Human Repentance, and Redemption (Lev 22, 26)

Deuteronomy 14–25

Laws of Holiness (Deut 14–15)

Dietary laws (Deut 14:3–20)
Tithes (Deut 14:22–29)
Sabbatical year (Deut 15:1–11)

Festivals (of Passover, of Weeks, of Booths) (Deut 16)

Institutions of Government (Deut 16:18–21:9)

Judges and supreme court, king, priests and Levites, and prophets (Deut 16–18)
Criminal law and laws of warfare (Deut 19–21:9)

Family Laws (Deut 21–25)

Marriage to a captive (Deut 21:10–14)
Right of first-born (Deut 21:15–17)
Disobedient son (Deut 21:18–21)

Miscellaneous Laws (Deut 22–25)

CHAPTER 7

The biblical view of God

We began this book with the Hebrew Scriptures because the interpretation of its words becomes the central focus of all subsequent developments in Jewish philosophy. The very topics that will concern Jewish philosophers all come out of these textual interpretations. When we introduced the study of the Scriptures themselves we said that they are not primarily philosophical, just as they are not primarily Jewish, because what develops through the ages out of these textual discussions is a Jewish people and a Judaism significantly different from the people, society, culture, and religion of the Bible. The same is true of the philosophy. What we will see emerge out of reflections on these texts as Jewish philosophy is significantly different from the philosophy of the Hebrew Scriptures. Nevertheless, the Hebrew Scriptures do contain at least one philosophy, and that is what we have summarized in the previous chapters. However, now, at the conclusion of this section, I am prepared to make an even stronger claim—the Hebrew Scriptures do not just contain philosophical claims; they are a philosophical text.

The Hebrew Scriptures as philosophy

This claim is highly controversial. Before the modern period rabbinic Jews believed that these words contained the answers to all questions, but they did not call it "philosophy." This was because they used this term referentially in a far more restricted way than I am using it here—for all speculative writings that come out of a specific canon of ancient texts other than the Hebrew Scriptures, viz., the works attributed primarily to Plato and Aristotle.[1]

Many Jewish thinkers in the late nineteenth century extended the term "philosophy" to the Hebrew Scriptures as well as to Judaism itself, precisely because both claim to provide answers to all questions about being human in the universe. However, since (at the latest) the middle of the twentieth century, this way of viewing the Scriptures and Judaism has been unpopular, primarily because it creates the false impression that both Judaism and the Scriptures are about beliefs to the exclusion of other factors in life, especially the ways that human beings (particularly Jews) ought to behave in relations with each other and with God. In contrast, I want to claim that a rich philosophy contains judgments not only about what one ought to believe but also about how one ought to behave, and that the more specific the philosophy is in spelling out these oughts, the richer the philosophy is. In this respect the Hebrew Scriptures do constitute a reasonably rich philosophy.

The data for this claim that the Hebrew Scriptures are a philosophy has been presented in the previous chapters. In this concluding chapter of the section I simply want to put together the general overview of that philosophy in a more coherent way. The "way" is to suggest that the Scriptures are primarily a philosophy of history that orders within it all conceptual subjects. In this respect the philosophy of the Hebrew Scriptures is very much like the philosophy of Hegel, but it is not Hegel's philosophy. The differences, of course, are obvious. Georg Wilhelm Freidrich Hegel lived in Germanic lands in the late eighteenth and early nineteenth centuries (1770–1831 CE) in Christian Europe, whereas our author(s)/editor(s) of the Hebrew Scriptures lived more than 2200 years earlier in a very different Mediterranean culture. However, Hegel's philosophy, much like Hebrew philosophy,[2] also ordered general conceptions about the universe and everything in it into a historical framework whose implicit central focus was the newly emergent (in this case German) state.[3]

The critical difference between Hegelian and Hebrew philosophy, beyond their different temporal and spatial contexts, is the way they organize their topics within history. This "way," in Hegel's case, is called a "dialectic." Hegel's dialectic, as we will see when we turn to modern Jewish philosophy (in Chapters 24 through 26), is a statement of the logic by which God thinks, and in thinking does what he does in his created world. It is a movement of thought from an affirmation (thesis) to a contrary affirmation formulated by thinking about the inadequacy of the first affirmation (antithesis), back to the original on account of the recognized inadequacies of the contrary affirmation, then back again over and over again until a new affirmation is formed (a synthesis) that solves the problem of how to combine in a coherent way what is thought to be good and bad about the earlier affirmation and its contrary. The new affirmation (the synthesis) then functions as a thesis in combination with an antithesis that leads to a new synthesis in a process that repeats itself over and over again.[4]

The Hebrew Scriptures also exhibit a dialectic, but it is different from Hegel's.

Chiasm and introversion

"Chiasm" is a literary structure in which two key things (be they terms and/or events and/or concepts), call them "A" and "B," are repeated with some variation (call the variant of A "A'" and the variant of B "B'") in the form ABB'A'. When more than two key things are involved, the structure is called "introversion." For example, if there are three things, the form would be ABCC'B'A' or ABCB'A'.

The chiasm/introversion structure is clearly one way that we order life. All living things are born, reach physical and/or mental maturity, decline from that maturity, and die. In the case of those animals, including the human, who are fortunate enough to live full, natural lives, the death parallels the birth, for the elderly, like infants, are largely dependent on others (often family), cannot walk unaided, and have difficulties with most bodily and mental functions. From this perspective a life is to be valued not by what it is at the end,[5] but by what it was in the middle, which is the apex (maximum point) of the curve of mental and/or physical development.

This inversion structure can be observed at almost every level of the biblical narrative, from small but independent units to the narrative as a whole at the most general level. The critical point is the middle element ("C" in our ABC example). Now, what "the middle" is depends on what we consider the total narrative to be, and there are several ways to answer this question, since each book of the Bible has a structure of its own which becomes altered when we make that book a part of a larger collection, which changes again when the collection is included into a larger collection. The largest collection is the Hebrew Scriptures themselves, which are codified sometime during the period of Hellenistic (Greek or Roman) occupation of Judea. However, our focus in this section has been primarily on the Pentateuch, which traditional rabbis believe was composed by God and presented to Moses on Mount Sinai, and modern academic Bible scholars believe was compiled from earlier sources some time near the beginning of the second Jewish state when Ezra was the High Priest.

If we focus on the Torah proper and add to it the Book of Joshua, then the structure in Figure 1 emerges. The central event is the theophany at

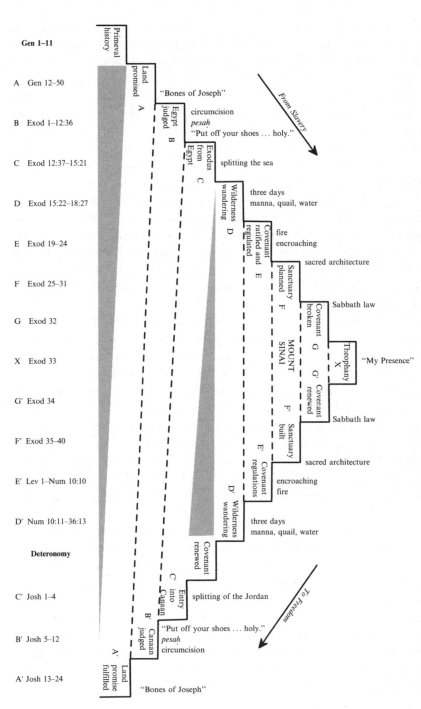

The theological-literary structure of the Hexateuch. From *The JPS Torah Commentary: Numbers*. Copyright © 1990 by the Jewish Publication Society. Used by permission.

Gen 1–11

A   Gen 12–50

B   Exod 1–12:36

C   Exod 12:37–15:21

D   Exod 15:22–18:27

E   Exod 19–24

F   Exod 25–31

G   Exod 32

X   Exod 33

G'   Exod 34

F'   Exod 35–40

E'   Lev 1–Num 10:10

D'   Num 10:11–36:13

Deteronomy

C'   Josh 1–4

B'   Josh 5–12

A'   Josh 13–24

Sinai (Exod 33) when God reveals his "presence" to Moses, in a story that begins with the creation of the world (Gen 1), on through the death and embalming of Joseph (Gen 12–50) in Egypt, and ends with the reburial of his bones in the promised land (Josh 13–24) and the creation of the first state of Israel. As such the biblical narrative is a celebration of the creation of the Jewish state. The problem, of course, with this application of the structure is that it includes either too much or too little. The Torah of Moses consists of five books and not six. Joshua is not included. Hence, the conclusion must be the death of Moses and not the creation of the Jewish state. In this sense, as Genesis, which ends with the patriarchs, is Hebrew history prior to Israel becoming a people (that story begins with the birth of Moses and concludes with the death of Moses), so the Pentateuch is an Israelite history prior to Israel becoming a nation situated in space as well as in time. The temporal–spatial story of the nation, beyond its primeval origins, begins with the conquest by Joshua and ends with the destruction of the Jewish state in its two forms in the Books of Kings and Chronicles.

Whichever choice we make, be it to see the story that begins with the creation of the world to end either with the creation of the state at the death of Moses or to end with the termination of the state in the Babylonian Exile, the philosophy is the same. There is no significant change (not, at least, at this general level) in what the Hebrew Scriptures say about the origin (cosmogony) and composition (cosmology) of the universe, how physical (physics) and animal (biology) nature is governed, how humans ought to live (ethics), how a good society should be structured (political science), what are the means to gain and the limitations of human knowledge (epistemology), and (most importantly) how God relates to the world in general and to human beings in particular (theology).

The origin of the universe is an event set in the prehistory of the world, for the measurement of time only begins with the dating[6] of the descendants of Noah after the division of humanity into distinct nations.[7] The universe is divided into distinct regions of light (day) and dark (night); land, water, and sky. The sky separates the water into two regions. The space of the earth and the lower waters is occupied by vegetation and life forms that eat that vegetation—animals, insects, and birds on the surface of the earth and fish in the sea. These living things are subdivided into a variety of kinds. Of the human kind, there is a further subdivision into nations, and within the nation there are further subdivisions. In general, people are noted by political office (monarch, elder, priest, and judge) and by qualification for military service. There is some evidence of the recognition of individuals as individuals, but for the most part there is no recognition of meaningful independent existence below the level of the family. Animals are, on the other hand, known as individuals, but their individuality is a function of their appropriateness as food for sacrifice. Fish must have fins and scales; land animals must have cleft hoofs and chew the cud.

The universe is run by the will of God expressed in speech. God creates the universe and its inhabitants and gives to each kind laws by which to govern and be governed. With the exception of the prophets, all people are expected to obey their authorities independent of whether or not the authorities are correct. If they are not, then they must answer to the people who are their authorities, but that has nothing to do with the individual's uncompromised obligation to obedience. Every individual is subject to the authority of his/her elder, who is answerable to the priest and king, who are answerable to God.

It is clear that one of the things that makes human beings different from all other kinds that God created is the ability to be disobedient. It seems that only human beings are sufficiently ignorant to do so, "ignorant" because disobedience always works against the self-interest of the rebel. Still, humans are rebellious, presumably by nature. Yet they seem to be loved by God as much as God is disdained by them. It is a flaw in creation out of which comes much of the drama of the biblical narrative. The repair of that flaw is the ultimate, cosmic hope for a final "day of the Lord" when all people in peace and harmony will worship God at his Temple mount in Jerusalem.

The central event in the history of both Israel and the world is the theophany at Sinai. The universe exists to support the priestly caste of the people of Israel in the regular, daily performance of the sacrifices in the Temple at Jerusalem. Nature exists to produce the living things (animal and vegetable) for sacrifice and the nation Israel exists to support those sacrifices and the highest level of quality control. Israel is a nation who in family units spends three times a day (and four times on the Sabbath) eating barbecues together with its deity in the open air at the top of the universe on Mount Zion in Jerusalem in the state of Israel on the surface of the earth, surrounded by a sea of nations on the earth and stars in the sky.

The convex curve of this history has two high points. The first (and highest) is the theophany at Sinai. The second is the reign of Solomon, built on the political success of David, when the nation as a whole worships its deity in the first Temple at Jerusalem. The high moment on Sinai declines into the sin of the golden calf (Exod 32), and the high moment of the single nation united in worship declines into the civil war between Israel and Judah. Are more high moments to come? The answer to that question, at least for the Hebrew philosophers, rests on the books of the prophets. Some of them (e.g., Jeremiah, parts of Isaiah, and early minor prophets like Amos) speak of the end of the nation without any hope of renewal, but others (e.g., Ezekiel, parts of Isaiah, and late minor prophets like Haggai) are prophets of return. Still, you can argue, the return of which they speak is the second Jewish state, and in that case their predictions were true. However, what about a third state? Given that the final compilation of the Hebrew Scriptures occurred during the period of Greek and Roman occupation, did the editors intend the prophecies of a renewal into a second Jewish state to apply to a third Jewish state, independent from foreign rule? The answer is undoubtedly yes, and that failed national hope is our key to the rise of rabbinic Judaism and the transformation of Jewish philosophy.

Notes

1 By this definition, a significant number of works in contemporary Anglo-American philosophy would also not be called philosophy.

2 I will use the expression "Hebrew philosophy" as a shorthand for the philosophy of the Hebrew Scriptures.

3 The separate German states (*Länder*) came together in a confederation of states in 1815. In 1870, the land of Prussia emerged as the dominant state in the confederation and its ruler became the emperor of all the German states except for Austria. The German lands became, in effect, two nation states—a northern Germany simply called "Germany" and a southern Germany called "Austria." I state the history in this way precisely to draw attention to the parallelism between the emergence of the nation Israel and the emergence of the nation Germany. That similarity has, I believe, an important role to play in understanding modern Jewish intellectual history, especially in terms of the German hostility to the Jewish conception of the chosen people.

4 Hegel scholars debate whether or not a final synthesis has or can be reached.

5 Which is what the case would be if we apply Hegel's dialectic in this way. (This is one, but only one, way that Hegel's philosophy can be seen to be Christian. It certainly is not Jewish.)

6 I.e., assigning numerical values to time by listing numbers of years from birth to death of the individuals listed.

7 I.e., following the story of the tower of Babel (Gen 11:1–9).

Suggestions for further study

Milgrom, Jacob. *The JPS Torah Commentary: Numbers*. Philadelphia: Jewish
Publication Society of America, 1990.

Key questions

1. What does it mean to claim that the Hebrew Scriptures are a philosophical text? Why is this claim controversial?
2. What is the philosophy of history of the Hebrew Scriptures? What are chiasm and introversion? How do these literary structures function in the historical narrative of the Hebrew Scriptures?
3. Compare and contrast Hebrew philosophy with the philosophy of Hegel.
4. From an introversive perspective on life, how is the value of a life to be judged?
5. In the historical narrative of the Hebrew Scriptures, how does the story begin and end? What are two different ways to answer this question?
6. State briefly how Hebrew philosophy answers the following philosophical questions:
   What are the origin and composition of the universe?
   What is the nature of the laws that govern nature and life?
   How it is possible to know and what are the limits on knowledge?
   Who and what is God?
   Who and what is the human being?
   How do and ought humans relate to each other and to God?
   How are fish, animals, and human beings classified?
   What is the central event of history? What are history's two high points? What is the hope for the end of history?
7. How do the Hebrew Scriptures value individualism and judge disobedience to authority? Are there any exceptions to these generalizations?

Early Rabbinic Literature

CHAPTER 8

Rabbinic history: from Alexander the Great to Muhammad

The story of the early rabbis

The Second Commonwealth

The Persian period

We know with some degree of reliability that a second Jewish political nation, called "Judea," was formed near the end of the sixth century BCE within the immediate area of the city of Jerusalem. Cyrus sat on the throne of Persia, the most extensive and powerful empire the world had known up to that time. A Babylonian Jew, named Nehemiah, had been appointed governor of Judea to oversee the foreign policy interests of the empire, and another Babylonian Jew, named Ezra, had been named "High Priest" and ruler over the internal affairs of the Jewish state.

In general, the foreign policy of the state was to have no policy. Within its national walls, which were among the first things it built, Judea remained isolated to pursue its divine destiny, which was to perform daily the sacrifices of the Temple cult. The rest of the world had little idea who these people were and no idea of the value of what they did, but the surviving descendants of Israel knew. God had revealed to them alone his true name, and in that revelation of himself he had made clear the meaning of all life in the universe. It was to serve God through meticulous obedience to the statutes given in the Torah that regulated every aspect of the life of this holy place upon this particular holy land and the lives of the holy people who lived and worshipped there.

In world politics it can be said that no news is good news, and if this is true then the news from Judea was good for close to two hundred years. From the perspective of the universe, within the walls of the city life did not change. Children were born, grew up to be either farmers or administrators within the Temple cult, married and had children, and died. Every day they worked and offered sacrifices to God on their Temple mount. They knew what a week was, because on the Sabbath the gates of the city were closed to foreigners. They knew what months were, namely periods of the moon's cycle around the earth's sphere, whose completed circuit was celebrated with special sacrifices. They knew what the seasons of the year were as well; they were periods of the sun's cycle around the earth, separated by significant changes in rainfall, and celebrated by special sacrifices: when the rainy season began (on the feast of Booths [Sukkot]); when the dry season began (on the unified feast of the Passover [Pesach] and Unleavened Bread [Matsah]), after which the annual planting of seeds took place; and at the time of the harvesting of the year's first crops, 50 days later, on the feast of Weeks (Shavuot). Finally, years themselves were distinguishable not by events in history but by numerical periods. Every seventh year was a Sabbath of years (the Sabbatical year), when the land itself was given a Sabbath rest, i.e., the land was allowed to remain fallow, and the year following each seven of Sabbatical years (the fiftieth year) was a Sabbath of Sabbaticals (the Jubilee year), when all trading of property was set aside and the land reverted back to its original owners.

The Greek period

This seemingly idyllic two-century period of tranquility came to an end because of international changes in a world of politics far removed from Judea. Persia's attempt to expand its empire onto the European continent failed in its wars with the confederated Greek city states at the end of the fifth century BCE (the Peloponnesian Wars). The invader then found itself invaded by those it tried to invade. By the fourth century BCE the Greek city states were dominated by their northern neighbor, Macedonia, whose ruler, Philip, declared his nation with its vassals to be an empire called Greece. Philip's son Alexander, who came to be called "the great" (Alexander the Great), extended his father's so-called Greek empire across the Mediterranean Sea and conquered much of the territory that had been Persian and more as well. Included in Alexander's empire was Judea, which the Greek army conquered in 333 BCE, displacing Judea's Persian garrison with a Greek one.

After Alexander's death, his empire was divided among his generals. Asia Minor became the Greek kingdom of Antigonus, Persia became the Greek kingdom of Seleucus, and Egypt became the Greek kingdom of Ptolemy. In a relatively short span of time, the territory of Antigonus was swallowed up by the Ptolemaic Egyptian Greek kingdom and the Seleucidan Persian Greek kingdom, and these first two world powers entered into a competition of their own which would not be resolved until, about three hundred years later, the Romans swallowed up both Greek kingdoms.

In this new world of geopolitics, the second Jewish state, the theocracy of Judea, found itself once again caught between two world powers (Seleucidan Syria and Ptolemaic Egypt), just as the first Jewish state, the monarchy of Israel, had been caught, without room for escape, on the battle line between ancient Mesopotamia and ancient Egypt. Judea became a vassal of the Ptolemaic kingdom in 320 BCE, only to be taken over by the Seleucidan kingdom five years later. It continued to be a Syrian Greek[1] vassal for most (but not all) of the next three hundred years.

On the surface it would seem that, although the Mediterranean world as a whole had in the fourth century BCE undergone dramatic change, within the very small, politically isolationist world of Judea nothing of great importance had happened. Before Alexander's conquest a Persian militia and governor had been stationed in Jerusalem to preserve Judea's military and geopolitical isolation. Now the militia and governor were to be Greek. However, given Judea's place and purpose in God's universe, this difference should have been trivial. The people Israel existed to worship God, and that collective worship was a full-time activity. Whether those foreigners observing and preserving them were Persian or Greek should have been of no importance. However, what actually happened was quite different.

The transition from the Persian to the Greek empire was more than a change of international banners, uniforms, and languages; it was a change of culture and world-view at a very deep level, caused, to a large extent, by the Greek empire's success in becoming a world empire, by integrating the peoples of its territory into an organic (i.e., mutually dependent) unit in every way and not just in politics, viz., in social structure, in economic structure, and (what is most important for our purposes) in philosophic outlook on every aspect of human existence in the world.

The Seleucidan Greeks took control of Judea at the beginning of the third century BCE, and in 175 BCE Antiochus IV became its king. It was during his reign that the imperial occupiers of Judah attempted to change the relationship initiated by Cyrus that had operated so effectively for all of those centuries. The Greeks tried to transform the Jerusalem Temple of the Lord of Israel into a Greek temple that incorporated Judea's deity into a pantheon of deities governed by the Greek deity Zeus. This change in the political status quo provoked the Jewish people into once again caring about the affairs of the world, a care that led to a national revolt against Greek hegemony.

Actually, the Greek-enforced change in worship was not only about worship. It was about political, social, and economic reform. It was about forcing the nation Judea to give up its relative autonomy and become integrated into the new empire, and the Jewish people had no interest in such integration.

Syrian Greece was involved in major conflicts with Egyptian Greece, and the shadow that was hovering over both old kingdoms was the nascent Roman Empire. Antiochus needed to commit his troops to those foreign wars rather than to maintaining garrisons within his own imperial borders. To free up its occupying troops Syrian Greece had to be able to trust its vassals not to revolt, i.e., not to act like vassals but to behave as if they themselves were part of the conqueror and not one of the conquered. In other words, the vassals had themselves to become Greek, i.e., to be "Hellenized."

If, or so it was implicitly argued, conquered states such as Judea would undergo Hellenization, i.e., would assume the same language, culture, and social and political structure as the Greeks, then they would see themselves as Greek, and therefore they would no longer be vassal nations who needed to rebel in order to become independent. If this vast political, social, and cultural transformation were to take place, then the Seleucidans would be free to reduce (even withdraw) their garrisons and could, in gratitude, grant to the transformed vassals the equivalent of what we today call a "most favored nation status" in trade. The only nation in the region that refused Hellenization was Judea, and that refusal condemned it to be one of the poorest and most backward nations in the region.

Being treated as a Greek in trade was no small matter. Alexander's empire in effect united the world of nations bordering the Mediterranean Sea into a single nation of extensive intercourse of every kind (physical and cultural as well as economic and political), whose cultural and trade routes extended beyond the Middle East into India and Africa. To be part of such a world meant great opportunity for wealth (through world trade) and for learning (in all disciplines).[2] However, there was a price to be paid for such an opportunity—Judah would cease to be the holy nation whose calling on the earth was to serve the creator of the universe by preparing the daily sacrifices that tie God to humanity and nature.

Judah fought a war to preserve its sense of uniqueness, but again the price it paid for that preservation was great, in terms of the new wisdom and of the new wealth. It was a trade-off that not everyone in the Jewish state was willing to pay. What followed Judea's revolt against the Syrian Greeks was a series of civil conflicts within the Jewish nation that laid the grounds for its transformation into what would become rabbinic Judaism.

From 167 to 164 BCE a group of priests from a suburb of Jerusalem called Modiin led a rebellion against the Syrian Greeks to preserve the purity of the Temple, which meant to preserve the Jewish state as a "Torah-true" theocracy. The leaders were called "Maccabees," which means "hammers," and their successful struggle was preserved in the two Books of the Maccabees and in the winter festival of Hanukkah.

One of the Maccabees, Jonathan, was appointed High Priest in 152 BCE, which began what is known as the "Hasmonean" dynasty. At the same time, a governing senate, called the "Sanhedrin", was established independently to administer the government of Judah. How this new institution came about is a matter of considerable speculation among academic historians, and this is a debate into which we need not enter here, other than to say that after the Maccabean revolt the government of Judea ceased to be centered in the priesthood and became centered instead in a form of parliament that at least had the form of the Greek city state (*polis*) government, and included as its legislators far more than just members of the priestly families.

Again, scholars debate just who sat in the Sanhedrin and how they were chosen, but everyone agrees that there were in this legislature at least two factions—those who supported the Hasmonean priesthood and those who did not. Of those who did not, the important group for our purposes was a political–religious party called the "Pharisees."[3]

While the Hasmoneans came to power in order to preserve the theocracy of the Torah, in fact, once in power, they were continually drawn in the direction of assimilation and integration into the politics and culture of the dominant Greeks. The force that stood against this national assimilation was the party of the Pharisees. The conflict between the Hasmoneans and the Pharisees produced two major civil wars. The first occurred when Alexander Janneus was the High Priest (103–76 BCE), and the second, after his death, when Alexander's wife, Salome Alexandra, became the ruler of the country. The conclusion was a draw between the forces of the priesthood, backed by the Seleucidan Greeks, and the Pharisees, backed by the ordinary people.

The conflict was primarily over religion and culture, but it was also over social class and economics. The priesthood had become an aristocracy with considerable wealth from commerce, gained independently of their clerical functions from investments in international trade made possible by their legislative functions. In contrast, the people were, as we say today, "dirt poor" farmers. The Pharisees represented these people in the conflict with the priests.

The result of the military draw between the two Jewish parties was a division of powers. The priesthood was given control of the external affairs of the Jewish state, which enabled its members to enter freely into trade agreements with other states in the empire, independent of the pressure of the Sanhedrin. In this sense, the priesthood constituted a kind of alternative senate that in many respects resembles the British House of Lords. The Sanhedrin itself became a Pharisee body that had control of the internal affairs of the nation, including the governance of the sacrifical cult administered by the priests.

It was a strange compromise. The Torah gave power to a priesthood to rule an agrarian nation whose all-consuming activity as a nation was to sacrifice animals and produce provided by the farming population. The priests themselves, however, whose sole authority to rule came from the provisions of the Torah, wanted as much as possible to free themselves of the Torah and to transform Judea into a contemporary commercial state. Whatever their reasons for wanting this transformation, they wanted it at the price of their political right to rule, because without the support of the Torah they had no political legitimacy. On the other hand, the Pharisees, whose political power had no source whatsoever in the Torah (whose only recognized ruling classes were priests, kings, judges, and prophets), used their power to preserve a system of government (the Torah's) that did not recognize their existence.

The paradox persisted as long as the Temple existed. Its destruction by the Romans brought the power of the priesthood to an end, and, with its end, the Jewish state was transformed into rabbinic Judaism. However, we are slightly ahead of our story. Let us first deal with the ascendancy of the Romans over the Greeks in Judea and then turn to the way that the Pharisees transformed the Jewish state in the Sanhedrin.

The Roman period

The Roman general, Pompey, completed his army's conquest of Greek Asia Minor and Syria in 65 BCE. Two years later, he entered Jerusalem to settle a dispute over the right of accession to the Jewish high priesthood and took control over the Jewish state. Internal strife within the Roman Empire itself (viz., the war of the western part of the empire under Octavian against the eastern part of the empire under Mark Anthony and his Egyptian wife, Cleopatra) misled Judea into a false sense of security that enabled it to declare independence from Rome in league with the then rising Parthian empire to the east. However, the independence was short-lived. The Hasmonean dynasty of High Priests came to an end in 37 BCE, and Herod I[4] was appointed by the Romans as the procurator or "king" of Judea.

Throughout the period of Judea's involvement in the politics of warring empires the internal affairs of the Jewish state continued, without interruption. The nation was ruled by a Sanhedrin whose members, called "sages" (*chachamim*) or "rabbis," totally reformed the nation, all in the name of preserving the nation from change. The Sanhedrin was broken down into two parties with two party leaders—a majority party headed by a Nasi (prince) and a minority party headed by an *av bet din* (father of the court). Decisions were made in the names of the two parties (called *zugot* [pairs; the singular, pair, is "*zug*"]), giving the majority view and the minority view.[5] These views governed the decisions of courts (*betai din*, the plural of *bet din*) spread throughout the land in administrative districts or providences over which the court had complete control in all matters. In many cases, these local courts made their own decisions about legislation based on their interpretations of the Torah, the national constitution. However, where a decision had been made by the Sanhedrin, its judgment took precedence over local rules.

The relationship with Rome continued to deteriorate until finally, in the year 66 CE, the Judeans, under the popular leadership of a party called the "Zealots," initiated an open military rebellion, which concluded when the Roman army, under the command of the emperor-to-be Vespasian, destroyed the rebel forces and, in the year 70 CE, tore down almost all of the walls of the second Temple.

As relations between Rome and Judea had deteriorated, the Romans assumed direct rule over Judea in 6 CE and dissolved the parliament of the Sanhedrin. During this period rabbis continued to assert authority in judgment over the Jewish people, but they did so as rebels, for their very activity as rabbis became a crime punishable by death.

Not long after the destruction of the Temple, the Romans permitted a reinstitution of the Sanhedrin, this time located outside Jerusalem in the village of Yavneh. However, there were no longer pairs (zugot). Rather, decisions were issued by individual rabbis in their own names. Authority was vested not in the rabbis themselves but in the Nasi who, while guided by the members of the Sanhedrin, was subject to the power of the Roman military governor.

Political discontent continued to grow and the rabbis themselves continued to be split over cooperation with the Romans. Some rabbis (probably the majority) encouraged compliance with Rome. They reasoned that the likelihood of achieving national independence by force of arms was unrealistic, and the result of a failed revolt would be further deterioration of collective and individual life.

However, others (probably a minority among the rabbis but a majority among the ordinary people ['am ha-aretz]) advocated a second revolt, because they believed in the literal word of the Torah. They believed that if they were true to God's word and followed the teachings of the Torah, then God would prosper them, materially and spiritually, in this life. Clearly, God would stand with the Torah-true Jews against the idolatrous Romans. Hence, given Judea's faithfulness to God, how could Judea lose? Certainly the military arms of the Romans, as awesome as they were, were no match for the power of the creator of the universe.

A second and a third revolt occurred—the second against Rome in 116 CE, and a third between 132 and 135 CE when Judea, under the leadership of Simon bar Kokhba, fought a Rome ruled by Emperor Hadrian (who reigned from 117 to 138 CE). This third defeat devastated the nation, because it went to the heart of biblical Judaism's faith. Most Jews believed in the literal word of the Torah and, by that literal word, the Torah-true Judeans should have been successful against the idolatrous pagan Romans. Judah's defeat on three separate occasions seemed convincing proof that the Torah as a philosophy simply was not true. However, the rabbis did not believe that the literal word of the Torah was its true meaning, and in its true meaning the Torah was true, which it in fact had to be if it was the word of the creator of the universe who is supreme in all virtues, including speaking truth.

Hence, rabbinic Judaism, unlike biblical Judaism, could survive the national catastrophe, since its interpretation of what it meant to say that the Bible is the word of God was not dependent on a literal interpretation of those words that would entail the prospering of the just (Israel) and the failure of the unjust (the Romans). However, biblical Judaism could not prosper, even survive, in Judea or, for that matter, anywhere else in the Roman Empire.

Jewish life in a second exile (galut)—the return to Babylonia

In the year 200 CE, the reigning Nasi, Judah I, published the Mishnah from the new seat of the Sanhedrin in Sepphoris in the Galilee. This code of Jewish law is the foundation document of rabbinic Judaism. However, Jewish life in Judea continued to deteriorate. Rome was at the beginning of a major period of social and economic decline that would last for about ninety years (193–283 CE). During this time Jews continually left Judea to live and settle elsewhere. Some went to more prosperous places, such as Alexandria in Egypt, within the Roman Empire itself. But most moved out of the Roman domain altogether into the territory of the Parthians. Hence, the Jews returned once again to Babylonia.

Throughout the period of Greek and Roman hegemony over Judea there had grown major Jewish settlements outside of the holy land, everywhere in the Greco-Roman empire and beyond, including Arabia. How large these communities were in comparison to the rabbinic community of Judea is debatable and a subject of serious historical research today. Of these communities, we know a little about the settlement in Arabia, which we learn from references to Jewish tribes in the Koran, a little about Jewish communities in Persia that we learn from archeology, and a great deal about at least the intellectual class of Alexandria in Egypt that we learn from the writings of the first Jewish philosopher, Philo (about 20 BCE to about 50 CE). What we learn from these sources is that all of the forms of Judaism were committed to the Torah as the word of God, none of them believed that what the texts say literally is what they really meant, and what these groups understood the texts to mean is radically different from what the rabbis understood the texts to mean.

Of these (what we would consider to be variant) interpretations, those of Philo are closest to what Christianity becomes. However, we will not concern ourselves here with any non-rabbinic interpretations of Judaism, no matter how important they are in themselves. Whatever they were, only one reformation of the philosophy of the Hebrew Scriptures other than rabbinic Judaism survived over the course of generations, and that was Christianity. However, since Christianity spread north of the Mediterranean in Europe as rabbinic Jewish life grew south of the Mediterranean in Babylonia, there was little contact between these two religious nations, and, therefore, little impact of one on the other at this stage of development. That situation would change with the rise of Islam in the seventh century CE. Then the Roman Christian territories would become part of a Muslim empire in which rabbinic Jewish life was centered, with the consequence that Jewish thinking would change Christianity, as Christianity would change Jewish thinking, as both world religions interacted with the third and then dominant world religion, Islam. However, none of this will concern us until we conclude our discussion of early rabbinic literature and turn in Part II to the classical Jewish philosophy of the so-called "Middle Ages." For now, let us focus only on the political and literary structures which developed with the spread of rabbinic Judaism in the non-Roman Middle East.

In the year 200 CE, Judah I redacted the Mishnah, and the first rabbinic academy was established in Babylonia in the city of Nehardea. Nineteen years later a second Babylonian academy was established, by Rav, in Sura. This occurred just before Arashir I, the first Sassanian ruler of Persia, overthrew the Parthians and revived the religion of Zoroastrianism in the empire, and his successor, Shapur I, confirmed Jewish religious autonomy in the Sassanid empire. It marked the beginning of a period of great literary productivity for the rabbis in Babylonia.

In 254 CE, Judah ben Ezekiel established a third rabbinic academy, in Pumpeditha, and six years later the academy of Nehardea closed, leaving again two academies—one in Sura and another in Pumpeditha. Whatever these academies had to do with learning, they were also (if not primarily) centers of government.

In general, there were three collective political institutions that governed Jewish life in the Sassanian empire, which would continue when this empire was succeeded by Islam in the seventh century. The institutions were the two academies and the Exilarch (*resh galuta*).[6] Presumably the Exilarch appointed the heads of the academies who appointed rabbis to administer the separate Jewish communities located throughout the Parthian and then Sassanid empires. At first the rabbis who served in these academies were trained in Judea and functioned as rabbis there as well. Later, as Judean Jewry declined and Babylonian Jewry prospered, the Babylonian rabbinate became more independent of a

Judean rabbinate and the two rabbinic Jewish communities became more distinct.

The starting point for all rabbinic discussions, in Judea and Babylonia, was the interpretation of the texts of the Hebrew Scriptures, especially the Torah, in the light of oral and written traditions of earlier rabbinic interpretations of the text. There were many texts that survived to guide the later rabbis' interpretations, especially the various collections of midrashic interpretations of the Bible. However, in the area of government and law, the single most important guide was the Mishnah. Rabbinic reflections in Judea on the meaning of the Torah under the guidance of the Mishnah are redacted into a work called "the Jerusalem Talmud" in the Galilee in the mid-fourth century CE. It was written as the rabbinic world of Roman Judea was coming to an end.

During the fourth century, Rome split into two separate empires, both of which were officially Christian. In this same century Christianity defined its distinctiveness from Judaism and from any other religion as it increased its control over the Roman empires. Christian states have had limited tolerance for a Jewish minority, at least until very recent modern times, so the plight of the Jews became especially precarious in a world that in its own right was undergoing continuous cultural, economic, and social decline. The final record of that Judaism was the Jerusalem Talmud, but, since rabbinic Jewish life continued primarily in the lands that would become Muslim rather than the lands that would become Christian, the Jerusalem Talmud had relatively little impact on the subsequent development of Judaism.

The Babylonian Talmud was redacted around 474 CE under the leadership of Rav Ashi in the academy of Sura. This work was polished into its present form during the next century by a group of rabbis called "Saboraim." Their product, completed in 540 CE, defines traditional Judaism to this day. It, together with the Mishnah and the Midrash, contain the early roots of the development of Jewish philosophy beyond the Bible.

Notes

1 A word about terminology here, which can be somewhat confusing. Alexander's general, Ptolemy, became the king of a territory of the Greek empire that was, for the most part, Egypt, whose seat of government continued to be in Egypt. This kingdom or empire can be referred to as

Ptolemaic Greece, Ptolemaic Egypt, Egyptian Greece, or simply the Ptolemaic kingdom. Similarly, Alexander's general, Seleucus, became the king of a territory of the Greek empire that was, for the most part, Persia, whose seat of government was located in an administrative district north of Israel that was called "Syria." Hence, this kingdom or empire can be referred to as Seleucidan Greece, Seleucidan Persia, Seleucidan Syria, Syrian Greece, or simply the Seleucid kingdom.

2   The unification of the worlds of Egypt and Persia into the world of the Greeks also enabled an integration of what each of these empires had known about astronomy, physics, and the mathematics that underlay both sciences. By the time of Antiochus IV, people who loved wisdom (i.e., philosophers) could learn from the written record of mathematicians such as Euclid of Alexandria (who, in 300 BCE, wrote *The Elements*) and Archimedes of Syracuse (287–212 BCE), and astronomers such as Aristarchus of Samos (310–230 BCE) and Appolonius of Perga (262–190 BCE), who used mathematical techniques to determine the charted motions of the stars. (Aristarchus applied trigonometry; Appolonius applied cycles and epicycles.) All of this work was brought together in the second century BCE as an unified mathematical picture of the universe by Ptolemy of Alexandria in his *Algamest*. Those very same people whose minds were open to foreign, Greek writings could also learn from the recorded traditions of the wisdom of natural philosophers such as Thales of Miletus (624–548 BCE), Anaxagoras (who died in 428 BCE; he was the teacher of Pericles of Athens), and (most importantly) the schools of Plato (427–347 BCE) and Aristotle (384–322 BCE).

3   Readers should be aware that what I will say below about the Pharisees is controversial. Traditional rabbinic Judaism sees them as a stage in the continuous development in Judaism that begins at the time of Ezra with the scribes and a group called "the men of the Great Assembly" and ends with the sages or "rabbis" whose judgments are incorporated in Judah I's Mishnah. Most academic scholars agree that the origins of the Pharisees are no earlier than the Maccabean revolt, but there is no consensus yet on how important they are until the time of the revolts against the Romans at the end of the first century CE. What is most at issue here is whether the Pharisees are nascent rabbis or something altogether different. I shall treat them as different from the scribes but not different from the rabbis.

4   Herod is the son of Antipater. Antipater was the administrator that the Romans set over Judea when they first entered the country in 63 BCE to support John Hyrcanus' claim to legitimacy as High Priest over the claim of his brother, Aristobulus II.

5   The most famous of these pairs were the Nasi Hillel the Elder and the Av Bet Din Shammai, who reigned from the years 31 to 4 BCE.

6   The term *resh galuta* means the head or ruler of the Exile. He was considered

to be a direct descendant of King David who would again rule as king with the establishment of a renewed Jewish kingdom in the land of Israel.

Suggestions for further study

Dodds, E. R. *Pagan and Christian in an Age of Anxiety.* Cambridge: Cambridge University Press, 1965.

Gerhardson, Birger. *Memory and Manuscript.* Copenhagen: E. Munksgaard, 1964.

Goldenberg, Robert. "Talmud," in Barry W. Holtz (ed.), *Back to the Sources: Reading the Classic Jewish Texts.* New York: Summit Books, 1984, pp. 129–75.

Hengel, M. *Judaism and Hellenism.* English translation by J. Bowden. Philadelphia: Fortress Press, 1974.

Lauterbach, Jacob Z. *Rabbinic Essays.* Cincinnati: Hebrew Union College Press, 1951.

Lieberman, Saul. *Hellenism in Jewish Palestine.* New York: Jewish Theological Seminary of America, 1950.

Mielzener, Moses. *Introduction to the Talmud.* New York: Bloch, 1968.

Neusner, Jacob (ed.). *The Formation of the Babylonian Talmud.* Leiden: E. J. Brill, 1970.

Neusner, Jacob. *A History of the Jews in Babylonia.* Leiden: E. J. Brill, 1966–70.

Neusner, Jacob. *Judaism, Christianity and Zoroastrianism in Talmudic Babylonia. Studies in Judaism.* Lanham, MD: University Press of America, 1986.

Neusner, Jacob. *There We Sat Down.* New York: Ktav, 1976.

Newby, Gordon Darnell. *A History of the Jews of Arabia: From Ancient Times to Their Eclipse under Islam.* Columbia, SC: University of South Carolina, 1988.

Rivkin, Ellis. *A Hidden Revolution: The Pharisees' Search for the Kingdom Within.* Nashville, TN: Abingdon Press, 1978.

Rivkin, Ellis. *The Shaping of Jewish History.* New York: Charles Scribner's Sons, 1971.

Sandmel, Samuel. *Philo's Place in Judaism.* Cincinnati: Hebrew Union College Press, 1956.

Seltzer, Robert M. *Jewish People, Jewish Thought: The Jewish Experience in History.* New York: Macmillan, 1980. Part II, "From the Hellenistic Period to Late Antiquity", pp. 171–314.

Simon, Marcel. *Jewish Sects at the Time of Jesus.* Philadelphia: Fortress Press, 1967.

Steinsaltz, Adin. *The Essential Talmud.* New York: Basic Books, 1976.

Strack, Hermann L. *Introduction to the Talmud and Midrash.* New York: Atheneum, 1969.

Winston, David. "Hellenistic Jewish philosophy", in Daniel H. Frank and Oliver Leaman (eds.), *History of Jewish Philosophy*, Vol. II of *Routledge History of World Philosophies*. London, Routledge, 1997, pp. 38–61.

Winston, David. *Logos and Mystical Theology in Philo of Alexandria*. Cincinnati: Hebrew Union College Press, 1985.

Zeitlin, Solomon. *The Rise and Fall of the Judean State*. Philadelphia: Jewish Publication Society of America, 1978.

Key events of rabbinic history

450–430 BCE	Pericles rules Athens; period of a new wave of immigration from Persia to Judah; social and cultic reforms in Jerusalem by Nehemiah and Ezra
431–404 BCE	Peloponnesian Wars
427–347 BCE	Life of Plato
384–322 BCE	Life of Aristotle
336–323 BCE	Reign of Alexander the Great
334–331 BCE	Greek army conquers Persia and the Near East
333 BCE	Greek army occupies Judah
320 BCE	Ptolemaic Greeks of Egypt take over Judea
315 BCE	Seleucidan Greeks of Syria capture Judea
3rd century BCE	Alexandria in Egypt becomes the major center of Hellenistic culture; composition of the Septuagint
201–198 BCE	Seleucidan Greeks of Syria take control of Judea
175–163 BCE	Antiochus IV Epiphanes rules Seleucidan Greece
167–164 BCE	Maccabean revolt in Judea against Antiochus IV
152 BCE	Appointment of first Hasmonean High Priest, Jonathan; establishment of Sanhedrin in Jerusalem
140 BCE	Simon is appointed High Priest and Ethnarch over independent Judea, establishing the Hasmonean dynasty
103–76 BCE	Alexander Janneus, son of John Hyrcanus, the High Priest and Ethnarch; borders of Judea extended to include most of Palestine and Transjordan. Civil war with Pharisees
76–67 BCE	Salome Alexandra, wife of Alexander Janneus, rules Judea
76 BCE	Civil war between Pharisees and Hasmoneans
63 BCE	Roman general Pompey enters Jerusalem to support Salome's son Hyrcanus II as High Priest against his brother. Antipater appointed administrator of Judea
40 BCE	Parthians take over Judea. Antipater's son Herod flees to Rome where he is recognized as King of Judea
37–4 BCE	Herod I reigns as King or procurator of Judea
6 CE	Rome assumes direct rule over Judea

c. 20 BCE–50 CE	Life of Philo of Alexandria
66–73 CE	First Judean war against Rome
70 CE	Jerusalem Temple destroyed by Vespasian
73–132 CE	Gamliel II Nasi of reassembled Sanhedrin at Yavneh
116 CE	Second Judean war against Rome
132–135 CE	Third Judean war, under Simon bar Kokhba, against Rome
135–170 CE	Simon II Nasi of Sanhedrin relocated at Usha in the Galilee
161–180 CE	Marcus Aurelius rules as Emperor of Rome
c. 170–217 CE	Reign of Judah I as Nasi (Patriarch) of Sanhedrin relocated at Sepphoris in the Galilee.
200 CE	Judah I redacts the Mishnah; first academy (at Nehardea) established in Babylonia
217 CE	Gamliel III becomes Nasi; Sanhedrin relocated at Tiberias in the Galilee
219 CE	Establishment of academy of Sura in Babylonia by Rav
225–255 CE	Judean patriarchate moves from Yavneh to Tiberias in the Galilee
226–240 CE	Arashir I, first Sassanian ruler in Persia, overthrows the Parthians and seeks to revive Persian power and Zoroastrian religion
240–271 CE	Shapur I confirms religious autonomy of Jews in Sassanian empire
254 CE	Establishment of academy of Pumpeditha in Babylonia by Judah ben Ezekiel
260 CE	Close of academy of Nehardea
286 CE	Roman Empire splits into western (Roman) and eastern (Byzantine) empires
306–337 CE	Emperor Constantine rules Rome; makes Christianity the legal religion of the empire
325 CE	Church Council of Nicea
340–420 CE	Jerome translates Bible into Latin
Middle 4th century CE	Redaction of the Palestinian Talmud in the Galilee
395 CE	At death of Theodosius I Rome divides permanently into a western and an eastern empire
410 CE	Rome sacked by Visigoths
425 CE	On death of Gamliel VI, Theodosius II abolishes the office of the Nasi
455 CE	Rome sacked by Vandals
c. 474 CE	Redaction of much of the Babylonian Talmud, under leadership of Rav Ashi at the academy of Sura
475–476 CE	Romulus Augustus the last Roman emperor in the west

500–540 CE	Saboraim of Babylonia add notes and comments to the Babylonian Talmud
520s CE	The King of Himyar in southwestern Arabia converts to Judaism
529 CE	Roman Emperor Justinian closes Greek schools of philosophy at Athens

Political leaders of the Jewish people: 1

High Priests of the Second Commonwealth: Onias II; Hyrcanus; Simon II; Jason (Jeshua); Menelaus; Alcimus (Jakin); (office vacant from 159 to 152 BCE); the Hasmoneans

The *Hasmoneans* (152–37 (BCE): sons of Mattathias of Modiin: Jonathan (152–142); Simon (142–135); John Hyrcanus (135–104) {Simon's son; converted Idumeans}; Aristobulus I (104–103) {king; semi-independence of Syrian and Egyptian Greece}; Alexander Jannens (103–76) {Aristobulus' brother; civil war with Pharisees}; Hyrcanus II (76–67)—Salome Alexandra {mother of Hyrcanus II, wife of Aristobulus I and Alexander Jannens, mother of Aristobulus II [head of army]}, Hyrcanus II and Aristobulus II fight to be king/High Priest (67–63); Judea conquered by Rome under Pompey [63]; Hyrcanus II (63–40) {High Priest = king = Ethnarch under Rome}; Mattathiah Antigonus (40–37) {High Priest = king under Parthians}

Judean Kings: Herod (37–4 BCE) {named High Priest/king by Anthony and Octavian; married Miriam [daughter of Aristobulus II's son Alexander and Hyrcanus II's daughter Alexandra]; son of Idumean Antipater; backed Hyrcanus II and Rome against Aristobulus II}; Archelaus and Sabinus (4 BCE); Archelaus (Ethnarch) (4 BCE–6 CE)

Roman Procurators: Pontius Pilate (26–36 CE); Agrippa I (41–44 CE), Fadus (44–48 CE); Camunus (48–52 CE); Felix (52–60 CE); Festus (60–62 CE); Albinus (62–64 CE); Florus (64–66 CE)

Zugot of the rabbinic Sanhedrin: Simeon the Just and Antigonus of Sokho; Jose ben Joezer of Zeredah and Jose ben Jochanan; Joshua ben Perachyah and Nittai of Arbel; Judah of Tabbai and Simeon ben Shatach; Shemaiah and Avtalyon; Hillel the Elder and Shammai

#Babylonian Exilarchs and Gaonim

Exilarchs	Nehardea Gaons	Pumpeditha Gaons
Huna Ukba (c. 170–217)	Shila: Rab, Karna, Samuel Samuel (219–247) Nahman Ben Jacob (247–260) *Sura Gaons* Rav (219–247) Samuel (247–254) Huna (257–297)	Judah ben Ezekiel (254–299) Rabbah ben Nahmani (309–330) Judah (330–333) Abaye (333–338) Raba [at Mahoza] (338–352)
	Ashi (375–427) Rabina II (474–499)	

CHAPTER 9

Major texts of rabbinic Judaism

The history of Jewish philosophy is a history of commentaries on texts that are commentaries of texts before them. The first texts are those of the Hebrew Scriptures. The second set of texts are those which we describe in this chapter as the writings of the *tannaim* and the *amoraim*. We have already mentioned three of them—the Mishnah and the two Talmuds. In this chapter we will introduce them all.

In the previous chapter we outlined the early history of Judaism. It began with the completion of most of the biblical texts with the establishment of the second Jewish state—a theocracy composed of farmers ruled by hereditary priests whose administration was guided by the now written record of the initial covenant established between the Lord of Israel and the people of Israel in an ancient desert past before the creation of the first Jewish state. It concluded with the composition of the foundational texts of rabbinic Judaism—an oligarchy composed of farmers and merchants living throughout the Middle East and Asia Minor, ruled by a class of sages whose wisdom was gleaned from written and oral records of earlier sages who lived and governed during the second Jewish state. In this chapter, I will go into more detail about what these early rabbinic texts were and the set of beliefs developed to support their claim of authority for the Jewish people.

The chain of tradition—oral and written Torah

In the previous chapter we briefly discussed the paradox of the Pharisees and rabbis, who are not mentioned in the Torah, governing in order to preserve the political order of the Torah, in opposition to the ruling dynasty of priests, whose authority lay in the words of the Torah. Those whom the Torah authorized to rule did not want to rule by its authority, while those who preserved the Torah's authority had no authority to do so from the actual words in the Torah. The resolution of this paradox was the doctrine that I will call here, for the sake of simplification, "the oral law." As we will see, it can also be called "the double law theory" and the doctrine of the chain of tradition.

The most central doctrine underlying biblical Judaism is the affirmation *torah mi-sinai* (literally, "Torah from Sinai") that the written Torah as we now possess it is an accurate record of the law that God revealed to Moses in the theophany at Sinai. To that doctrine rabbinic Judaism adds that God revealed not only the words but what those words mean. The revelation of the meaning of the written Torah is the oral Torah. It is a tradition of interpretation that God revealed to Moses, that Moses reported to Joshua, that Joshua passed on to the elders of the new nation, that the elders transmitted to the priest Eli, who transmitted it to others, including his son Pinchas and the prophet Samuel, who transmitted it to King David and his court, from whom it was transmitted through the subsequent prophets and their courts, on to Ezra and his court (who are called "the men of the Great Assembly"), the last of whom was Simon the Just. From Simon the transmission continues through a chain of rabbis in an unbroken chain of transmission to the *zugot* of the Sanhedrin—Shemaiah and Avtalyon, Hillel and Shammai, Jochanan ben Zakkai and Shimon—on through the separate rabbis, on to Judah I and his colleagues in the Sanhedrin.[1] What is critical in this list is that from the time of Ezra and the men of the Great Assembly on, the continuous transmission of what the words of the Torah means was transmitted through rabbis, not priests. Therefore, while the Torah gave the priests the authority to administer the sacrificial cult and govern the nation, it was the rabbis and not the priests who possessed the knowledge necessary to direct decisions that the priests had to make. Hence, by the rules of the Torah, the governing priests were subject to the decisions of the rabbis. Consequently, the Torah-true nation should have been governed by the rabbis.

There is no paragraph in the Torah, no sentence in any one of its paragraphs, and no word in any one of its sentences whose meaning is in itself clear. The Bible is a rich text, and because of its richness it is subject to many interpretations. However, not every interpretation is the word of God; only the true interpretations are. By reason alone there is no way to deduce what the text means; for that you need an authentic tradition— one in which the author explained what he meant to say to someone of sufficient intelligence to understand the explanation and sufficient integrity to report faithfully what he had learned, and the intelligent and honest witness passed on what he witnessed to other faithful and honest witnesses in an unbroken chain of transmission.

It is a fundamental claim of rabbinic Judaism, as critical as the doctrine of *torah mi-sinai* is for biblical Judaism, that the chain of tradition from Moses to Joshua on through the judges, priests, and prophets, on to Ezra, and from Ezra on through the rabbis is an authentic chain of transmission, a chain that is continuous, where every link is a rabbi of indubitable intelligence and integrity.

Mishnah and *Baraitot*

The authority of the Mishnah is first and foremost that it is the product of an authentic chain of transmission from Moses to the time of Judah I. The Mishnah itself does not summarize the entire chain. Rather, it limits itself to decisions made by a group of rabbis who become known as the *tannaim* (*tanna* in the singular), viz., the members of the Sanhedrin over the previous four hundred years—from the second century BCE through the first two centuries CE. Judah organized their decisions by conclusions in categories. The categories are quite different from those of the Hebrew Scriptures themselves, and that new way of organizing the law, in and of itself, constitutes the Mishnah as a philosophic work, for it transforms the categories by which the Jewish people had formally organized everything in life and in the world into a new set of categories.

The new categories are presented as six "orders" (*sedarim*, *seder* in the singular). They are the following topics of law: agriculture (*zeraim* [seeds]); the Sabbath and festivals (*moed* [festival]); marriage, divorce and other vows (*nashim* [women]); civil and criminal law (*nezikim* [damages]); the objects of ritual slaughter and sacrifice, and other kinds of holy objects (*kedashim* [holy things]); and ceremonial purity (*tohorot* [purities]).

In all probability, Judah I intended the Mishnah to be a code of all Jewish law, viz., a summary of four hundred years of legal decisions that legislated out of the different decisions reached by rabbis whose decisions constitute the law. In practice, however, the Mishnah served more as a legal collection than a code, for all of the positions recorded, be they the ones that Judah tells us is the law or not, serve equally as authorities for subsequent legal decisions. In fact, positions other than those recorded in the Mishnah are also authoritative. Almost all legal decisions by *tannaim* are equally authoritative, whether or not they are in the Mishnah. Those remembered judgments that are not in the Mishnah are called *baraitot* (*baraita* in the singular), and, again, in subsequent Jewish law, in most cases a *baraita* is as authoritative as a judgment from the Mishnah.

Midrash and Aggadah

The specific legal judgment in the orders of the Mishnah is broken down into distinct paragraphs. Each paragraph of the Mishnah is itself called, in Hebrew, a "teaching" (*mishnah*). However, a *mishnah* is not just any teaching. It is a statement by a *tanna* (a rabbi who lived between the second century BCE and the second century CE) that is independent of any biblical text. Hence, every paragraph in the Mishnah (Judah I's second-century CE code of Jewish law) is itself a *mishnah*—a tannaitic statement that is not in literary form about the biblical text. I say "in form," because, in principle, every transmitted statement by a rabbi, whether or not it is stated, is understood within rabbinic Judaism to be an interpretation. In fact, one of the important concerns in the rabbinic literature after the Mishnah is the attempt to specify the biblical texts of which the statements in the Mishnah are an interpretation.

The kind of tannaitic literature whose primary concern is to interpret the biblical text or to discover the biblical basis that the rabbinic statement expresses is called *midrash*. The Midrash itself is a collection of different books that present both general and detailed tannaitic interpretations of the Bible. It contains two kinds of material—*halakhah* and *aggadah*. The term *halakhah* (literally, a "way") refers to all discussions and determinations of Jewish law. Its opposite, *aggadah* (literally, "saying") refers to all discussions and determinations of anything other than law.

Jewish philosophy is not law, because the rabbinic discussions of what is true are not binding in the same way that the rabbinic discussions of what is good are binding. This distinction is not clear at first. In fact it was not worked out until the end of the Middle Ages.[2] However, even in the period of the *tannaim*, it is clear that there is a difference in how these rabbis discussed questions of belief and questions of actions.

The Mishnah and the *baraitot* are restricted to questions about what we Jews are to do, both individually and collectively, in every sphere of religious and civil life. Here decisions are relatively concrete and particular, and differences are marked as differences or resolved, with a clear understanding that one should do what is right, what is right is a specific, concrete judgment, any variant from the right judgment is wrong, and most wrong judgments are subject to punishment (divine and/or human). However, the Mishnah and their related *baraitot* say nothing about proper belief, one way or the other. Issues of belief are simply not in their domain.

Issues of belief are presented as interpretations of biblical texts and they appear as such as *midrashim* in different midrashic collections. Here the organization of materials is dictated by the formal structure of the Bible and not by topics. Hence, for example, the midrash on Genesis (like the midrashic collections on every other book of the Bible) begins with tannaitic comments whose main focus is the first word or word group of the first verse of the first chapter of Genesis (Gen 1:1), goes on to the second word or word group, and then to the third word group, bringing series of word groups together in between particular word groups in phrases, on to the meaning of the entire verse.[3] The collection then proceeds in the same way to the second sentence, and the third sentence, until it completes what is called the "portion of the week" (*parasha*).[4]

In these presentations no apparent effort is made to reconcile or to priorize apparent differences of interpretation. So, for example, in discussing Gen 1:1, we are told without attribution that the Torah and the Throne of Glory were created before creation, and the creation of the people Israel, the Temple, and the name of the Messiah were contemplated before creation. Rabbi Ahabah ben Rabbi Ze'ira adds "repentance" to the list of things whose creation precedes creation and asks whether the Torah precedes the Throne or the Throne precedes the Torah. Rabbi Abba ben Kahana says the Torah, but Rabbi Huna reports that Rabbi Jeremiah said that Rabbi Samuel ben Rabbi Isaac said that the people Israel was created before both. Rabbi Banayah argues that the Torah was first, and Rabbi Huna says that Rabbi Mattenah said that the world was created for the sake of three things, all kinds of offerings in Temple sacrifice—*hallah* (a kind of bread), tithes, and first fruits. No attempt is made to prioritize these different views, to say how they do or do not agree with each other, and, where they disagree, who is right. As such the books of midrash are more like collections of sayings than like a doctrinal code that legislates proper from improper belief.[5]

The two Talmuds

Our primary source for discussions of what the biblical sources for judgments in the Mishnah were and what these judgments mean are the

Jerusalem (also called the "Palestinian") and the Babylonian Talmuds. These works, edited in the sixth century by rabbis known as "thinkers" (*saboraim* [*sabora* in the singular]) read formally as commentaries on the Mishnah. In fact, the only formal structure that the Talmuds have is dictated by the Mishnah. The Talmuds begin with the first *mishnah* (i.e., the first paragraph) of the first of the six orders of the Mishnah. What follows is a discussion by rabbis who lived at some time after the completion of the Mishnah before the completion of the Talmud, i.e., between the years 200 CE and 500 CE. These rabbis are known as *amoraim* (*amora* in the singular), and the section of commentary on the Mishnah that contains their attributed words is called the *gemara*.

Once the *gemara* is finished, the next single paragraph of the Mishnah is introduced, with an amoraic discussion of it in the *gemara*. The Talmuds proceed this way through the entire Mishnah. The number of books involved in this discussion, because the *gemarot* (the plural of *gemara*) can be very long, is sixty-three. Each book is called a "tractate" (*massekhet* [*mesekhot* in the plural]).

In literary form every *gemara* is a discussion of a particular *mishnah*, but the literary form in this case does not reflect the actual content of a *gemara*. For example, the first *mishnah* of the first tractate of the Talmud, whose order is agricultural laws (*zera'im*) deals with the time limit of reciting evening prayers. A Jew is obligated to pray three times each day— morning, afternoon, and evening (with a fourth, *musaf*, service between the morning and the afternoon services on the Sabbath). The question is, beyond what time is it too late to say evening prayers? As the discussion in the *gemara* proceeds, a number of issues arise, not all of which bear directly on the Mishnah's question. For example, are priests subject to different laws from ordinary Jews (p. 2b)? Why should a person not reside alone at night in a ruin and what do Jews believe about demons (p. 3a)? How did King David pray (p. 3b)? Did David consider himself to be "pious" (a *hasid*) (p. 4a)? What is the proper order of prayers, e.g., does the *shma'* (the declaration of God's unity) precede or follow the primary, petitional, "standing" prayer (the *'amidah*) (p. 4b)? Does the recitation of the *shma'* have the power to enable a person to subdue his "evil inclination" (*yetser ha-ra'*) in support of his "good inclination" (*yetser ha-tov*) (p. 5b)? And so on, on through the rest of the *gemara*.

In other words, a text that seems to be a discussion of the limits on evening prayers turns out to include, among other subjects, important questions about idolatry (the issue of demons), the nature of the development of the prayer book by the time of the completion of the Talmuds (the issue of the relationship between the *shma'* and the *'amidah*), the power of prayer, and the nature of human beings (at their most excellent in the case of King David and in general in the case of the nature of human good and evil inclinations). Note also that the distinction between *halakhah* and *aggadah* that seemed somewhat rigorous in the case of the tannaitic literature has for all practical purposes collapsed in the amoraic period, for aggadic and halakhic discussions are all intertwined, as are discussions of law as law and midrash in the form of either stories of biblical interpretation or the use of biblical interpretation to determine law.

Notes

1   For a full list of the asserted transmission of the tradition up to the time of Maimonides (in the twelfth century), see his *Introduction to the Mishneh Torah* in *hilchot yesodei hatorah* (The Foundation Laws of the Torah) in Eliyahu Touger's English translation of *Maimonides' Mishneh Torah* (New York/Jerusalem: Moznaim Publishing Corporation, 1989, pp. 12–34).

2   Cf. Chapter 20.

3   For example, the topics of the paragraphs in *bereshit rabbah* (the collection of tannaitic *midrashim* [textually oriented discussions of the Bible] of the Book of Genesis [*bereshit*]) begin as follows: (1) "In the beginning God created", (2) "heaven and earth", (3) "Now the earth was *tohu* (unformed)", (4) "And God said let there be light", (5) "and God saw the light", etc.

4   The Torah is read on an annual cycle, with portions of the text divided into weekly readings. These weekly portions are called *parashot* and are the major way texts from the Torah are identified beyond verses in chapters. Most portions are named from the first critical word in the portion. Hence, for example, the portion that runs from Gen 1:1 to Gen 6:8 is called *bereshit* (in the beginning), which is the first word in the portion.

5   I say nothing here about what any of these statements mean. What is at stake in this determination of the order of creation? Do terms like "Torah" and "Throne of Glory" refer to objects as the terms "Temple," "Messiah," and the "people Israel" do? What kind of thing is "repentance"? Etc. I do not claim to be able to answer these questions. Nor can scholars of midrash, although many, very different ways of understanding these judgments are being proposed in academic journals and books. My own relatively uninformed view is that the different midrashim are precisely what they appear to be, relatively crude attempts to interpret the meaning of the biblical text. I say "crude" because these forms of commentary undergo rigorous

change in the form of the medieval biblical commentaries after the rabbis have absorbed more of the formal rules of formal rhetoric, linguistics, and logic. The new (and, for our purposes, more philosophic) forms of commentary began to appear in the tenth century.

Suggestions for further study

Babylonian Talmud. English translation by I. Epstein. London: Soncino Press, 1935–48.

Blackman, Philip. *The Mishnah.* An English translation. New York: Judaica Press, 1964.

Boyarin, Daniel. *Intertextuality and the Reading of Midrash.* Bloomington: Indiana University Press, 1990.

Braude, William G. *The Midrash on Psalms.* New Haven: Yale University Press, 1959.

Danby, Herbert. *The Mishnah.* An English translation. Oxford: Oxford University Press, 1933.

Daube, David. *Collaboration with Tyranny in Rabbinic Law.* London: Oxford University Press, 1965.

Eichler, Barry and Tigay, Jeffrey (eds.). *Studies in Midrash and Related Literature.* Philadelphia: Jewish Publication Society, 1990.

Eilberg-Schwartz, Howard. *The Human Will in Judaism: The Mishnah's Philosophy of Intention.* Brown Judaic Studies No. 103. Atlanta: Scholars Press, 1986.

Feldman, David M. *Marital Relations, Birth Control, and Abortion in Jewish Law.* New York: Schocken Books, 1974.

Fraade, Steven D. *From Tradition to Commentary: Torah and Its Interpretation in the Midrash Sifre to Deuteronomy.* New York: State University of New York Press, 1990.

Glatzer, Nahum N. *Hammer on the Rock.* New York: Schocken, 1962.

Glatzer, Nahum N. *Hillel the Elder: The Emergence of Classical Judaism.* New York: Schocken, 1966.

Goldenberg, Robert. "Talmud", in Barry W. Holtz (ed.), *Back to the Sources: Reading the Classic Jewish Texts.* New York: Summit Books, 1984, pp. 129–75.

Halivni, David Weiss. *Mishnah, Midrash and Gemara: The Jewish Predilection for Justified Law.* Boston: Harvard University Press, 1986.

Halivni, David Weiss. *Peshat and Derash: Plain and Applied Meaning in Rabbinic Exegesis.* New York: Oxford University Press, 1991.

Hartman, Geoffrey and Budick, Sanford (eds.). *Midrash and Literature.* New Haven: Yale University Press, 1986.

Holtz, Barry. "Midrash", in Barry W. Holtz (ed.), *Back to the Sources: Reading the Classic Jewish Texts.* New York: Summit Books, 1984, pp. 177–211.

Kadushin, Max. *A Conceptual Approach to the Mekilta.* New York: Jewish Theological Seminary of America Press, 1969.

Maimonides, Moses. *Introduction to the Mishneh Torah* in *Maimonides' Mishneh Torah: hilchot yesodei hatorah* (The Foundation Laws of the Torah), translated into English by Eliyahu Touger. New York/Jerusalem: Moznaim Publishing Corporation, 1989.

Midrash Rabbah. English translation under the editorialship of H. Freedman and Maurice Simon. London: Soncino, 1939. Reprinted in 1977.

Mielzener, Moses. *Introduction to the Talmud.* New York: Bloch, 1968.

Montefiore, C. G. and Loewe, H. (eds.). *A Rabbinic Anthology.* New York: Meridian, 1963.

Neusner, Jacob. *Comparative Midrash: The Plan and Program of Genesis Rabbah and Leviticus Rabbah.* Atlanta: Scholars Press, 1986.

Neusner, Jacob. *Form-Analysis and Exegesis: A Fresh Approach to the Interpretation of Mishnah.* Minneapolis: University of Minnesota Press, 1981.

Neusner, Jacob (ed.). *The Formation of the Babylonian Talmud.* Leiden: E. J. Brill, 1970.

Neusner, Jacob. *Invitation to Midrash: The Workings of Rabbinic Bible Interpretation—A Teaching Book.* San Francisco: Harper and Row, 1989.

Neusner, Jacob. *The Mishnah.* New Haven: Yale University Press, 1988.

Neusner, Jacob. *The Mishnah: An Introduction.* Northvale, NJ: Jason Aronson, 1989.

Neusner, Jacob. *The Modern Study of the Mishnah.* Leiden: Brill, 1973.

Neusner, Jacob. *The Philosophical Mishnah.* Atlanta: Scholars Press, 1989.

Neusner, Jacob. *There We Sat Down.* New York: Ktav, 1976.

Neusner, Jacob. *What Is Midrash?* Philadelphia: Fortress, 1987.

Steinsaltz, Adin. *The Essential Talmud.* New York: Basic Books, 1976.

Stern, David. *Parables in Midrash: Narrative and Exegesis in Rabbinic Literature.* Cambridge, MA: Harvard University Press, 1991.

Strack, Hermann L. *Introduction to the Talmud and Midrash.* New York: Atheneum, 1969.

Wright, A. G. *The Literary Genre Midrash.* New York: Alba House, 1956.

Key questions

1. What is the most fundamental doctrine of rabbinic Judaism? What problem does this doctrine solve?

2. In what sense is the Mishnah a philosophical work? How is the logical thinking of the Mishnah a radical break with the logical thinking of the Hebrew Scriptures?

3. Why did the Mishnah not succeed as a code? How instead does it function authoritatively vis-à-vis rabbinic Judaism?

4. Describe the formal or literary structures of the Mishnah, the two Talmuds, and the collections of midrash. How well do these forms match the content of these books?
5. Why is there a separation between Jewish philosophy and Jewish law in the tannaitic period? How does that distinction begin to collapse in the amoraic period?

CHAPTER 10

The God of the early rabbis

The distinctiveness of rabbinic philosophy as philosophy

We have already noted that the names of the orders of the Mishnah constitute a philosophical way of thinking, viz., forming most general categories under which all of reality is ordered into an intelligible model of the life, the universe, and everything in it. A consequence of this judgment is that the subject headings that we recognize as philosophical categories are not those of the early rabbis. For us, influenced primarily by a tradition of philosophic writings that comes out of the schools of Plato and Aristotle, philosophical categories are subjects such as theology and physics, astronomy, life sciences, earth sciences, psychology, epistemology (theories about how we human beings know), linguistics and logic, and (last but by far from least) ethics. For the tannaim the categories were agriculture, liturgy, oaths, marriage, holiness and profanity (what is not holy), and purity and impurity. Nevertheless, all of the kinds of questions we recognize as philosophical are discussed in the early rabbinic literature, even though the format of its discussion is not one that we of the modern West commonly recognize as philosophical.

What would be the best way to introduce the philosophy of the early rabbis? If our goal is to be as accurate as we possibly can in presenting their thought as representative of their history, then we should not restructure the literature into our categories, but present it in its own terms. Certainly, that is the primary way those scholars of the Midrash present it today.[1] However, it is not the approach that we will follow in our summary of midrashic philosophy. Instead we will use an older model that restructures what the rabbis said in terms of traditional western categories. We do so not to impose a Christian model of philosophy on Jewish philosophy, but to highlight the place that the philosophy of the tannaim and the amoraim plays in the history of Jewish philosophy itself as a transition from the philosophy of the Hebrew Scriptures (the subject matter of the first subsection of Part I, Chapters 2 to 7) to the classical

Jewish philosophy of the Middle Ages (the subject matter of Part II, Chapters 14 to 22).

The reader should know that this last claim is controversial. Many academic scholars today believe that the kind of thinking revealed in the texts of the Midrash and the gemara of the Talmuds reflects a distinct way of thinking, qualitatively different from the thinking exhibited in the Bible and the thinking expressed in the body of texts of classical Jewish philosophy. Furthermore, some of them want to argue that the kind of thinking found in the earlier rabbinic literature expresses an authentic form of Jewish thinking that in itself distinguishes Judaism from any other religious community in the world. This claim plays an important role in some of the modern Jewish philosophy that we will discuss at the end of this book (especially in Chapters 26 and 30). I do not share this view, and the history summarized here will reflect the belief that I think is historically more accurate. The view is that the early rabbis were the first to raise the critical philosophical issues about biblical philosophy that will dominate the agenda of subsequent classical philosophy.

The tannaim and amoraim pose serious answers to their profound questions, but the answers are only provisional. What they lack, besides the advantage of a tradition of thought about them that extends over several centuries, are the critical tools needed to sharpen the questions and sharpen the answers. The philosophers of the Muslim world were to develop those tools in the ninth and tenth centuries, which absorbed and further developed the textual inheritance from the Mediterranean world in every field of what we today call science. For the moment, the critical tools were logic, grammar, and rhetoric. However, what the Muslims and the Jews participating in Muslim civilization absorbed was more than these formal studies—it was a model for understanding everything, a model that they used to reinterpret the biblical text in the realized expectation that (armed with these tools) they could advance interpretation beyond what the early rabbis achieved.

My judgment is that classical Jewish philosophy was primarily that: an improvement on the methods of textual interpretation of the early rabbis based on the later rabbis' absorption of the new sciences of the golden age of Islam. Hence, in the chapters of this section (Chapters 10–13) my emphasis will not be on the answers that the rabbis state, but on the problems that their discussions highlight, problems that will become the primary subject matter of classical (medieval) Jewish philosophy.

A textual example: God's glory

Let me give one illustration of my claim that the Midrash primarily raises good questions that are resolved in a certain distinctive way that is unsatisfying in itself but does point the way to the kinds of solutions that the medieval Jewish philosophers would propose.

The Torah portion named *ki tissa* (Exod 30:11–34:35) begins with the concluding discussion of the first laws that Moses received from God on Mount Sinai, continuing with the story of Israel's idolatry with the golden calf, the sight of which provoked Moses to destroy the first set of tablets of the covenant, only to return up the mountain to bring down a second pair of tablets of the covenant. The portion concludes with Moses returning to the camp a second time, this time with his face aglow from the experience.

After the golden calf incident, "the Lord speaks to Moses face to face, as a man speaks to his friend" (Exod 33:11). Moses complained that despite the fact that God said that Moses knows him by his "name" and that he "has also found grace in (God's) sight," he still did not know who would go up with him out of Egypt, the Jewish people or some other nation that God might decide to form out of Israel (leaving Israel to die in the wilderness in punishment for the sin of the golden calf) from Moses' descendants (as he formed a human species out of the descendants of Noah, leaving the rest of humanity to die out because of its sins) (cf. Gen 6 and Exod 32:9–14). Moses wants to know God's "ways" that he (Moses) may "know" him (God) (Exod 33:13). God's answer is that his "presence" will go with him and he should set his mind at ease. Moses distrusts this promise, for he adds "If your presence go not with me, carry us not up hence" (Exod 33:15). (Moses' fear is that God is still angry with the people, as he was in Exod 32:9–14, and that he plans to lead the nation further into the Sinai wilderness only to destroy it once it rebels again against God's word.) God reassures Moses by saying he will be with Israel because "you (Moses) have found grace in my sight and you know me by name" (Exod 33:17). Then Moses says, "Show me, please, your glory?" (Exod 33:18) and God promises, "I will make all my goodness pass before you, and I will proclaim the name of the Lord before you; and I will be gracious to whom I will be gracious, and will show mercy on whom I will show mercy" (Exod 33:19). Next God warns that no one can look upon his face and live (Exod 33:20) and offers instead to let his "glory" pass by while he uses his "hand" to cover Moses, so that Moses will see God's "back" rather than his "face" (Exod 33:21–23). God then descends in a fiery cloud and passes by before Moses, asserting

> The Lord, the Lord God, merciful and gracious, long-suffering, and abundant in goodness and truth; keeping mercy for a thousand generations, forgiving iniquity and transgression and sin, but that will by no means clear the guilty, visiting the iniquity of the fathers upon the children, and upon the children's children, unto the third and fourth generation. (Exod 34:6–7)

God's proclamation in Exod 34:6–7, which begins his second statement of the covenant between God and Israel, is interpreted to be an expression of thirteen distinct attributes of God. The first problem is how you get the text to name thirteen attributes, and the answer is as follows: (1) The Lord (YHVH), (2) the Lord (YHVH), (3) God (*El*), (4) merciful and (5) gracious, (6) long-suffering, and (7) abundant in goodness (8) and truth; (9) keeping mercy for a thousand generations, (10) forgiving iniquity (11) and transgression (12) and sin, (13) but that will by no means clear the guilty, visiting the iniquity of the fathers upon the children, and upon the children's children, unto the third and fourth generation. Now, just what it means to call these thirteen attributes of God "attributes" is also not clear, especially with Nos.1–3. But that question only begins to explore the problems with the interpretation of this biblical text.

How is God related to his attributes? They seem to correspond to the divine "back" that God promised to show Moses instead of his "face" (Exod 33:23), but how are attributes (viz., sets of moral or character qualities) a back? Furthermore, if this is God's back, why does it say at the beginning of the story that Moses spoke with God "face to face," which is interpreted in the biblical passage to be (at least) analogous to intimate speech between two friends (Exod 33:11). Furthermore, if Moses is so intimate with God, why is he so distrustful of God's promise that he needs constant reassurance from God that God will keep his word?

In any case, what God and Moses say to each other makes little sense. When Moses asks to see God's "ways," God says that his "presence" will go up with him and Moses knows God's "name." What do divine presence and name have to do with God's ways? Furthermore, when Moses asks to see God's "glory," God promises to show his "goodness" and "back" but not his "face." What do divine face, back, and goodness have to do with God's glory? What sorts of things are the references of these appellations, and how are they related to God, since in some sense the answer to these questions reveals just who or what God is.

As for the direct commentary on this passage, the *midrash rabbah* collection focuses exclusively on the term "glory" in Exod 33:18. In summary, what it says is the following: One explanation of this term (given by Rabbi Tanhuma ben Abba as well as by Hillel) is that a wise man will always humble (even humiliate) himself in the presence of others so that they can promote (even exalt) him. How this applies to the text is not explained. The most obvious answer is that in so humbling yourself you act as God acted before Moses. God was so humble that Moses had to ask God to show his glory, i.e., show himself to be who he is and not some lesser being.

A second explanation, given by Rabbi Judah ben Nehemiah, is that God humbled himself when he first appeared to Moses at the burning bush so as not to frighten him. Hence he appears to Moses in the voice of Moses' father rather than in his own voice.

In both explanations the one who is humbling himself is God, and he is doing so on account of his greatness. God is so great that if God were to appear as he truly is to a human, even one of the excellence of Moses, then the human would not be able to relate to God. Moses, now more experienced in prophecy, is telling God that he is prepared to know God as he really is. But the Midrash does not tell us, who are not Moses, what that appearance means, so our questions have to remain unanswered.

A radically different line of interpretation is taken by Rabbi Joshua ben Karhah. It is not God who is being too humble, but Moses. Moses, in fear, had hidden himself from God, so God pacified him by appearing as less than he is. However, if Moses had been more courageous and self-confident, God would have revealed to him the deepest mysteries of the universe, viz., "what is above and what is below, what had taken place in the past, and what will happen in the future." Now Moses is prepared to see God as he is, and God is reluctant to show him because of Moses' initial lack of trust.

Rabbi Joshua of Siknin then reports that Rabbi Levi added that, despite Moses' initial humility, God still does reveal himself as he is (i.e., without concealment) to Moses because of Moses' past humility. In this way Rabbi Levi reverses the counter reading of Joshua ben Karhah and returns us to the initial lesson of Judah ben Nehemiah, viz., to act with humility is always a virtue, as it always was for Moses.

A different line of interpretation is then presented by an unnamed commentator who says that "glory" means the reward of the righteous, so that what Moses is doing is asking to learn why the wicked prosper now but only now, and what the reward is that the righteous will eventually receive. In other words, what Moses means when he asks to see God's glory is to foresee the coming of Israel's redemption in the days of the Messiah. (The interpretation is based on an application to our text of how the term "glory" functions in Prov 3:35 and Isa 24:23.) Hence, God's response in our text, that no one can see his face and live, means that no one, even Moses, can know the details of the nature of the world to come that will be our redemption.

Note that the answers given in the Midrash do address real questions in the biblical text, but that the answers given are totally unsatisfying as answers. Note furthermore the use of stories, metaphors, and analogies as explanations. And note finally that answers to questions about God end up as statements about human virtues and moral questions about our material world, which presumably are knowable, as opposed to statements about God's nature, which presumably are unknowable.

Some generalizations about the God of the early rabbis

The short passage we looked at is, I believe, typical of the philosophy of the Midrash. Hence, it is clear why it has been so difficult for scholars—both traditional rabbinic and modern academic—to make sense out of the conceptual content of the Midrash. It is far easier to understand any other kind of traditional Jewish literature, including both Jewish philosophy and Kabbalah, than it is to understand the Midrash. We would not even attempt to do so if it were not for the fact that the Midrash provides an irreplaceable link between the Hebrew Scriptures and classical Jewish philosophy in this history of the discipline.

The passage cited exemplifies some of the features of rabbinic theology (i.e., philosophy about God). In the Torah the emphasis on God's activity is on creation of the world and revelation to prophets; to these actions midrash adds an emphasis on divine redemption. What we know is what God has revealed to us. From that revelation we know that God created the world but we know nothing about its nature. What it means is revealed, at least in principle, in the Genesis account of creation (the *ma'ase bereshit*),[2] but we have no real idea of what the words mean, and furthermore we should not try to uncover their meaning. The same can be said of the world to come, viz., we know of redemption through revelation, especially in the Ezekiel account of the chariot (the *ma'ase merkavah*),[3] but we have no real idea of what the words mean, and furthermore we should not try to uncover their meaning. (Uncovering the meaning of creation was to become a major preoccupation of medieval Jewish philosophy, as uncovering the meaning of the end of days was to become a major preoccupation of the Kabbalah.)

While the Midrash seems to claim to know less about God than the Hebrew Scriptures claim, it says much more about him. First he has inherited an entire court, even city, of angels. In general the Torah is free of any divinities other than the Lord of Israel, although at times there are references to divine "messengers" (*malakhim*), who come in subsequent generations to be understood to be divine angels. Some of them serve God's will directly and others (demonic forces) serve God's will only indirectly. But every force in the universe serves the will of God.

Furthermore, the deity of the Hebrew Scriptures is known only by what he says and four names—*Elohim, El, El-Shaddai*, and *YHVH*, and only the fourth is a proper name. The list of expressions for God increases exponentially in the Midrash. Of the many ways of speaking of God, five names in particular emerge, two of which are biblical and three of which are post-biblical. The two biblical terms, *Elohim* and *YHVH*, express names of God with reference to specific divine properties, divine justice and divine mercy respectively. To these two is added a rabbinic term, *ha-shechinah* (the Presence), which is a name for God with reference to the property of divine presence, i.e., self-revelation. Next, there is the term "the Place" (*ha-makom*) which situates God in the physical world as its place. Finally there is the term "the holy one blessed be he" (*ha-kadosh baruch hu*). This expression is added to every written reference to God. It expresses that God is holy just as he is just, merciful, present, and where the world is situated. However, what the "is" in each case here means (whether it is an expression of identity [as in "1 + 2 is 3"] or an expression of predication [as in "John is a boy"] or something else is not unpacked in the Midrash.

We are told sometimes that the ways used to refer to God are only analogies. In these cases the statements are said to be *kiv'yachol*, whose meaning is the counterpart of the English expression "so to speak." We are not told how extensively the "so to speak" qualification applies. It certainly applies to physical predications of God, viz., that he has body parts like a face, a back, a hand, and a finger. It may also apply to motions in space like ascending and descending. However, we are told nothing else about this use of statements about God as analogies other than the general judgment that we know nothing about God. On one hand we can and should speak about God, especially in prayer; on the other hand we know nothing about the one of whom we speak. No way is suggested to resolve this dilemma. All of these questions of theology await the rise of classical, medieval Jewish philosophy.

Notes

1 The best summary of early rabbinic thought as history, i.e., preserving its own form and categories of presentation, is Ephraim E. Urbach's *The Sages: Their Concepts and Beliefs* (English translation by I. Abrahams. Jerusalem: Magnes Press, 1971).
2 Genesis Ch 1.
3 Ezekiel Ch 1.

Suggestions for further study

Ginzberg, Louis. *The Legends of the Jews*. Philadelphia: Jewish Publication Society, 1909–39. One-volume abridgment published under the same name in 1956.

Kadushin, Max. *A Conceptual Approach to the Mekilta*. New York: Jewish Theological Seminary of America Press, 1969.

Kadushin, Max. *Organic Thinking*. New York: Jewish Theological Seminary of America Press, 1938.

Kadushin, Max. *The Rabbinic Mind*. New York: L. Bloch, 1952.

Moore, George Foote. *Judaism in the First Centuries of the Christian Era*. Cambridge, MA: Harvard University Press, 1927. Reprinted New York: Schocken Books, 1971. See especially Part II (pp. 357–442).

Neusner, Jacob. *Between Time and Eternity: The Essentials of Judaism*. Encinco, CA: Dickenson, 1975.

Neusner, Jacob. *Symbol and Theology in Judaism*. Philadelphia: Fortress Press, 1991.

Novak, David. "The Talmud as a source for philosophical reflection," in Daniel H. Frank and Oliver Leaman (eds.), *History of Jewish Philosophy*, Vol. II of *Routledge History of World Philosophies*. London and New York: Routledge, 1997, pp. 62–80.

Ochs, Peter (ed.). *Understanding the Rabbinic Mind: Essays on the Hermeneutic of Max Kadushin*. South Florida Studies in the History of Judaism No. 14. Atlanta: Scholars Press, 1990.

Rabinovitch, Nachum L. *Probability and Statistical Inference in Ancient and Medieval Jewish Literature*. Toronto: University of Toronto Press, 1973.

Rabinowich, Nosson Dovid. *Talmudic Terminology*. Jerusalem and Brooklyn:

Moznaim, 1988. Contact Rabinowich at 1529 56th St., Brooklyn, NY 11219.
Soloveitchik, Joseph B. *Halakhic Man*. Philadelphia: Jewish Publication Society, 1983.
Urbach, E. E. *The Sages: Their Concepts and Beliefs*. English translation by I. Abrahams. Jerusalem: Magnes Press, 1971. See especially Chs. 2–5, 7, 9, and 11 (pp. 19–96, 124–34, 184–213, 255–85).

Key questions

1. What are the similarities and differences between biblical, midrashic, and medieval Jewish philosophy?
2. How is early rabbinic philosophy distinct from any other kind of western philosophy and what are the problems entailed by its distinctiveness?
3. How is early rabbinic philosophy a transition from the philosophy of the Hebrew Scriptures to the classical Jewish philosophy of the Middle Ages?
4. What are the thirteen attributes of God? From where do the rabbis derive them?
5. What new names does the Midrash apply to God? What do and do not these names tell us?
6. Can we legitimately make any generalizations about what the Midrash says about God? What might they be?

CHAPTER 11

The Torah of the early rabbis

The Torah as ethics

A fundamental distinction in (at least) tannaitic literature is the division between questions of law (*halakhah*) and everything else that is not about law (*aggadah*). It is a distinction that cuts across the division between *midrash* (tannaitic literature whose formal intent is to interpret biblical texts) and *mishnah* (any tannaitic literature that is not *midrash*). Almost all mishnaic literature, like the Mishnah, is halakhic, i.e. almost all discussions of questions of Jewish law by the tannaim (rabbis who lived between 200 BCE and 200 CE, the period of Judah I's Mishnah) are not centered on the meaning of biblical texts. However, not every midrashic collection is aggadic, i.e., some collections of tannaitic commentaries on books of the Bible deal with questions of law. Notable examples in this case are the *Mekhilta* (a halakhic midrash collection on Exodus), the *Sifra* (a halakhic midrash collection on Leviticus), and the *Sifrei* (a halakhic midrash collection on Numbers and Deuteronomy).

The kind of midrash we looked at in the last chapter was aggadic, i.e., a non-legal discussion that focuses in overt form on the biblical text while its content is about the nature and human perception of God. Let us look now at non-midrashic halakhic texts and see if the philosophical nature of the presentations have a different character. In this case the conceptual focus of the chapter is on how the early rabbis understood the concept of Torah.

We have already discussed in Chapter 9 the related doctrines of *torah mi-sinai* and the oral law. At Sinai God revealed to the people of Israel his Torah in two forms—a written text that has been preserved unchanged by the rabbis since the time of Ezra, and an authentic, continuous oral tradition that transmits the correct interpretation of the written text for all situations. That the Torah is complete in the sense that the correct answer to all moral questions can be found in the proper interpretation of the words of the double law (the written and the oral Torah) is a fundamental principle of Judaism at least since the time of the amoraim. There are no moral precepts, be they general or particular, that do not fall within the domain of Jewish law.

One way to express this fundamental doctrine is that the written text of the Torah functions as a constitution for the rabbinic state, the oral tradition of legal rabbinic judgments is the record of the state's case law, and in principle the case law is a set of consistent and coherent consequences that can be deduced or inferred from the constitution. To make such inferences requires a form of logic, and the early rabbis at least began to develop it. In this respect the philosophic state of Jewish law was seriously more advanced than every other area of Jewish philosophy. Not only were the judgments of the tannaim and the amoraim about civil and moral questions more detailed and determined than their statements about every other topic of theological and philosophical interest; they also were based on a conscious use of methods of inference that did not apply directly to their other discussions.

The rabbis offered many suggestions as to what were the principles of legitimate inference from the statement of specific laws in the written constitution (the Torah) and the previous case law (the Mishnah, its related *baraitot*, and the *midrashim*). The list of principles that gained the broadest acceptance in subsequent generations of rabbinic philosophers of law was Rabbi Ishmael's list of thirteen rules. It is presented in the introduction to the *Sifra* and appears today as part of the daily morning blessings (*birchat ha-shachar*) in every traditional rabbinic prayer book, usually placed just before the recitation of what is called the "rabbi's kaddish" (*kaddish de-rabbanan*).

Ishmael's rules of inference

As stated, there are thirteen rules. (1) "From minor to major (*mi-kal ve-chomer*)," which means that a strict ruling can be inferred from a lenient ruling and a lenient one from a strict one. (2) "From a similar ruling (*migzerah shavah*)," which means that the sense of the use of words in one legal context can be used to interpret the legal intent of similar expressions in another legal context. (3) "From a major foundation built from one or two texts," which means the inference of a general principle from one or two biblical verses. (4) "From something general and particular," which means that the application of the statement of a general ruling is limited to the domain specified in a subsequent statement.

(5) "From something particular and general," which means that the domain of a specific judgment is broadened when it is followed by a general judgment. (6) "A general (judgment followed by) a particular (judgment, followed again by) a general (judgment)" restricts the range of applications to the particular case. (7) "From a general judgment that needs a particular one (to clarify its meaning) and from a particular that needs a general (to clarify its meaning)" in order to specify an exception to the rules defined in (4) and (5). (8) "Anything included in the general (judgment) that is singled out of the general to teach (something) not only teaches about itself, but teaches (something further) about the entire general (principle)." (9) "Everything that is (part of) the general (judgment) and is singled out to give an argument for something whose meaning is similar is singled out to make (the general ruling) more lenient, not more strict." (10) "Everything that is (part of) the general (judgment) and is singled out to give an argument for a (very) different (case) that is not similar is singled out to make (the general ruling) stricter, not more lenient." (11) "Everything that was (part of) the general (judgment) and singled out to judge a new case can only be returned to (the) general (judgment from which it was singled out) if Scripture (explicitly) interprets it as (part of) the general (judgment)." (12) "The (meaning of some) thing is learned from its context, and the (meaning of some) thing (else) is learned from its end (i.e., from the passage that follows it)." (13) "Similarly, two (biblical) verses contradict each other until the third text comes and reconciles them."[1]

Scholars debate just what these thirteen rules are. In my judgment they are all variations on a single logic form, viz., argument by analogy. They are all different ways of saying that when two statements are alike, valid inferences can be made from one statement to the other insofar as they are alike. Of course this is a principle of rhetoric, i.e., a formal rule intended to convince people, or "show them," something. As such they are the kind of reasoning that people in the same profession of the rabbis—lawyers, judges, and legislators—must use. However, they are not examples of the kind of reasoning that philosophers and scientists use—principles of logic whose intent is to learn something new from something already known. As such, the rules of rhetoric of the rabbis are rules for forming reasonable opinions or beliefs, but not rules for gaining knowledge, and this is the epistemic situation appropriate to questions of conventional law and government rather than science. In different words, what the early rabbis developed is a systematic study of the moral politics of Judaism; what awaits development in the next stage of Jewish philosophy after the rise of Islam is a systematic study of what we will call the sciences of Judaism.

Lifnim mi-shurat ha-din

The application of rhetorical argument by analogy within a legal system permits stipulated laws in the system to be extended possibly without limit to all contexts of lived life between human beings. However, it can be asked, can the legal rulings of a political regime (even one created by God) ever be complete in the sense that its rulings are identical with what is ethics, so that anything required by the law is moral, anything prohibited by the law is immoral, and anything excluded from the domain of the moral is morally neutral? A category of judgment that suggests that the rabbis believed that the domain of morality is broader than the domain of Jewish law is the principle of *lifnim mi-shurat ha-din*, which literally means judgments that are beyond the boundary of legal judgment. However, scholars—both rabbinic and academic—have debated whether or not the most obvious interpretation that I have suggested is correct. Let us focus our discussion of it on a single case of halakhic midrash which highlights the difficulty in answering this question as well as other features of rabbinic civil and moral ethics.

The case of Joshua ben Levi

The Jerusalem Talmud[2] relates a story that is set during the time between the second and third Jewish war for independence from Rome when Hadrian was the emperor and instituted a general policy of oppression against the Judeans, including the rabbis, in the vain hope that punishment was the way to overcome the people's desire for independence. It was a time when popular Zealots were carrying out guerilla attacks on the Roman occupying troops and then hiding. One such "freedom fighter," Ulla bar Qoosheb, was hiding in the attic of Rabbi Joshua ben Levi's home in Lyddia. The Romans surrounded the rabbi's home, asked him to turn Ulla over to them, and threatened that if he did not then hostages would be taken and executed. Joshua then went into his house, told Ulla what had transpired, and Ullah on his own surrendered himself to the Romans. Up till that time, Joshua used to communicate regularly with the prophet Elijah, but afterwards Elijah stopped appearing to him. Joshua then prayed and said in his defense that everything he did was "according to the law" (*ki-halakhah*) but Elijah responded that he did not communicate with people who merely followed the law; rather, he appears only to people who have the moral characteristics of the pious (*midot ha-hasidim*).

The first question about the tale is, what is the "law" in accordance with which Rabbi Joshua acted, and there are a number of answers. Joshua himself cited one in his own defense. First, he gave what we would recognize as a straight utilitarian argument based on the principle of consequences. He said that it was better that the one man, Ulla, die than the entire community that the Romans would execute instead. Secondly, he cites the case of "the company of men." Let us take the second argument first.

A different gemara in the Babylonian Talmud (bt Terumot 7:19) discusses the case in the second Book of Samuel, Chapter 20, of Sheba ben Bichri. Sheba led a rebellion of Benjaminites against King David. David sent his military commander, Joab, with troops to quell the rebellion. David's forces besieged Sheba's forces in the walled city of Abel. A "wise woman" spoke to Joab on behalf of the city, which she saved by cutting off Sheba's head and throwing it over the wall to where Joab's men had the city surrounded. The question discussed in the gemara is whether or not the wise woman's action was proper under Jewish law. Rabbi Simeon ben Johai, who was a supporter of the rebel action against the Romans, said absolutely not. Under no circumstances is it ever right to turn a rebel over to the enemy in order to save the city. However, Rabbi Judah bar Ilai, who was against the rebellion, said that she acted properly because Joab had the city surrounded. Hence, this argument (the so-called "company of men" argument) is a variation of Rabbi Joshua's first utilitarian argument. Since the city was surrounded there was no chance for the wanted person to escape. Hence, no matter what was done, he would be killed. The only question is, would he alone be killed or would the entire city die with him. Hence, in this case, viz., when the city is surrounded, the law permits handing over the wanted person.

This then is the argument that Rabbi Joshua gave, but the story also indicates other ways that he acted according to the law. The most important one is that Joshua did not actively (unlike the wise woman of the Bible) turn Ulla over. His deed is passive rather than active; he simply told Ulla the hopelessness of the situation and let him act on his own. If there is a sin involved here, it is one of omission only. The case he could have recited in his own defense was the case of the men carrying dedicated loaves (in bt Terumot 7:19). According to this story, men were carrying loaves of bread that had been dedicated for use in sacrifice in the Temple and hence could not be eaten by anyone else in any other context. They were stopped by heathens and threatened if they would not turn the bread over to the hooligans. Rabbi Eliezer ben Hyrcanus (a man who communicated with God and who often presents the voice of moral absoluteness) said that under no circumstances should the men turn the bread over, but his legal nemesis, Joshua ben Hananiah (a man who was not noted for any spiritual qualities but who enjoyed considerable political success in the rabbinic parliament of the Sanhedrin) said that they should place the loaves down on a rock and let the hooligans take the bread on their own. It was Joshua who introduced the moral distinction between passive and active actions. To let an evil happen is not the same thing as committing an evil. For those most spiritual people who communicate with divine voices (who are the very few), perhaps it is not enough merely to avoid doing evil, but for the ordinary people (who are the many) simply not to sin actively is a major accomplishment. Hence, Joshua ben Levi could have invoked the legal precedence of Joshua ben Hananiah, to which the story, as it is told, alludes.

These then are two of the arguments that Joshua could have been invoking in his claim that what he did was legal. Note, however, that the prophet Elijah, who will at the proper time initiate the redemption of the world by proclaiming the coming of the messiah, granted Joshua his argument and retorted that it did not matter. The prophet lives (eternally) by a much higher standard. His ethics are not the ethics of this world. They are the absolute messianic standards for those seeking to invoke the messianic age and human perfection. Those to whom Elijah speaks do not settle for merely being good. They strive to become perfect.

In summary, the case of Joshua ben Levi and Ulla bar Qoosheb highlights a number of interesting principles of philosophical ethics. They are the following: (1) The principle of consequences that will play a critical role in the development of modern utilitarian ethics which appears in our gemara in a reasonably sophisticated sense, far from the simplistic judgment that the welfare of the many takes precedence over the welfare of the few. It is this principle more than any other that guides the moral judgments of "ordinary people" who, like our two rabbis Joshua, simply seek to live and get by in this world. (2) There is an important moral distinction between considering the good from the perspective of what is permissible and judging the good from the perspective of what is best. The difference is one between the morality of the ordinary human being, which is the subject of law, and the morality of the extraordinary human being, which is the subject of the characteristic moral traits of the pious. The latter reflects the morality of the religious extremist who seeks perfection. The former conditions are the focus of the early rabbis; the latter is the focus in our texts of rabbis such as Eliezer ben Hyrcanus, Simeon ben Johai, and the prophet Elijah. It is a messianic focus upon which the ethics of the medieval philosophers and mystics would fix.

Is Jewish law complete?

How then are we to answer the question about the completeness of rabbinic law? In my personal opinion there are contradictory answers and both seem to me to be true. As the case of Joshua ben Levi illustrates, there are situations when the morally right thing to do is not identical with how the law distinguishes the legal from the illegal. When Joshua argued that what he did was in accord with the law, he was right. On the other hand, doing what is right in the legal sense of the term is not the same thing as doing what is right in the moral sense of the term. Joshua was permitted under law to turn Ulla bar Qoosheb over to the authorities, but to do so was not the best moral thing he could do. In Elijah's word in our halakhic Midrash, it is not how someone who is pious (a *hasid*) will act.

In general, law differentiates between what is permissible and not permissible even when the law of the state is also understood to be a moral law, as it is in the case of rabbinic Judaism. However, this distinction is not sufficient for ethics. Ethics does not just draw a line between what is good and bad; it distinguishes what is the worst from what is merely bad, and (far more important) it distinguishes what is best from what is merely good. The rabbis as lawyers could settle for the simpler distinction between the good and the bad as the permissible and non-permissible, as what is, in the language of the rabbis, "according to the *halakhah*." However, these rabbis were more than lawyers. They were also philosophers, who, as philosophers, knew that this legal distinction was not sufficient. The Jewish people were understood by them to be a "holy nation" and, as such, they were expected to strive to do what is best, to act in the language of the rabbis "according to the character of the *hasid*," whose standard is more than what is good but is rather what is best. The higher standard becomes the emphasis in rabbinic philosophy in the ethics of the Middle Ages. There the focus becomes (in the language of the Aristotelian sciences) the attainment of happiness, which the rabbis understood to be identical with the religious obligation to achieve a human perfection that will invoke the realization of the messianic age. This understanding of ethics and human psychology has its source in the early rabbis' legal ethics, discussed in this chapter, as well as in their understanding of human psychology, which is our next topic of discussion.

Notes

1   For an example of how each rule works, see the commentary on these rules in any Orthodox prayer book such as *The ArtScroll Siddur: Weekday/Sabbath/ Festival*, commentary by Nosson Scherman Brooklyn, NY: Mesorah Publications, 1984, pp. 48–52), and/or *The Daily Prayerbook*, commentary by Philip Birnbaum (New York, NY: Hebrew Publishing Co., 1949, pp. 41–5).
2   In 46b.

Suggestions for further study

Bleich, J. David. "Is there an ethic beyond Halakhah?" in Norbert M. Samuelson (ed.), *Studies in Jewish Philosophy: Collected Essays of the Academy for Jewish Philosophy, 1980–1985*. Lanham MD: University Press of America, 1987, pp. 527–46.
Daube, David. *Collaboration with Tyranny in Rabbinic Law*. London: Oxford University Press, 1965.
Feldman, David M. *Birth Control in Jewish Law*. New York: New York University Press, 1968.
Lichtenstein, Aharon. "Does Jewish tradition recognize an ethic independent of Halakha?" in Menachem M . Kellner (ed.), *Contemporary Jewish Ethics*. New York: Sanhedrin Press, 1978, pp. 102–23.
Schreiber, Aaron M. *Jewish Law and Decision-Making: A Study through Time*. Philadelphia: Temple University Press, 1979.

Key questions

1. Explain how rabbinic Judaism understood the fundamental belief that *halakhah* is complete?
2. What are Rabbi Ishmael's thirteen principles? For what are they useful? How can they not be used?

3. For the early rabbis, are there any moral principles that extend beyond the law?
4. What two radically different kinds of ethics are found in early rabbinic philosophy? Are they compatible or mutually exclusive?
5. How are rabbinic legal ethics tied to rabbinic understandings of human psychology and redemption?

CHAPTER 12

The Jewish people of the early rabbis

We have now looked at all three forms of rabbinic literature. In the chapter on the concept of God we looked at an aggadic midrash (the explanation of Exodus' thirteen attributes of God) in the tannaitic collections of *midrashim*, and in the chapter on the concept of the Torah we examined a halakhic midrash (the story of Sheba ben Bichri in 2 Sam 20) and two mishnaic forms of literature in the amoraic gemara—one in the Babylonian Talmud (Ishmael's thirteen principles) and another in the Jerusalem Talmud (the story of Rabbi Joshua ben Levi with Elijah). Now, on the question of the Jewish people, we will look at examples of these forms as they came to be incorporated into the rabbinic prayer book.

Actually, it is too early in our history of Jewish philosophy to speak of a prayer book as such. This kind of religious text would not be formalized until the next period of Jewish life under the hegemony of the Muslim empire. However, the roots of formal Jewish prayer go back to biblical Judaism when prayers were formulated for priests to recite in the Temple while sacrificing the offerings that the people brought. Scholars debate when the rabbinic institution began, either before or after the destruction of the second Temple. However, whenever that was, the rabbis began to formalize some of the prayers that the congregation should recite within the context of fixed days and times for prayer and a fixed order of prayers.

If we consider the modern traditional rabbinic prayer book, it is an evolving text around a fixed core, with additions set either at the beginning or the end of the liturgy. The core was fixed early in the Muslim period, and many (if not most) of its prayers were composed in either biblical times (e.g., the many psalms used liturgically) or in the time of the tannaim and amoraim. The prayers we will focus on here were composed in these two early rabbinic periods.

What is a human being?

The first thing to say about the Jewish people is that they are people, i.e., human beings, so that whatever the rabbis believed about human nature they also believed about Jewish nature. Hence, the first topics to be considered have to do with what human beings are. Afterwards we will ask what marks distinguish Jews within this more general classification.

The first liturgical acts of a Jew in every day are acts that in no way distinguish Jews from any other human beings other than the blessings uttered that accompany the act. They arise, wash their hands, and go to the bathroom. The prayers recited are found in Berakhot 11a and 60b of the Babylonian Talmud. The prayer recited for washing the hands thanks God for the commandment to wash our hands. It is a standard formula that transforms any natural human action into a commanded action. As such, it is an address to the God of creation whose philosophic context is that nature runs by physical laws that are themselves spoken commandments from God. As God orders the stars to move in a fixed periodic order in the heavens and the animals to reproduce, so he orders human beings to rise in the morning and wash their hands. In this context all that is unique about a human being is that the act is voluntary, and what is distinct about Jewish human beings is that they praise God for this commandment. Hence, the Jewish human says, "Blessed are you O Lord our god who sanctified us by his commandments and commanded us to wash hands."

The prayer recited with going to the bathroom is the following:

> Blessed are you O Lord our god, king of the universe, who created the human being in wisdom by creating in him holes and orifices. It is clear and certain before your Throne of Glory that if you were to open or close any one of them it would be impossible (for the human being) to exist and they would perish before you. Blessed are you O Lord, who heals all flesh and does wonderful things.

This prayer, too, is an address from the universal human being to the God of creation. It highlights a standard human function that in no way distinguishes a human being from any other animal, bird, or fish in the sphere of God's created earth, for all living things take in other living things through one hole (a mouth), and then, having ingested all the life force from their food to perpetuate their own life, expel what remains through another hole (an anus) for, if the refuse remained within the body, it would poison and thereby kill the body.

Living is a miraculous act because, if any hole is added to the body, then the internal fluids will escape the body, killing the person, and if any existing hole in the body is closed, the body will die. If the mouth is closed, then food cannot be taken in. The living thing has no permanent source of energy within itself. It lives only by killing something else that is alive. Yet this act of taking life for the sake of preserving life is not a crime, because it is something that God commands. The judgment, building on the preceding prayer for hand washing, presupposes that all natural functions are acts of obedience to divine law, and transforms the presupposition into an expression of wonder—wonder at what God can do that goes beyond anything within human capacity.

What distinguishes human beings as distinct from other animals is that they are so much like God, which here simply means that their actions are voluntary. But what distinguishes them from God is their lack of perfection. What God wills in his mind occurs in physical reality, whereas what human beings will rarely occurs as they will it. All that is human is imperfect and therefore subject to decay. In this respect the human being is the same as every other creature who in the beginning comes into existence from nothing, grows to become something, and then declines to return in the end to the nothing from which each creature came. Hence, the traditional Jewish funeral service begins by reciting the line from the biblical Book of Psalms (Ps 144:3–4):

> O Lord, what is a human (*Adam*) that you know him, a son of man (*ben enosh*) that you think of him. (For) a human is like a vain breath (*hevel*), his days passing by like a shadow.

Humans may create, but what they create exists only for a moment, whereas what God creates, like God himself, exists forever. It is this recognition of the difference between God and his creatures, and the wonder that the recognition in nature produces, that marks off human beings from all other living things.

What is a Jew?

What marks the Jew, at least in the eyes of the rabbis who composed the liturgy, as chosen from other human beings is what they next recite in their daily liturgy. Having washed their hands and gone to the bathroom, the Jews say "Blessed are you O Lord our god, king of the universe, who sanctified us by his commandments and commanded us to be occupied with words of Torah." The "us" commanded when washing the hands were human beings; here the "us" commanded are the Jewish people. The theme repeats and expands what was clearly implied in the philosophy of the early rabbis but was not so clearly stated in the philosophy of biblical Judaism. All that makes the Jews a people is that God commanded them and only them to obey the laws of the Torah.

The prayers that now follow are commanded for Jews and only for Jews. Next they say the following:

> Please O Lord our god make pleasant the words of your Torah in our mouth and the mouth of your people, the house of Israel. May we, our descendants, and the descendants of your people the house of Israel, all of us, become knowers of your name and learners of your Torah for its own sake. Blessed are you O Lord who teaches Torah to his people Israel.

The previous prayer repeats but adds nothing to the biblical under-standing of chosenness. This prayer goes beyond the biblical injunction for Jews to obey the Torah's commandment to command Jews to understand what is commanded. The ultimate commanded act is the obligation to study. In so doing the prayer hints at the biblical understanding that there is nothing special about the Jewish people as compared with any other people except the fact that, for no apparent reason, God chose them to be so commanded. The present generation of the descendants of Jacob have no more natural capacity for holiness than did the children of Jacob who sent their brother Joseph into slavery in hope of his death, or the descendants of those twelve sons who showed little capacity in their first polity to obey God's word. Nor have they any special capacity for study. The blood-related citizens of rabbinic Judaism are commanded to study the Torah, but they need to pray for God to make that study "pleasant" since it is not something that they would by nature enjoy—neither they nor their descendants. The present Jewish people have no more capacity for wisdom than did their ancestors in the second Jewish polity. Hence, that they in fact do study and learn the wisdom of the Torah is as miraculous an expression of what God wills (now as the revealer of the Torah) as the fact of going to the bathroom is a miraculous expression of what God wills (then as the creator of the universe). All exists, including the Jewish people, to praise the one God of the world whose actions, as creator as well as revealer, are wondrous.

What is the human end?

All things exist to fulfill the word of God. For those who are born Jewish the completion of their nature is to do something beyond nature—to understand what God commands. This end is the study of the Torah, now understood to include not only the written words of the text of the Hebrew Scriptures but also the correct interpretation of those words in the chain of tradition. However, this understanding cannot be completed in any human lifetime.

The levels of interpretation are infinite. The law can only be understood when it is creatively applied to every real situation in lived life. However, nature is endlessly innovative. No new situation is precisely like any past situation. The bridge here between past and present into the future is the creative application in the particular of the laws specified through past rabbinic applications of the Torah. Each new application by a rabbi becomes a precedent for every new situation in the future, and each application is a specification of what the Torah means. Hence, no human being who can die can ever fully understand the meaning of the Torah—not even a prophet such as Moses, whose like in wisdom never has and never again will exist until the end of days when the Messiah will appear.

The end of Jewish existence is to know the Torah, and this end can only be fulfilled in messianic terms. Life in the present is about understanding the past, and understanding the past requires living in an expectation of a future redemption. This hoped-for end and perfection to creation is the last major theme we will examine in this summary of early rabbinic philosophy.

Suggestions for further study

The Daily Prayer Book (ha-siddur ha-shalem). English translation by Philip Birnbaum. New York: Hebrew Publishing Co., 1949.

Neusner, Jacob. Judaism: The Evidence of the Mishnah. Chicago: University of Chicago Press, 1981.

Neusner, Jacob. The Life of Torah: Readings in the Jewish Religious Experience. Encino and Belmont, CA: Dickinson, 1974.

Neusner, Jacob. The Way of Torah. An Introduction to Judaism. Belmont, CA: Wadsworth, 1992.

Key questions

1. When was the Jewish prayer book composed? What existed by the time of the completion of the Hebrew Scriptures? What existed by the time of the completion of the Talmuds?
2. What do Jews first do when they awake in the morning and what are the prayers they recite?
3. What do the morning prayers in the prayer book tell us about human beings in comparison and contrast to God and to other living things?
4. What do the morning prayers in the prayer book tell us about Jews in comparison and contrast to other human beings?
5. Why is merely living a miraculous act? What does your answer say

l nature?
What does your answer say

id that the Jews are God's
essed in the early morning

wish liturgy, why did God
ist? Why do Jews exist?
can understand the Torah?
What is the rabbis' solution

SAMUELSON, NORBERT
ORDER NO: 66881
ORDER DATE: 22JUN2004
JEWISH PHILOSOPHY : AN HISTORICAL INTRODUCTION
/ NORBERT M. SAMUELSON.
CONTINUUM INTERNATIONA 2003   1 VOLS
34.95 USD PAPER
0-8264-6141-7 2003-43524
R5-417783
QTY ORDERED: 001
QTY SHIPPED: 001
190201/0018
GERBER
ACQUISITIONS
BLACKWELL BOOK SERVICES
SYRACUSE UNIV
NLSY
120350009I

CHAPTER 13

The rabbinic view of ethics

We saw in the last chapter that what distinguishes the Jews as the chosen people is that God gave to them, for no apparent good reason, the Torah to obey and, more importantly, to understand. While to understand the Torah has a higher status than merely to observe what it says, the two are not unrelated, for the attainment of the wisdom of the Torah is conditional on its observance. In general, the regimen of the laws of the Torah came to be understood as a discipline whose intent is to inculcate in its observers dispositions toward correct behavior. These cultivated dispositions, called moral characteristics (*middot*; *middah* in the singular), are also necessary for an individual to acquire "wisdom" (*chochmah*), and it is wisdom that comes to be understood as the ultimate human good or perfection (*shelemut*).

Rabbinic virtue ethics

The identification of wisdom (*sophia* in Greek and *chochmah* in Hebrew) and happiness (*eudaemonia* in Greek and *osher* in Hebrew) is clearly expressed in the virtue ethics of Plato and Aristotle, and the rabbis' adoption of this kind of ethics may be a consequence of the influence of Hellenistic philosophy on them. However, the source for this kind of ethics is no less biblical than it is Hellenistic, for at least one book of the Hebrew Scriptures—the Book of Proverbs—is a work of virtue ethics in which obedience to the precepts of the Torah is understood to be a way to attain a certain kind of wisdom, identical with happiness. The clearest book in all of early rabbinic literature that expresses this kind of ethics is the tractate "Sayings of the Fathers" (literally, chapters of the fathers [*pirkei avot*]), which is found in the fourth order of the Mishnah (on "damages" [*nezikin*]).

A discussion of this tractate combines our earlier focus on the explicit forms of early rabbinic literature (in this case on mishnaic *aggadah*, i.e., non-legal material whose form is not that of commentary on verses of the Bible) with the focus on rabbinic liturgy in the last chapter, because these six chapters of early rabbinic aphorisms about human virtue are recited on the Sabbath afternoons between the Passover (*pesach*) and the Jewish New Year (*rosh hashanah*). We will look, in some detail, at the beginning of this tractate as a reflection of the whole six chapters of the treatise.

The Sayings of the Fathers

The text in this tractate in the Mishnah opens with the dogma of the chain of transmission of the two interdependent laws—the written and the oral. Here both are simply called "Torah." The chain of transmission runs from God to Moses, to Joshua, to the elders, to the prophets, to the "men of the Great Assembly" (*knesset ha-gedolah*). According to rabbinic tradition, the Great Assembly was the beginning of what would become the Sanhedrin. It was a legislative body of Jewish scholars that was formed at the time of Ezra (about 500 BCE) and lasted until the rise of the Pharisees (around 300 BCE), who are identified with the first generations of rabbis.[1]

The rest of the paragraphs and chapters of the "Sayings of the Fathers"[2] attribute moral aphorisms to different early rabbis in a presumed historical succession that begins with the last wise priests who are also men of the Great Assembly and ends with third-generation tannaim who live in the middle of the second century CE, i.e., who were rabbis in the last generation before the Nasi Judah I edited the Mishnah.

The first quoted aphorism is attributed in general to the men of the Great Assembly. We are told that

> they said three things: Be patient in making judgment, develop many disciples/ students (*talmidim* [*talmid* in the singular]), and make a fence around the Torah.

The text begins with political advice for judges to succeed. The principle of the "fence" is an important one that needs a word of explanation. As we saw in the last chapter, law (*halakhah*) distinguishes what is good from what is bad, but not what is good from what is best or even better. In different words, law maps out a territory and draws a line; what is on one side of the line is bad and what is on the other side of the line is good. Hence, where the line itself is drawn is at a point of what is least good and least bad. Now, the tendency in human nature is to settle for the mere good (as opposed to pursuing the best) and to go as close to the line of moral separation as possible. However, in so doing there is always the danger that the moral agent will unintentionally go too far and cross over the line. Therefore, to protect an agent from this normal tendency a fence is drawn, which is a line removed from the threshold, so that when individuals in error cross the line, they have not done anything seriously wrong.

In this way our statement of rabbinic ethics begins with very practical political advice for people in power who rule by means of law. As we shall see, the aphorisms become increasingly more expressions of what the Greek philosophers called "theoretical (even theological) judgment" (*theoria*) and less "practical (even political) judgment" (*phronesis*).

In the second paragraph Simeon the Just says that

> the world stands (*'omed*) on three things—on the Torah, on service (*'avodah*), and on deeds of piety (*gemilut chasadim*).

Simeon the Just is identified in the Mishnah as one of the last members of the Great Assembly. Tradition marks him as a miracle worker who reigned as a High Priest in the penultimate dynasty of the Onias family that was replaced in the Maccabean revolt against the Syrian Greeks in the second century BCE. Simeon himself is either Simeon I (who reigned around the beginning of the third century BCE) or Simeon II (who reigned around the end of the third century and the beginning of the second century BCE).

It is not clear what Simeon is saying here. The most difficult term is the operative verb, "stands." Clearly it is not intended to be understood literally. These three "things" are not really things; they are behavioral ideals which, as such, do not literally "stand" anywhere. However, just what the verb means is subject to more than one interpretation. Whatever its clear meaning, equivocally what the verb expresses is that the value of the world itself and human life within it (both collective and individual) depends on at least striving to attain these three ideals. However, this interpretation is intentionally vague. We have not sufficient textual evidence to be more precise in our interpretation. (Those who give these kinds of early rabbinic judgments a clear meaning are the classical Jewish philosophers whom we will begin to study in the next chapter.)

The "service" here means, minimally, the activities of sacrifice in the Temple cult. Maximally, it means doing whatever God desires—behaving like a good "slave" (*'eved*, which has the same Hebrew root as "service") of God. In this maximal sense of the term, there is no clear separation between "service" and "Torah," since both have to do with obedience to God's word. However, even in this broad sense a distinction can be made, where the emphasis on the term "Torah" is the study of God's will and the emphasis on the term "service" is the performance of what has been studied. However, in both cases, what we are talking about is studying and observing the law, something that every ordinary person is obligated to do. The third technical term, "deeds of piety," moves us beyond what is merely "according to the law" to the pursuit of the moral ideal.

In general, all of the aphorisms have in common at least two levels of operative meaning. The first, what I would call "simple," meaning is practical and legal. The second, what I would call "deep," meaning is ideal and theoretical. In Simeon's aphorism, the simple meaning is to study and obey the sacrificial provisions of the Torah as the rabbis interpret them, while the deep meaning is to go beyond the letter of the law to acquire a moral and intellectual perfection, the attainment of which is the very purpose for which the universe exists.

In the third paragraph Antigonus of Sokho says the following:

> Do not be like servants ('avadim) who serve the master on condition of receiving a reward; rather be like servants who serve the master without a condition of receiving a reward. Let the fear/awe of heaven (more shamayim) be upon you.

As Simeon is the last member of the Great Assembly in the chain of the transmission of torah mi-sinai, Antigonus is one of the first of the rabbis in the chain whom the later rabbis identified with the Pharisees. He was active as a judge during the first half of the third century BCE. Here the simple meaning of the saying attributed to him is that servants who perform their service solely for the sake of a reward will serve with less excellence than servants who serve for less self-serving reasons, whatever they are, be they the love of the master or simply the desire to do whatever you do with excellence. At a deeper level, the "servants" are those who worship God, the service is worship, and the master who is served is God. Hidden here is a judgment about the rabbinic belief in divine providence.

"Divine providence (hashgachah)" is a theory about the wisdom and justice of God's governance of the world. In a just universe, all good deeds and thoughts will be rewarded in proportion to their goodness, and all bad deeds and thoughts will be punished in proportion to their evil. However, that does not appear to be the way God runs the world. It seems that human beings can choose what they do, which means that God has not determined it, and those choices do involve consequences for them, for others, and for the world. However, it is not clear just what those consequences are and how they are administered. The rabbis speak often about this question, but what they say about it is not often clear. For example, in Chapter 3 we are told that Rabbi Akiba said,

> Everything is foreseen (*tsafui*), permission (*ha-reshut*) is given, in goodness the world is judged, and everything is according to the majority of the action (*rov ha-ma'aseh*).

What I have given is a literal translation of the original Hebrew. However, that is not the way most translators translate it. For example, Herbert Danby, in his translation of the Mishnah (Aboth 3:16) says "All is foreseen, but freedom of choice is given; and the world is judged by grace, yet all is according to the excess of works [that be good or evil]." Now Danby's translation is clear. God foresees everything, but despite that human beings have free will. How that is possible is not clear. If God foresees how you will choose then how you will choose seems to be determined, in which case you do not have free will. Danby's translation suggests that the early rabbis recognized the paradox between affirming God's perfect knowledge of everything, including human choices, and affirming that there is free will to make or not to make these choices. Furthermore, even though they recognized the conceptual problems, they made the affirmation anyway.

   This is certainly what the text says on Danby's translation, but it is not what the Hebrew itself says. What it says is that, while everything is foreseen, there is still "permission." It says nothing about either divine determinism (just divine foresight) or freedom of choice. *Reshut* is a legal term, not a psychological term. It says nothing about how we choose, be it freely or not freely; it simply says that human beings are authorized under the law to make some choices. Just what "authorized" means here is not explained.

   The second part of Akiba's statement is equally problematic. Danby takes "goodness" to mean grace. In so translating he has in mind *midrashim* in connection with the creation of the world that speak about God creating the world by balancing both justice and mercy or grace. God creates as both *Elohim*, understood to be God acting with respect to justice, and as YHVH, understood to be God acting with respect to mercy or grace. God creates by balancing both, because by either one alone the world would be destroyed. If the world were governed solely by justice, then the laws of justice would require God to destroy the world because of all the sin in it. On the other hand, if the world were governed solely by grace, then sin would be so widespread (because there is no punishment to deter evil behavior), the world would self-destruct. Hence, the only way the world can "stand" (here meaning persist), in the view of these authors of the Midrash, is by a balance of the two divine persona.

Danby's rendition of Akiba's statement makes sense in the light of these *midrashim*, but it is not what the text says. It does not say the world is judged by "grace"; it says it is judged by "goodness," and the goodness is determined according to the "majority of the action," whatever that means. Whether or not the early rabbis themselves knew more clearly what they were saying is open to debate, by both academic and rabbinic scholars. In either case, this doctrine of divine providence is determined in detail by the classical Jewish philosophers whom we will study next. Clearly the rabbis were concerned about the issue, as our primary text by Antigonus of Sokho indicates. But that does not mean that he or any other rabbi had worked out a clear solution to their philosophical/theological problems. Again, that work was left for the classical Jewish philosophers.

All of our remaining paragraphs can be read in this way. They all possess a simple meaning that is practical and legal, but beyond the simple meaning is a deeper meaning that is conceptual and philosophical. The deeper meaning points to an important lack of clarity in rabbinic philosophy of which the rabbis were aware, but their awareness does not mean that they had an equally perceptive answer to their problems. The solutions, most of which had to do (directly or indirectly) with questions of religious ethics, awaited specification and clarification in the classical period of Jewish philosophy.

Redemption and the end of days

The rabbis quoted next in our text, after Antigonus of Sokho, are the five generations of pairs (*zugot*) who governed the Pharisaic Sanhedrin as majority party leader (*nasi*) and minority party leader (*av bet din*). They are, as they are quoted in the Sayings, listed in chronological order. In each case the Nasi is mentioned first and then the *av bet din*. First are Jose ben Joezer of Zeredah and Jose ben Jochanan, who lived in the first half of the second century BCE at the time of Maccabean revolt against Antiochus IV. Next are Joshua ben Perachyah and Nittai of Arbel, who lived in the latter half of the second century BCE during the reign of John Hyrcanus as High Priest. Next are Judah of Tabbai and Simeon ben Shattach, who lived at the beginning of the first century BCE during the reigns of Alexander Janneus (John Hyrcanus' son) following a civil war between the Pharisees and John Hyrcanus' forces. Next are Shemaiah and Avtalyon, who lived in the middle of the first century BCE when Judea fell under Roman hegemony. Finally there were Hillel and Shammai, whose reign is recognized in rabbinic tradition as the beginning of the period of the Tannaim. They governed at the end of the first century BCE, at the time when the Hasmonean dynasty of priests came to an end and Rome reestablished a monarchy (albeit puppet) with Herod.

Jose ben Joezer of Zeredah said that you should make your house a place for scholars where you sit at their feet and learn. The deeper meaning turns on the ambiguity of the term "house" (*bayit*) which, among its many meanings in rabbinic literature, means the Temple. In this sense Jose is making a judgment about the political authority of the Torah study of the Pharisees over the sacrifices of the Jerusalem priests as a form of appropriate worship of God.

Jose ben Jochanan also speaks about the "house." He says it should be a place that is open to everyone and not just to some. He also says that you should treat the poor as you would treat members of your own family, and you should not gossip with women, including your wife. He notes that the earlier "sages" (*chachamim*) said that

> anyone who has a great deal of speech with a woman/wife (*ha-ishah*) causes evil to himself, neglects the words of Torah, and (in) his end he inherits *gehinnom*.

The attitude that Jose's saying correctly reflects is a significant decline in the status of women in the rabbinic period below what it was in the biblical Jewish states. Certainly the women of the Bible were judged in many respects as inferior to men, but they had at least the possibility of high political office (as in the case of the judge, Deborah) and even prophecy (as in the case of Moses' sister, Miriam). However, that possibility disappeared under the reign of the rabbis where women were generally (although not always) excluded even as witnesses in a trial. That situation further deteriorated in the classical philosophical period when the medieval rabbis, armed with the judgments of Aristotelian science on the inferior status of women over men, further reduced the position of females. In brief, women were not considered physically capable of serious intellectual activities, so that speaking with women necessarily had to be about frivolous topics. This judgment was made at a time when the rabbis, early rabbinic and medieval, continually strengthened the tie between the activities of the intellect and moral virtue. Hence, here Jose discourages most association with women (except as is necessary with a wife to manage the household and to fulfill the commandment to procreate), because such association detracts from what really matters in life—the study of Torah.

Neglect of study leads to serious practical harm. In keeping with the lessons of the biblical Book of Proverbs, Torah guides a man to prosperity, success, and happiness in this world of practical concerns. And thus it also guides him to prosperity, success, and happiness in the world to come where continued human society transcends all practical involvement. *Gehinnom*, first mentioned in Jeremiah 32:35, is a term initially used to name a valley near Jerusalem that the prophet notes as a place of major idolatry. However, here the reference is to another place of evil in the next world, not in this world. It is the place where the evil in this world will suffer for their evil, and for rabbis like Jose there is no greater evil, or at least no greater cause of evil, than ignorance of the Torah.

Joshua ben Perachyah, following in the tradition of the two Joses, said that you should be sure to get both a teacher (*rav*) from whom to learn Torah and a companion (*chaver*) with whom to discuss Torah, and you should judge every human being (*ha-adam*) according to his merit, i.e., favorably. The implication may be that as you dedicate yourself to the study of Torah so that in the world to come you will dwell in the heavens (*ha-shamayim*) rather than in the underworld (*gehinnom*), so should you apply your knowledge to others in the very generous manner that you hope that God will judge you.

A further implication is that, though the study of Torah is the path to redemption, there are no guarantees that the study will be sufficient. Creature imperfection applies as much to the pursuit of knowledge as it does to any other pursuit. The hope again is expressed that God's governance of the universe, even in the world to come, is regulated not just by justice but by mercy or grace as well.

Nittai of Arbel provides a counterbalance to Joshua's saying. Like his predecessors Nittai tells one to keep away from evil influences—in this case a bad neighbor rather than a woman/wife. However, there is a difference in emphasis between what Nittai says and Joshua said. Joshua's message was positive—find a friend and hope for mercy. Nittai gives the corrective, negative flip side of Joshua's saying—do not associate with an evil person, and do not abandon belief (*tityaesh*) in retribution. Joshua sees the good human beings do and hopes/prays that it will be good enough for humanity to earn salvation; Nittai sees the evil and hopes/prays that those who deserve to suffer will in fact suffer. Remember that Joshua and Nittai were governing after the Maccabean revolt when both the Hasmoneans and the rabbis ascended to power and just before major conflict erupted between the rabbinic sages and the Hasmoneans. Joshua's conception of divine justice focuses on the sages/rabbis, and their followers among the people of Judea; Nittai's focus is on the Syrians and/or the Hasmoneans and their followers. The tradition in general recognizes that the truth of proper justice lies in a balance of both of these rights—the necessity to reward the good and to punish the evil.

Judah of Tabbai said that while standing in judgment the judge should view each defendant as guilty until proven innocent, but immediately after the trial, when he is no longer formally acting as an agent to enforce the justice of the court, he should regard each defendant as innocent. Beyond the simple practical advice for judges, Judah also proposed his mental picture of what it means to say that the God of Israel—who, as the God of redemption, is the final judge of the earth—can be understood to balance his character as the creating God of justice with his character as the Torah-revealing God of mercy. Hence, Judah's saying is as much a mental picture of the hope for the end of days as it is practical advice for living in this world.

Simeon ben Shattach, however, plays down Judah's emphasis on mercy after judgment. His focus is more on justice as it is more on the role of the judge in this world. He says that witnesses should be examined thoroughly and careful attention should be paid to what they said, lest "they learn from (the witnesses') words to tell lies."

Shemaiah and Avtalyon continued with the practical advice for life in this world. Shemaiah said that men should love work, despise political office, and not associate with politicians. Avtalyon said that they were, as a sage (*chacham*), to be careful about what they said. If they were not careful they would say things that would harm themselves and all who paid attention to them. The sages and their listeners would suffer exile, and their students would suffer more. They "will drink and die, and the name of heaven (*shem shamayim*) will be profaned." The suggestion is that what human beings, especially rabbis, do in this world has in itself cosmic significance for the universe as a whole and/or for the world to come. Just what Avtalyon means is not stated explicitly and it is not by itself clear. The meaning could be simply that you are judged by what you do and believe and not by what you intended to do and intended to believe. Error and sin are not forgivable just because you intended to know the truth and do the good. However, there is probably more to what this rabbinic text, like most other early rabbinic texts, means. That deeper meaning still occupies the attention of both rabbinic and academic scholars, as it certainly occupied the attention of many of the classical Jewish philosophers.

Finally, we look at the sayings of the last of the ruling rabbinic pairs with whom tannaitic Judaism begins. Hillel said they were to be disciples of Aaron, loving and pursuing peace. Just what this means he next explained. First it means to love your fellow creature, which alludes to the so-called "love commandment," viz., to love your neighbor as yourself (Lev 19:18). Second, it means to draw near (*mekorban*, whose noun-form, *korban*, also means a sacrifice) to the study of the Torah. Hillel's words combine in an unexplained sense of synthesis the practical altruistic virtues of serving your fellow human being with the theoretical/theological intellectual virtues associated with Torah study, which, through his choice of language, is further associated with sacrifice. Rabbinic Judaism replaces the emphasis in biblical Judaism on sacrifice with Torah study and good deeds. As for the now-discredited biblical Jewish philosophy sacrifice was the *raison d'être* of the universe, in the newly emerging rabbinic philosophy the foundational purpose for the existence of the universe will become the human activities of altruistic behavior and/or theoretical study of the Torah. How this relationship, like the others mentioned, will be made clear is a task left for classical Jewish philosophy.

To these words of Hillel, Shammai merely added that study must be regularized, which means that, given Hillel's balance of deed and study, Shammai gives priority to the study. This argument was to be continued in medieval Jewish philosophy with even greater subtlety. As we shall see, the issue will be transformed into a question of the epistemological priority of *theoria* over *phronesis* or *phronesis* over *theoria* in an ethics that judges *sophia* to be the highest good, which has consequences for the rabbis' philosophical conception of the nature of the universe, in both this world of physics as well as in the transcendent, promised messianic world to come.

Notes

1   These historical claims are debated among contemporary academic scholars of this period. In part the debate turns on the legitimacy or illegitimacy of

identifying what the rabbinic texts call "sages/wise men" (*chachamim*) with "masters/teachers" (*rabbim*). The Pharisees are the "sages." The question is, are the sages the master teachers. For traditional rabbinic Judaism this identity is beyond doubt.

2   Henceforth called "the Sayings."

Suggestions for further study

ArtScroll Siddur (*siddur kol ya'akov*): *Weekday/ Sabbath/Festival*. English translation by Nosson Scherman. Brooklyn, NY: Mesorah Publications, 1990. *Pirkei avos*, pp. 545–87.

The Daily Prayer Book (*ha-siddur ha-shalem*). English translation by Philip Birnbaum. New York: Hebrew Publishing Co., 1949. "Ethics of the Fathers," pp. 477–534.

Danby, Herbert. *The Mishnah*. An English translation. Oxford: Oxford University Press, 1933.

Neusner, Jacob. *From Politics to Piety: The Emergence of Pharisaic Judaism*. Englewood Cliffs, NJ: Prentice-Hall, 1973.

Neusner, Jacob. *The Philosophical Mishnah*. Atlanta: Scholars Press, 1988.

Key questions

1. List and identify the five *zugot* quoted at the beginning of the "Sayings of the Fathers."
2. What are the "deep" and the "simple" meanings of a rabbinic aphorism in the "Sayings of the Fathers"? Give an example.
3. How did the early rabbis connect the precepts of the Torah with ethics?
4. How did the early rabbis connect Torah and ethics with wisdom?
5. How does early rabbinic Jewish philosophy pave the way for the medieval classical Jewish philosophy that follows? Give concrete examples of this claim of continuity between these two forms of Jewish religious thought.
6. What is the problem with the rabbis' understanding of how God governs the world, and how did they propose to solve it?
7. What did the early rabbis believe about redemption and the world to come?
8. What did the early rabbis believe about the nature and character of women? How do these beliefs compare with the beliefs of the earlier biblical Judaism and the later classical Jewish philosophy of the Middle Ages?

II. CLASSICAL JEWISH PHILOSOPHY

Jewish Philosophy before Maimonides

CHAPTER 14

Medieval history: from the rise of Islam to the expulsion from Christian Spain

The rise of Islam

The geographic focus of our survey of biblical Judaism was the eastern end of the Mediterranean Sea, running from the basin of the Nile River in the south to the mountains at the source of the Tigris and Euphrates rivers in the north.

Our focus expanded in our survey of early rabbinic Judaism to include the lands bordering the entire Mediterranean Sea, both in what is today the southern limits of Europe and the northern limits of Africa, for Jews lived everywhere that the Roman Empire expanded. However, by the end of the period surveyed, with the completion of the Babylonian Talmud, our focus again narrowed specifically to the rabbinic Jewish communities living in the Sassanid empire.

Jews continued to live everywhere in the Roman Empire as it expanded to include all of the western territories of Europe, but these Jews cease to concern us. Here we only note that they existed and had a life (and therefore a history), but that life is not our concern for two reasons, the second of which is more important than the first. First, because of the conditions of life in the lands north of the Mediterranean (i.e., what later became known as Europe), no significant developments in Jewish life occurred until the tenth century at the earliest. Second, because of these same conditions, nothing important happened for the history of Jewish philosophy until the end of the thirteenth century.

In general the reason for this difference has to do with the ultimate fate of the Roman Empire. The empire became two, one overtaken by the native peoples of western and central Europe and the other by the native peoples of Arabia. Culture and civilization thrived and grew under the Muslim Arabs, while it radically declined under the Christian Europeans. Hence, the cultural future for the Jewish people in all fields, especially philosophy, was in the world of Islam and not in the world of Christianity.

By the time of the reign of Theodosius I (379–395 CE), Christianity had been fully integrated as the official religion of the Roman Empire. By his death, the empire split in two, western and eastern empires. Both empires continued to experience some periods of imperial growth. However, for the most part the trajectory of history was one of decline in every respect. By the beginning of the seventh century there was no longer a western empire. In its place were the beginnings of a European civilization, with a Visigoth kingdom in Spain and Portugal, Frankish kingdoms in what are today France and Germany, and various small kingdoms of people such as Basques, Lombards, Bavarians, Saxons, Frisians, Anglo-Saxons, and the Irish, Scots, and Picts at the northern extremities of what had been Rome. The eastern Roman Empire, however, continued to exist. At first it became the empire of all of the Mediterranean, excluding the coasts of modern Spain, Provence, and much of Italy. However, by the early part of the eighth century this empire, now called "the Byzantine Empire," was radically reduced in size to what is today modern Greece and Turkey. The cause of the decline was the emergence of Islam, the third religion to develop out of the spiritual and intellectual resources of the Hebrew Scriptures.

Islam developed around an Arab prophet from the south of the Arabian Desert named Muhammad. Under his leadership and the immediate circle of his extended family, Islam formed an army that first conquered all of Arabia from the Persians and then went on to take over Egypt, Palestine, and Syria from the Byzantines. By the second decade of the eighth century, Islam had become a world empire whose territory ran along the Mediterranean Sea from Spain and North Africa to the basin of the Tigris and Euphrates rivers.

There are three notable differences between the inheritors of Rome and of Byzantium. First, while Rome was a political capital of the Roman Empire, it was never a cultural center (in many ways, like Washington, DC, in its relationship to the United States [excluding the Library of Congress]); rather, the cultural centers were places such as Antioch, and Alexandria (in many respects, like Boston and New York in relation to at least the eastern half of the U.S.A. [adding to them the Library of Congress]). Antioch (located in the region of Syria) and Alexandria (located in the region of Egypt) were the more important centers of learning because they were also major centers of international commerce that carried natural goods (such as resins, spices, and ivory) from Asia and Arabia into the empires. Both of these cities fell into the territories of the Muslims rather than the Europeans. Hence, the finest libraries of the Hellenistic world (the equivalents of the Harvard University's library, the New York City Public Library, and the Library of Congress in contemporary American civilization), which were the repositories of the collective learning in all of the sciences in western civilization (including Egypt, Babylonia, Greece, and Rome), became the property of the Muslims.

In contrast, the only libraries of significance in the West were the private libraries of Christian monks. These monks spread their Roman learning throughout western Europe, but that learning was primarily about language and literature rather than about science and philosophy. The monks were, first and foremost, missionaries, which meant that they were the salesmen of the Church. Selling, like politics and law, is about convincing people of what is believed to be true rather than about proving what ought to be believed to be true. In other words, it is an occupation that has great need for expertise in rhetoric but minimal need for expertise in science. The western European libraries of these clerics reflected that professional interest. They were strong, for example, on the collected works of the Aristotelians in the fields of poetry, drama, rhetoric, and logic, but weak on the collected works of the Aristotelians in fields such as biology, botany, geology, astronomy, and physics. To be sure some kinds of ancient philosophies could prosper in Roman Christendom, but they were not philosophy of the natural sciences. Hence, Neoplatonism thrived, but Aristotelianism was barely known.

In summary, because early Christian Europe was not a good place for philosophy in general, it was not a good place for Jewish philosophy, and because the world of Islam was a good place for philosophy in general, it was a good place for Jewish philosophy. This conclusion illustrates a general principle about all of Jewish intellectual history that is worth emphasizing now.

The Jewish people are always a minority civilization and never a majority civilization in every generation of their history. Now the important cultural difference between majority and minority cultures is that the historical development of the former is influenced primarily by its own past; hence it experiences continuous development as long as it is a majority culture. Such is not the fate of a minority culture. It too is influenced by its own past, but that influence is combined with the present influence of the majority culture. Hence, as we have already seen, biblical Judaism grew out of an interaction between the earlier cultures of the Hebrew people in dynamic interaction with the dominant cultures of Egypt and Mesopotamia. Similarly, early rabbinic Judaism grew out of the interaction of biblical Judaism with the dominant cultures of Persia, then Greece, then Rome, and finally the Persian Sassanid Empire. The result is that the development of the cultures, including philosophy, of minority civilizations such as the Jewish people is never continuous for very long, since the development is disrupted into radically new directions when it becomes subject to radically new influences as old empires die and new empires are born. There is no clearer evidence of this thesis than the different fates of rabbinic Judaism in Christian European civilizations and the same rabbinic Judaism in imperial Muslim civilizations. Certainly between the sixth and the eleventh centuries, when there was little significant contact between them, this difference is most clear, and it is the reason why, for these five hundred years, our interest is in the Jews of Islam and not the Jews of Christendom.

The synthesis of classical rabbinic practical philosophy

Still, despite the differences between Jewish life and thought in Christian Europe and the Muslim Middle East, we can speak of both Jewish civilizations as "Jewish" in much the same way, and that is very different from what we have seen so far. We have called the Jewish religion of the ancient Near East "biblical Judaism" and the Jewish religion that develops out of the sources of the literature of the tannaim and the amoraim "rabbinic Judaism." These are radically different kinds of Judaism, so different in fact, that, if we were to reserve the term "Judaism" for rabbinic Judaism, then, properly speaking, the religion of the Hebrew Scriptures is not Judaism. (It is a "proto-Judaism.") In much the same way, the other religions that develop as Jewish responses to the destruction of the second Temple and the failure of the three wars for independence from the Romans, the most notable example being early Christianity, are also not Judaism. However, the significantly different religions that emerge out of the Jewish experience of Christian European civilization, especially in the lands bordering the North Sea (the Judaism of the "Ashkenazim") and the Jewish experience of Muslim civilization, especially in the lands bordering the Mediterranean Sea (the Judaism of the "Sephardim") are both the same rabbinic Judaism. The commonality is because the practical side of rabbinic philosophy—i.e., the side that deals with personal, familial, and national ethics and politics—was established before the rise of Islam. These critical works of pragmatic Jewish philosophy were what we have just finished surveying—the philosophy of the Mishnah, the Midrash, and the Talmud.

Let us say here a final word about the legal structure of Judaism before we turn to the questions of speculative or theoretical philosophy that will become our primary focus in the rest of this book. Jewish ethics, especially political ethics, did grow in the subsequent ages of Jewish intellectual life, and there were changes, but, at least until the twentieth century, those changes were not radical. The practical side of Jewish philosophy was so well developed that, despite enormous changes in the majority cultural environment of Jewish life, Jewish practical ethics and morality remained constant.

In theory, the Hebrew Scriptures, especially the Pentateuch, is the constitution of rabbinic Judaism in the sense that the foundation doctrine of rabbinic Judaism is that the Torah contains within it all truth, so that what rabbinic law is is a process of teasing out from the words of the holy text their specific application to the continuous and endless new situations that arise in the lived life of the people in the concrete. In practice, however, the Hebrew Scriptures do not function this way, because "Torah" is understood not to be the written Scriptures but the proper understanding of what the written texts say in a chain of tradition that passes from God through the men of the Great Assembly to the rabbis. The works that systematically bring together the first nine centuries of this oral tradition, in a single, systematic way, are the published works of the tannaim and the amoraim. Of them the most important is that of "Rabbi," viz., the Nasi Judah I. However, it does not stand alone as an authority. Equal in status are the *baraitot* (other mishnaic, halakhic statements of the tannaim not stated in the Mishnah) and various collections of halakhic midrashim—especially the *Mekhilta* on Exodus, the *Sifra* on Leviticus, and the *Sifrei* on Numbers and Deuteronomy. Together these works constitute the teachings of the tannaim. Next in order of importance are all three to four hundred years of rulings and judgments by the amoraim that are recorded in the gemara of the Jerusalem and the Babylonian Talmuds. In combination with the writings of the tannaim, these early rabbinic works so structure Jewish life into a coherent political, social, and spiritual whole that, despite differences, all forms of Judaism, from the sixth to the twentieth centuries, can be recognized simply as "Judaism." This tradition of using the rabbinic rulings of past rabbis to specify rulings in new situations in the present continued into the period of Muslim hegemony over Jewish life.

In 750 CE the Ummayad dynasty, whose capital was Damascus in Syria, was overthrown and a new dynasty, the Abbasid dynasty, was established in Baghdad in modern-day Iraq. At its greatest point of expansion, the Muslim empire reached from all but the furthest northern regions of Spain (in what was the territory of the Basques) through North Africa, the entire Middle East, into India and the most eastern and southern islands off the peninsula of Asia. By the eighth century this new empire (the largest territorially in the history of the West) also began to decline, as regions at the empire's extreme broke away and formed Muslim governments of their own, under "emirs" rather than "caliphs." Notable among them was the establishment in 756 of an Ummayad emirate in Muslim Spain.

As the Muslim empire declined, a new Christian imperial stage began in Europe. In the end, conditions of life in the Muslim world declined to such a point that Jews in very large numbers emigrated out of the more hospitable Muslim world into the far less hospitable world of Christian Europe. They did so for economic reasons that took precedence over the cultural deficiencies of the new home. The choice, as we shall see, was inescapable, but nonetheless, minimally from the perspective of cultural development, a disaster. However, that gets us ahead of our story. For now we need only point out that the Muslim caliphate began a process of decline at the end of the eighth century, but the Abbasid Empire itself survived these setbacks into the thirteenth century. Throughout all of these five centuries there was a thriving Jewish community in which major contributions were made to Jewish life. Those contributions included the further formalization of Jewish liturgy into its present universally recognizable form (at least in Orthodox circles), a golden age of Kabbalah and Jewish mysticism, and (most important for our purposes) a golden age of philosophy.

When the Jews first returned to the world of Babylonia after the failed wars for independence against the Romans, the dominant Jewish authority was a professed descendant of King David who was called an "Exilarch" (*resh galuta* [head of the exile" in Aramaic]). Along with these hereditary rulers there emerged in the middle of the eighth century rabbinic "academies." In general, there were always two academies at the head of each of which was a rabbi known as a "Gaon." Rabbis out of these academies were appointed to be the rulers of Jewish communities.

These rabbis were first elected by the communities themselves on the solicited recommendations of either Gaon or the Exilarch, but once elected they ruled for life. They were both the chief executive and legislative officials in the communities where they served. In theory, their decisions were answerable to the authority of the chain of tradition and the Torah; in practice, they were not answerable to anyone, but generally they deferred authority, especially in difficult cases, to the academies from which they were appointed, especially their Gaonim. In practice, what this meant was that, when a rabbi was given a difficult question to solve for his community, he would write a letter to his Gaon and receive a response (responsum) from the Gaon. The Gaon would keep copies of his responsa which in time he would publish. These published letters had legal authority not only for the communities they addressed but for all Jewish law in all places at all times.

This process of publishing responsa was the primary way that Jewish law continued to progress in the centuries after the Talmuds. The first such notable collections were written by the gaonim. Later, from the eleventh century on, other rabbis would publish their responsa. This process continues into the present in traditional Jewish circles, both Ashkenazim as well as Sephardim, and (in the twenty-first century) in liberal as well as traditional Jewish religious communities.

Other Sephardic rabbis wrote codes of Jewish law. Of these, two of the most notable products were the *halkhot gedolot* of Rabbi Isaac al Fasi in North Africa (1013–73) and the *mishneh torah* of the Rambam (Rabbi Moses ben Maimon or Maimonides, 1135–1204). Similar work was done by the Ashkenazi rabbis. Among the authors of responsa collections are Rabbi Samuel Ha-Naggid of Granada and Rabbenu Gershom of Mayence in the eleventh century, their contemporary in France, Rashi (Rabbi Shelomo Yizhaki, 1040–1105), and the Tosafot (Rashi's descendants, of whom the most important are Rabbenu Yaakov Tam [Rashi's grandson, Rabbi Jacob ben Meir of Romeru who published *sefer ha-yashar*], Ri [Rabbenu Yaakov Tam's nephew, Rabbi Isaac of Dempierre], and Tosafot Rid [Rabbi Isaiah da Trani from thirteenth-century Italy]). Of particular interest were Ramban (Rabbi Moses ben Nachman or Nachmanides, who lived in Spain, 1194–1270), and Rashba (Ramban's student from Barcelona, Rabbi Solomon ben Adret, 1215–1310). Among the authors of codes are Asher ben Yehiel (1250–1327, who published *halakhot*; he was known as "Rabbenu Asher," "Asheri," or "Rosh") and his son Jacob ben Asher (1270–1340, whose published *arba'ah turim* [four towers] gave its author the name of Tur).

These post-amoraic authorities are collectively known as the *rishonim* (early ones). Together they constitute a third rank of rabbinic legal authorities, after the tannaim and the amoraim. Beyond them are everyone else through the present, who are called *acharonim* (later ones). The work that separates these last two categories of rabbinic authorities is the publication of a code at the end of the fifteenth century by a Sephardic Kabbalist from Safed in Palestine named Joseph Caro. Caro first published a code, called the *beit yosef* (the house of Joseph). There he presented the views of al Fasi, Rambam, and Asheri, and represented his own view as the majority decision between these three codifiers. He then published a summary that presented his final decisions without documenting the three sources for it. This summary of his code, called the *shulchan arukh* ("prepared table"), functions, at least in Ashkenazi lands and at least until the end of the twentieth century, as the primary source of authority for Jewish practice by all so-called "Orthodox" (literally, "right-thinking") Jews.

The golden age of classical rabbinic theoretical philosophy

Taken as a whole, these collections of rabbinic decisions, based ultimately on a tradition of common law that extends back through the Talmuds to the first generation of rabbis, were intended to govern every aspect of every Jew's lived life in the concrete, from the moment he arises in the morning to the moment he falls asleep in the evening. All of it is understood to be the word of God in the sense that it expresses the details of the relationship between the God who created the world and revealed the Torah and the people Israel who received the revelation as his agents in redeeming the world. The practical side of this central dogma that specifies the obligations of every Jew under their covenant with this God of creation, revelation, and redemption is for the most part clearly specified as a philosophical ethics by the time that the Jewish people enter under Muslim hegemony. What became developed in this Muslim period, as developed as the practical philosophy that was developed in the Roman and Sassanid periods, was the theoretical philosophy upon which rabbinic ethics rest.

The seminal figure in developing this theoretical side of classical rabbinic philosophy was Moses Maimonides. We have already noted his stature in ethics as a seminal member of the class of *rishonim* who determined Jewish law beyond the Talmuds. Without question, that legal stature contributed to his authority as a philosopher as well. He is also without question one of the most original Jewish philosophers of all time. In fact, this statement is far too humble. He is without doubt one of the most original as well as most influential philosophers ever to live, think, and record what he/she thought. We will consider in the next chapter the rabbinic philosophers of the Muslim world who preceded him. Then we will turn to Maimonides' philosophy itself and to that of the classical Jewish philosophers who responded to his written word, almost all of whom lived in Christian Europe.

Because the important Jewish philosophers who come after Maimonides lived and were influenced by Christian Europe, Maimonides and his contemporaries will be taken to represent the culmination of Jewish intellectual life in the Muslim world. Hence it will be referred to, as it commonly is, as a "golden age."

Whether or not it is *the* golden age of Jewish philosophy in general remains to be seen. It certainly has been judged that way by Christians, and many Jews today, especially in Orthodox circles, share this judgment. However, we will keep an open mind on the claim. Jewish philosophy will be seen in this book as something in decline until the early twentieth century. There will be a number of high points beyond Maimonides, which will include the philosophies of Levi Gersonides and Baruch Spinoza. However, they will also be seen as special cases in ages of general Jewish philosophical decline.

Jewish philosophy underwent a major revival in early twentieth-century Germany that continues today in the early twenty-first century to have an influence on Jewish thinking in both Israel and North America. Whether or not this renaissance of German Jewish philosophy will lead to a more general renaissance of Jewish thinking remains to be seen. A tentative answer to this question will be defended in the concluding chapter of this book.

Suggestions for further study

Ashtor, Eliyahu. *The Jews of Moslem Spain*. English translation by Aaron Klein and Jenny Machlowitz Klein. Philadelphia: Jewish Publication Society of America, 1973–79.

Broadie, Alexander. "The nature of medieval Jewish philosophy," in Daniel H. Frank and Oliver Leaman (eds.), *History of Jewish Philosophy*. Vol. II of

Routledge History of World Philosophies. London and New York: Routledge, 1997, pp. 83–92.

Fakhry, M. *A History of Islamic Philosophy*. New York: Columbia University Press, 1983.

Freehof, Solomon B. *The Responsa Literature*. Philadelphia: Jewish Publication Society of America, 1955.

Goitein, Shlomo D. *Jews and Arabs: Their Contacts Through the Ages*. New York: Schocken, 1955.

Lewis, Bernard. *The Jews of Islam*. Princeton: Princeton University Press, 1984.

Newman, Abraham A. *The Jews in Spain: Their Social, Political, and Cultural Life*. Philadelphia: Jewish Publication Society of America, 1942.

Rahman, Fazlur. *Islam*. Chicago: University of Chicago Press, 1979.

Rosenthal, Erwin I. J. *Judaism and Islam*. London and New York: Yoseloff, 1961.

Seltzer, Robert M. *Jewish People, Jewish Thought: The Jewish Experience in History*. New York: Macmillan, 1980, Part 3, Chs. 7–8, pp. 323–72.

Sharf, Andrew. *Byzantine Jewry: From Justinian to the Fourth Crusade*. London: Routledge and Kegan Paul, 1971.

Sirat, Colette. *A History of Jewish Philosophy in the Middle Ages*. Cambridge: Cambridge University Press, 1985.

Walzer, Richard. *Greek into Arabic*. Cambridge, MA: Harvard University Press. 1962.

Wasserstrom, Steven M. "The Islamic social and cultural context," in Daniel H. Frank and Oliver Leaman (eds.), *History of Jewish Philosophy*. Vol. II of *Routledge History of World Philosophies*. London and New York: Routledge, 1997, pp. 93–114.

Wolfson, Harry Austryn. *Philo: Foundations of Religious Philosophy in Judaism, Christianity and Islam*. Cambridge, MA: Harvard University Press, 1982.

Wolfson, Harry Austryn. *The Philosophy of Kalam*. Cambridge, MA: Harvard University Press, 1976.

Wolfson, Harry Austryn. *The Philosophy of the Church Fathers*. Cambridge, MA: Harvard University Press, 1970.

Wolfson, Harry Austryn. *Repercussions of the Kalam in Jewish Philosophy*. Cambridge, MA: Harvard University Press, 1979.

Zimmels, H. J. *Ashkenazim and Sephardim: Their Relations, Differences, and Problems as Reflected in the Rabbinic Responsa*. London: Oxford University Press, 1958.

Key questions

1. Why does the history of Jewish philosophy continue beyond the fall of the Roman empires with Jewish life in the Muslim world but not with Jewish life in Christian Europe?

2. What is the difference between being a dominant culture and a minority culture? How does this difference apply to the Jewish people in general and Jewish philosophy in particular? Give examples.
3. Why is Jewish intellectual life in tenth- to twelfth-century Cordova called a "golden age"?

Key events of medieval history

c. 570–632	Muhammad
661–750	Ummayad caliphate
711–715	Muslim conquest of Spain
c. 740	Beginning of Khazar conversions to Judaism
750–1258	Abbasid dynasty
756	Breakaway Ummayad caliphate established in Spain, centered in Cordova
762–767	Anan ben David establishes Karaite tradition
780–800	Western North Africa becomes independent of Abbasids
800	Charlemagne crowned Roman Emperor by the Pope
813–833	Reign of Al-Mamun as Abbasid caliph. Period of cultivation of arts and sciences in Baghdad; authority of Exilarch declines among Jews
830–860	Growth of Karaism
915–970	Hisdai Ibn Shaprut cultivates arts and sciences among Jews in Cordova
993–1056	Samuel Ibn Nagrela cultivates arts and sciences among Jews in Cordova
969–1171	Fatimid dynasty in Egypt
980–1037	Ibn Sina (Avicenna)
1085	King of Castile captures Toledo from Muslims; Almoravides sweep through Muslim Spain from North Africa
1095	Pope Urban II calls for the First Crusade
1020–57	Solomon Ibn Gabirol of Cordova
1033–1109	Beginning of western Scholasticism
1040–1105	Rabbi Solomon ben Isaac (Rashi) of Troyes, France
1055–1135	Moses Ibn Ezra of Cordova
1075–1141	Judah Halevi of Cordova
1089–1164	Abraham Ibn Ezra of Cordova
1100–71	Jacob ben Meir Tam (one of first Tosafists)
1110–80	Abraham Ibn Daud of Cordova
1126–98	Ibn Rushd (Averroes) of Cordova
1135–1204	Moses Maimonides of Cordova and Cairo

#Political leaders of the Jewish people: 2

Exilarchs	Sura Gaons	Nehardea Gaons
Bustani (618–670)		
	Yehudah (757–761)	
	Joseph ben Abba (814–816)	
	Abraham ben Sherira (816–828)	
	Paltoi (842–858)	Natronai (853–856)
		Amram (856–874)
	Zemah ben Hayim (882–887)	
David ben Zaccai (927–939)	Yom Tov Kahana (926–938)	Cohen Zedek II (917–936)
	Saadia (928–30; 937–42)	Hananiah ben Judah (936–943)
Judah ben David (c. 940)	Joseph ben Jacob bar Satia (930–937; c. 943)	
Solomon (c. 943)		Aaron ben Joseph Ibn Sarjado (943–960)
		Nehemiah ben Cohen Zedek (960–968)
		Sherira ben Hanina (968–998)
	Zemah ben Isaac (998–1003)	Hai ben Sherira (1004–38)
	Samuel ben Hophni (1003–13)	
	Samuel ben Saadia (1013–17)	
Hezekiah (c. 1038)	Closing of academy (mid-11th century)	Hezekiah (c. 1038)

CHAPTER 15

Major texts and themes of Jewish philosophy

The rise of Muslim and Jewish theoretical philosophy

The classical period for the writing of theoretical Jewish philosophy begins in the tenth century in Muslim Spain and Egypt. It happened there and then because the Jews were full participants in the life and culture of their Muslim hosts who were also experiencing their own golden age of theoretical philosophy. We will not say too much about the philosophy of the Muslims here in this book, since it is a work on Jewish philosophy. However, Muslim philosophy can no more be ignored in understanding classical Jewish philosophy than European Christian and post-Christian philosophy can be ignored in understanding modern Jewish philosophy. In both cases it is the intellectual developments in the science and culture of the host civilization that provides the setting for the intellectual developments in Jewish science and culture.

The story of Muslim philosophy begins with Islam's absorption of the philosophies of the Greek and Roman empires after its territories were conquered, and its libraries were absorbed into Muslim civilization, i.e., after the works in Greek and Latin from the conquered libraries were translated into Arabic. The work of translation began in Egypt in the second half of the seventh century under the direction of the Ummayad prince, Halid Ibn Yazid. It reached its conclusion in Baghdad during the reign of the Abbasid caliphs, especially al-Mansur (754–775) and Harun al-Rashid (786–809).

Many scholars treat Muslim philosophy and science as a holding action, bridging the gap between the fall of the Roman Empire and the rise of modern Europe. To these modern scholars, the Muslims merely translated the great works of Greek and Roman culture, but did nothing more. The reality was very different. In almost every respect, Muslim philosophy, grounded in Greek and Roman philosophy, marks a significant advance beyond (and often even a transformation of) its Hellenic origins.

Literally everything was translated, and, once translated, was absorbed, but it was more than absorbed. It was integrated with what the Muslims learned from other regions of the world that they conquered, notably Hindu India, and combined with what they learned themselves from empirical observation.

Let one example suffice. In the ninth century, during the Abbasid caliphate of al-Man'mun (813–833), Muhammad Ibn Musa al-Kihwarizmi wrote a treatise on arithmetic and algebra using Arabic translations of and commentaries on Euclid's *Elements* together with al-Fazari's eighth-century translation of the Hindu *Siddhanta* (composed in the sixth century), making explicit use of Hindu positional numerical notation (what we commonly call "Arabic numerals"). In this work he introduced the notation of the sine function, which was totally unknown in Greek and Roman trigonometry. This kind of example could be given in every field of academic learning—especially mathematics, astronomy, physics, the life sciences, medicine, and engineering.

The major schools of theoretical philosophy

At a more general level, philosophy—here in the sense of an overall world-view and life-view that both directs and builds on the work in more specific areas of natural and empirical study (what we today call "science")—builds from five inherited traditions that go back to specific schools of philosophy in ancient Greece. The oldest is the Pythagorean school founded by Pythagoras (570–497 BCE) and made systematic by Philolaos of Thebes (*c.* 480–400 BCE). The second is the so-called "Megarian" school of philosophy founded by Eucleides of Megara in the fifth century BCE. The third is the Academy of Plato (*c.* 427–347 BCE). The fourth is the school of atomism founded by Democritus of Abdera (465–370 BCE). And the fifth and last (but not least) is the Lyceum of Aristotle (*c.* 384–322 BCE).

It is possible, in terms of content, to speak of these five Greek schools as distinct, and they are often presented that way. However, to present them thus is artificial. In reality, the later schools were all influenced by the earlier ones, and ideas that were featured in one school at one time became prominent in a different school at another time. For example, the positivism of the Megarians was absorbed into the atomism of the school of Democritus, especially in the development of atomism's astronomy by Eudoxus of Cnidus (408–355 BCE). Similarly, Plato himself, especially in a late dialogue called the *Timaeus*, adopted Pythagoreanism as if it were his own philosophy (which probably it was), as a corrective to problems he himself saw (in works like the *Parmenides*) in more youthful writings like the *Republic*. (The *Republic* is the work that we today most commonly associate with the phrase "Plato's philosophy." This was not the case for the medieval Muslims and Jews, for whom Plato's most important work was the [clearly Pythagorean-influenced] *Timaeus*.)

By the Muslim period the interaction of these different philosophical traditions became even more confused. First, Aristotle was known to be a student of Plato, and both the Muslims and the Jews did not believe that a morally and intellectually good student (such as Aristotle) would disagree with his teacher. Hence, it was taken for granted that what Aristotle said was coherent with what Plato said. Furthermore, in reading both, they incorporated Eudoxus' astronomy as well as elements of Democritus' physical atomism.

These combinations were certainly not "authentic" representations of what the Greek sources said, but they were not intended to be. The Muslim and Jewish philosophers who studied these texts did so as philosophers, and not as intellectual historians. They were read not as representative examples of a past age to be studied, as a historian would read them. Rather, they were read as works of wisdom from which the readers themselves could gain wisdom. What mattered is what was true in these words, not who said them. Furthermore, they also believed that truth is one in the sense that all truth claims will necessarily be consistent and coherent with each other. Therefore, what these Muslims and Jews presented as philosophy was presented as a more or less coherent world-view and life-view, and this view was drawn from a constructive reading of historical texts in the light of empirical observations. Hence, what, for example, the Jewish astronomer Mash'allah (754–813) said about astronomy reflects much that both Aristotle and Eudoxus said, but also what he learned personally and from his colleagues who were actively engaged at the great Baghdad observatory collecting data with the help of the plane astrolabe for astrological measurements that Eudoxus had invented.

Still, it should not be thought that everything could be blended with everything else. Clearly there were differences in philosophic world-view, and these differences were associated with certain philosophical schools of

Greek origin. However, the differences were not pure, or, at least, not as pure as they will seem in the presentations given in this book.

Three kinds of philosophical positions emerged in Muslim and Jewish intellectual life. The first was that of atomism, which was adopted by the Kalam (the first great school of Muslim philosophy), as well as by the first notable Jewish philosopher, the tenth-century Gaon of Sura, Saadia ben Joseph al-Fayyumi (892–942) in his *Book of Beliefs and Opinions*.[1]

The second was a version of Platonism called "Neoplatonism," which emerged in Andalusia in the eleventh century. Its most important Jewish exponent was Solomon Ibn Gabirol (1021–58) in his *The Fountain of Life*.[2] It had considerable influence in its Latin translation on European Christian Scholastics, and may have even had some influence on European Kabbalists, but it had minimal influence on the Jewish philosophers, primarily because his speculation had no consequences for natural science.

The third kind of philosophical position was Aristotelianism, which emerged for Muslims in Baghdad in the ninth-century writings of al-Kindi (*c.* 801–866) on a variety of subjects, including psychology, geometry, and optics. It emerged for the Jews in twelfth-century Andalusia in the writings of Abraham Ibn Daud (1110–80, in his *The Exalted Faith*). Of the Muslim advocates of Aristotelianism, the most notable philosophers were al-Farabi (*c.* 870–950), Ibn Sina (980–1037; the Christians called him "Avicenna"), and Ibn Rushd (1126–98; the Christians called him "Averroes"). Of the Jewish advocates, the most notable philosophers were Moshe ben Maimon (1135–1204; the Jews called him "Rambam," and the Christians called him "Maimonides") in his *Guide of the Perplexed*[3] and Levi ben Gershon (1288–1344; the Jews called him "Ralbag," and the Christians called him "Gersonides")[4] in his *Wars of the Lord*.

Aristotelianism emerged late because it had no strong following in the Roman intellectual circles that fell to the Muslims. In the late days of the empires, especially in Antioch and Alexandria, the popular life-views were Epicureanism and Stoicism.[5] These philosophies drew their world-view from the science of the atomists (especially Eudoxus of Cnidus [408–355 BCE]) as well as their life-view from the spiritualism of Plato. However, Aristotelianism played no role, and therefore, at the level of non-technical intellectual Roman culture, Aristotelianism was not a factor. Consequently, Aristotelianism was a "latecomer" into Muslim and Jewish consciousness, and when it did emerge it was important only to those committed Muslim and Jewish religious leaders who also had the strongest commitment to a technical, expert (i.e., "scientific") understanding of the universe.

Aristotelianism emerged late, but not too late. Its most influential expression as Jewish philosophy was presented by Moses Maimonides. His *Mishneh Torah* (on practical philosophy) and his *Guide* (on theoretical philosophy) become not only the dominant expression of Jewish Aristotelianism but of Jewish philosophy in general for at least the next seven hundred years. We will devote the next five chapters (Chs. 16 to 20) entirely to summarizing his philosophy. First, however, in this chapter we will present a more general summary of examples of the major categories of philosophy named above through one spokesman for each. For an atomist Jewish philosophy, in the tradition of the Muslim's Kalam, we will summarize Saadia's *Book of Beliefs and Opinions*. For a critique of philosophy that presupposes philosophy as atomist, we will look at Judah Halevi's *Khuzari*. Finally, for an overview of Aristotelian Jewish philosophy we will look at Abraham Ibn Daud's *Exalted Faith*.

Atomism, Kalam, and the Jewish philosophy of Saadia

Saadia's *Book of Beliefs and Opinions* (*emunot ve-deot*) is primarily a rhetorical (rather than demonstrative) apology for rabbinic Judaism against the Karaites. The Karaites' major contention against rabbinic Judaism was the legitimacy of the doctrine of the oral law. They, like the Sadducean opponents of the Pharisees before them, accepted the authority of the written text of the Torah but rejected the claim that the chain of tradition through the rabbis was an authentic tradition.

The term "authentic" here reflects the Islamic cultural context of the dispute. Islam, no less than Judaism, was facing internal religious struggles of its own over which political religious community correctly understood the words of Islam's sacred Scripture, the Koran. In their case the dispute was between the Sunnis and the Shiites. Both sects claimed that the prophet Muhammad was the greatest prophet and his book of prophecy was the greatest sacred Scripture. Both sects also claimed the authority of what in rabbinic terms was an oral Torah. In the case of Islam this meant first, the Sunna, which, like the mishnah, midrash, and gemara of the early rabbis, both filled in and expanded the meaning of the written sacred text, and second, the Ijma, which was general consensus in judgment. The point of contention was over the Sunna, which, like the Talmud, consisted of judgments attributed to a chain of earlier religious authorities. The authority of any link of transmission in the Sunna rested on the authority of each preceding authority cited, and the Sunnis and Shiites disagreed about the moral integrity of the earliest traditional authorities. Similarly, the Karaites raised moral and intellectual charges against the first generation of Pharisees that called into question the entire authority of the rabbinic chain of tradition. Furthermore, following the example of the Karaites, the Muslims and the Christians adopted attacks on rabbinic Judaism, again, accepting the authority of the law of Moses as the word of a true prophet of God, but denying that the rabbinic tradition was an authentic interpretation of what the prophet had said.

Following the model of the Mu'tazilite school of Kalam, Saadia's work is divided into two primary divisions, the first dealing with divine unity and the second with divine justice. The section on unity begins with questions about epistemology. It argues that there are three ways to know truth—by human reason, by revelation, and by tradition. "Human reason" consists in using the logical powers of the intellect to interpret correctly what one experiences through the five senses and in making the logically proper inferences from those experiences. Revelation is also a process of using intellect to make inferences from experience, but in this case the experience is prophetic experience of the word of God. The first way is that of the philosopher, and the second way is that of the prophet. The third way is the path to truth of most people who, lacking the excellence of reason of the philosopher and the prophet, accept the written witness of the true philosophers and prophets to discover through them what is true. Saadia argues that the domains of all three ways of knowing are identical. With perfect reasoning a philosopher could know everything from the data of physical nature and a prophet could know everything from the data of divine revelation. Both sources are open to the ordinary human being, and both sources, properly understood, will always be in agreement. The necessity of agreement is a consequence of God's oneness, for God, who is true, is also absolutely one.

The demonstration of God's oneness, as well as of his existence and incorporeality, follows the discussion of epistemology. In this case the most important philosophical contention is God's incorporeality. While we today take it for granted that God has no body, that was not the case in the tenth century. The Bible (and similarly the Koran) speaks about God having bodily parts, such as a hand and a face, and it speaks about God doing things that literally require a body, like going up and down.

The rabbis raised questions about these attributions, but they continued to speak about God having a body that does physical acts, only with the qualification of *kivyachol*. Just what this qualification means is never fully spelled out. What does it mean to have a body, so to speak? Is that having a body or not having a body, or something else, and, if something else, what? Saadia is the first in a long tradition of Jewish philosophers to argue, in accord with Islam, that God is in no sense corporeal, and that all of the biblical statements whose literal meaning is that God has a body cannot properly be understood literally.

The second section of Saadia's work deals with questions of human volition, ethics, and dogmatics. In the case of Kalam philosophy, free will was a major issue that was denied by the religious purists. For conservative Islam, real free will compromises the absoluteness of God's power. These Kalam philosophers argued that, except for the will of God, everything in the universe happens by the necessity of laws of chance. It is God's will and God's will alone that orders this universal chance and mechanical necessity into a moral order. Hence there is at the cosmic level real free will, but it is only the will of God. Saadia did not deny this contention, which can be called fatalistic determinism, but neither did he affirm it. As a rabbinic Jew he was committed to the reasonableness of the laws of the Torah because they are an expression of the will of God. But if there is no real human choice then there can be no reasonable human responsibility, and if there is no human responsibility then it is unreasonable to demand of humans obedience. Hence, humans must have sufficient volition to be morally responsible to obey God's law. He, like those Jewish philosophers who followed him, called this human power *bechirah enoshit*, "human choice," but he tended to preserve the expression of free will, *ratson chofshi*, for God.

Saadia's discussion of human choice places the question of the moral status of the Torah at the center of his theology. Saadia argued that the laws are divisible into two primary groups—those that the sound reasoning of any human being would recognize as morally correct, and those which, while not contrary to reason, could not be known by the use of reason alone. The former he called "rational" laws and the latter "traditional" laws. In the case of the rational laws, their moral value is known in general but not in their particular applications. Similarly, the traditional laws are laws that by reason alone are not morally objectionable, but armed only with reason there is no way to know whether or not they are morally obligatory. Such knowledge is obtained only through the testimony of the prophet, and of all the prophets (contrary to Islam) none is equal to Moses. In general, the issue between Islam and Judaism turned on one and only one critical point—who was the most authoritative of prophets, Moses or Muhammad?

The final question that Saadia deals with is the issue of divine providence, i.e., how God governs the world. It is the key question about divine justice. The issue is that a perfectly good, all-knowing, and all-powerful deity should govern his realm in such a way that all who are good should receive reward for their goodness and all who are evil should receive punishment for their evil, and that does not empirically seem to be the case. Saadia argued that the good and the evil of a process must be judged by its end, and the end of this process that is the created world has not yet come. That it must come is a demand of moral reasoning. Hence, reason no less than revelation requires that there shall come a day when the messiah will come and those who have died will be resurrected for the final judgment of their eternal reward and punishment.

Judah Halevi and the critique of Jewish Kalam

Judah Halevi's objections to the kind of synthesis of Judaism and philosophy that Saadia initiated were not to its conclusions. Halevi, no less than Saadia, believed that God exists, is one, is incorporeal; the Torah is the word of God revealed through Moses, the greatest of the prophets, and was transmitted to us through the authentic tradition of the rabbis (whom he calls "friends" [*haverim*; *haver* in the singular]); and that at the end of days the messiah will appear to resurrect the dead of the world for a final judgment of eternal reward for the good and eternal damnation for the evil. He, no less than Saadia, believed that the road to redemption, both individual and collective, was through the rabbinic tradition of the Torah. His argument instead was only with the role that human reason has to play in this process. For Halevi, in clear opposition to all of the philosophers of his day—Christian, Muslim, Karaite, and rabbinic—attributed hardly any value whatsoever to human reason as an aid to achieving redemption.

Halevi presented his critique of philosophy as a story in *The Kuzari*. It is based on a legend surrounding the apparent reality that at one time the King of the Khazars[6] converted to Judaism and transformed his empire into a Jewish state. As Halevi told the story, the king had frequent dreams in which an angel appeared to him and told him that "your intentions are acceptable to God, but not your practice." Concerned for what the dream meant, he called to his court a philosopher to interpret it. He listened but was not satisfied with what the philosopher said. All the philosopher could tell him was what he should believe (the intentions of the heart), but he had no ability to tell him in the concrete what he ought to do (the practice) to bring about redemption for both himself and his people. Furthermore, what made the king especially doubtful of the professed wisdom of the philosophers was that no philosophers were prophets, but clearly the highest level of human existence was that of the prophet.

Next he spoke with a Christian and then a Muslim doctor, but they no more satisfied him than did the philosopher. However, the Christians and Muslims, in speaking of their own prophets, mentioned an earlier prophetic source, Moses, and that those who still followed Moses' teachings were the Jews. Curious at the apparent fact that there was a consensus (*ijma*) over the truth of the prophet Moses but no such consensus over the truth of the professed prophets Jesus and Muhammad, the King of the Khazars called a Jewish "friend" to the court. What the *haver* told the king constitutes the rest (and major part) of Halevi's book. His central contentions are the following:

True religion must be based on religious experience; it cannot be gained from reason and natural experience alone. The inadequacy of philosophy is that it is founded on a Greek tradition of wisdom, but these wise men were from a nation not privileged to have prophets of its own. In contrast, the nation Israel and Israel alone knows God intimately through collective national experience. The experience is so intimate that Israel and Israel alone knows God by his true proper name. All of Israel's laws are derived from the religious experience of Moses, who was the world's greatest prophet. As such, its truth claims are beyond reasonable doubt. Israel's law is perfect because, in the hierarchy of species in the created world, Israel is the most excellent nation, its land is the most excellent land, its language (Hebrew) is the most excellent language, and its time (the theophany at Sinai) is the most excellent time. All these factors come together in the life of Moses at the time he stood with God at Sinai. In the curve of the history of the universe, that moment is its moral apex. Hence, since Moses there never has been and can never be, in principle, a prophet like unto Moses. As such there is no real distinction between the so-called rational and the ceremonial laws of the Torah; they are all of supreme importance as the ultimate word of God. Obedience to them is the ultimate path to the final salvation at the end of days when the immortal souls of all humans will be physically resurrected to stand in the final judgment.

Aristotelianism and the Jewish philosophy of Ibn Daud

The question could be raised, just what philosophy is the philosophy of Halevi's "philosopher"? In general it is the philosophy that Saadia assumed, viz., the atomistic philosophy of Muslim Kalam. However, it is far removed from a pure atomism. Clearly recognizable in it is the then growing influence of the Muslim Aristotelians al-Farabi and Ibn Sina. Similarly, one can find in this philosopher's philosophy elements of atomist astronomy and a Neoplatonic doctrine of cosmic emanation of this world from the One who is the Good to Intellect, to Soul, to Nature, to Matter.

Halevi lived in Cordova, Andalusia, at the time that the Aristotelian revolution was taking place in Islam, with Cordova at the center of intellectual activity in the then "new" science. For all of Halevi's opposition to it, Aristotelianism was gaining ascendancy in educated people's thought, Jews no less than Muslims. The earliest Jewish Aristotelians focused on what we today call "natural sciences" such as astronomy and physics without any attempt to synthesize these studies into a total world-view and life-view. The first Jewish philosopher to propose such a synthesis, i.e., the first Jew who in philosophy was a Jewish philosopher (as opposed to a philosopher who was Jewish) was Abraham Ibn Daud (Rabad) in his *The Exalted Faith*.

Rabad's work is divided into three books. The first deals with Aristotelianism, the second with Jewish doctrine, and the third with moral questions. We will summarize here only the first two books, because the third is not in good enough shape as a manuscript to summarize. It purports to be a book on "the healing of the soul," which means practical philosophy or ethics.[7]

The first book is a series of eight chapters that deals with the basic presuppositions of Aristotelian natural science and the order of the universe. The chapters summarize Aristotle's ontology, physics, theology, and astronomy. The ontology posits a universe of substances with a variety of kinds of qualities. The substances are composed out of prime form (what makes something to be what it is) and prime matter (what makes what can be something into something definite with spatial and temporal location) into elements from which are composed compounds subject to a variety of laws of motion in a chain of teleological causation whose ultimate cause is a first mover who is God. (Hence physics and theology are mutually dependent.) The movers are all souls (non-material substances that govern material bodies), the highest (both spatially and in terms of moral perfection) of which are intellects. Beyond the level of the human these intellects are independent of the bodies they influence, which are celestial spheres of space some of which (but not all of which) contain material globes. These globes within these otherwise empty spherical spaces are the heavenly bodies.

The second book of *The Exalted Faith* uses the summarized Aristotelian world-view of Book I to lay out and interpret the basic principles of Judaism. Those principles are five. The first deals with what Ibn Daud calls the "sources of faith or belief" (*emunah*), by which he meant the affirmation that the one, existent God of the universe is incorporeal.

The second principle interprets the root doctrine that God is one, which he understands in Aristotelian terms to mean that God is a necessary (rather than a contingent) existent and that he is uniquely so, which entails that oneness is an essential characteristic of God. The third principle deals with other divine attributes, especially those mentioned in the Bible, to argue that whatever it is that they mean it is not what we literally understand them to be. Ibn Daud is the first Jewish thinker to argue for the kind of radical negative attribute theology that we will see in greater detail in the chapters on Maimonides (Chs. 16 to 20). It is almost identical with Maimonides' theory except for one difference. Whereas Maimonides was to restrict what can properly be affirmed of God to his actions, Ibn Daud restricted these kinds of statements to his actions and his relations. It is in denying affirmations about divine relations and only about divine relations that Maimonides' theory is more radical than Ibn Daud's, and it is precisely this one point of difference that raises the most serious problems for Maimonides' theology in subsequent generations of Jewish philosophy. As we shall see (in Ch. 21), Gersonides, who at least as a philosopher and an astronomer is probably the greatest classical Jewish philosopher, was to criticize and reconstruct Maimonides in such a way that he returned Jewish Aristotelianism to the more moderate negativity of Ibn Daud's theology.

The fourth principle deals with God's actions, which here means an explanation of the intelligence that governs the sublunar world (viz., what in the language of Aristotelian science is called "the Active Intellect" that is identified with what in the language of the early rabbis is called the *shechinah*), as well as the other incorporeal entities or separate intellects that govern God's order in the celestial universe. In connection with this fourth principle on divine action, what Ibn Daud presented is a summary of the scientific astronomy of his age that drew heavily on both a Neoplatonic theory of divine overflow (or emanation) of the universe as well as the Eudoxus tradition of geometric astronomy. In general, spheres are contained within spheres, in such a way that the lesser spheres are subject to governance by the motion of the greater spheres, and each sphere itself is nothing more than a three-dimensional vector sphere whose rotation has a distinct direction and speed. What that direction in correlation with speed is depends on empirical observations of the heavens, for there are as many but only as many spheres as vector geometry requires to make intelligible the observed periodic motions of celestial bodies. Just how many such spheres there are determines how many angels there are, since angels are the intelligences that move (i.e., determine the speed and direction of) the spheres.

The fifth principle deals with the nature of prophecy, an argument that Moses is the paradigm philosopher, and finally an argument that rabbinic tradition is the true interpretation of the Torah. Torah is here presented in Aristotelian terms as the consequent propositional and imperative affirmations of the prophet Moses from his intellectual conjunction with the Active Intellect. Tradition is defended against Karaites, Muslims, and Christians as an authentic tradition in historical terms, viz., as an unbroken tradition whose links are all men whose authority as witnesses is beyond question, because of both their moral and intellectual excellence.

The last fundamental principle presented deals with divine providence. Rabad himself said that the entire architectonic of his Jewish philosophical system was constructed solely to deal with this question. He used it to argue that God is/can be perfect and humanity does/can have voluntary choice without intellectual compromise. Both affirmations, understood in coherent terms, are, or so Ibn Daud argued, the ultimate rational foundation upon which the intelligibility of the philosophical system of Torah depends.

All of these issues—in ontology, physics, theology, psychology, astronomy, epistemology, and ethics—we will visit again in more detail in Maimonides' *Guide of the Perplexed*.

Notes

1 Other atomist works by Jewish philosophers worthy of mention are Isaac Israeli's *The Book of Elements* and David ben Merwan al-Mukammas' *Twenty Chapters*.

2 Other works of Jewish philosophy from the same period, which are worthy of mention but less easy to classify in this typology, are Bahya Ibn Pakudah's *Duties of the Heart*, Abraham bar Hiyya's *Logic of the Soul*, Joseph Ibn Zaddik's *Microcosm*, and Judah Halevi's *The Kuzari*. Of these works the most important for our purposes is Halevi's *Khuzari* as a critique of philosophy.

3 Henceforth simply called "the *Guide*."

4 The thirteenth and fourteenth centuries are major periods of philosophical productivity by rabbis, most of which are not major works as philosophy. However, some of them are. Especially worthy of mention are Hillel ben Samuel's *The Rewards of the Soul*, Hasdai ben Abraham Crescas' *Light of the Lord*, and Joseph Albo's *Book of Roots*. Of these works, Crescas' *Light of the Lord* is most important as a critique of philosophy.

5 Epicurus of Samos (342–270 BCE) established Epicureanism. Stoicism was established by Zeno of Citium (*c.* 335–263 BCE), Cleanthes of Assos (*c.* 330–232 BCE) and Chrysippos of Soloi (*c.* 281–208 BCE).

6 An ancient Turkic people who arose in Transcaucasia in the second century CE, settled in the lower Volga area, and grew into an empire of major importance in the seventh century CE. Between the eighth and tenth centuries this empire reached from the northern shores of the Black Sea and the Caspian Sea as far west and north as Kiev. In the tenth century, the empire allied with the Christian Byzantine Empire to war with and defend itself against the incursion of Islam. The empire may in fact have been Jewish in the eighth century.

7 Unlike the first two books it consists of only a single chapter that supposedly deals with virtue, family life, and the law. However, as it now stands, it is a series of relatively independent and largely incoherent aphorisms. All of this suggests that, if Ibn Daud actually did complete his third book, we no longer possess an adequate version of it.

Suggestions for further study

Abraham Ibn Daud. *The Exalted Faith*. Translated into English by Norbert Samuelson. Rutherford, NJ: Fairleigh Dickinson University Press, 1986.

Ben-Shammai, Haggai. "Kalam in medieval Jewish philosophy," in Daniel H. Frank and Oliver Leaman (eds.), *History of Jewish Philosophy*. Vol. II of *Routledge History of World Philosophies*. London and New York: Routledge, 1997, pp. 115–48.

Booth, Edward. *Aristotelian Aporetic Ontology in Islamic and Christian Thinkers*. Cambridge: Cambridge University Press, 1983.

Dhanani, A. *The Physical Theory of Kalam*. Leiden: Brill, 1994.

Duhem, Pierre. *Medieval Cosmology*. Translated into English by Roger Ariew. Chicago: University of Chicago Press, 1985.

Dunlop, D. H. *The History of the Jewish Khazars*. New York: Schocken, 1967.

Goodman, Lenn E. "Judah Halevy," in Daniel H. Frank and Oliver Leaman (eds.), *History of Jewish Philosophy*. Vol. II of *Routledge History of World Philosophies*. London and New York: Routledge, 1997, pp. 188–227.

Guttmann, Julius. *Philosophies of Judaism*. English translation by David Silverman. New York: Schocken, 1973.

Hourani, George F. *Reason and Tradition in Islamic Ethics*. Cambridge: Cambridge University Press, 1985.

Husik, Isaac. *A History of Mediaeval Jewish Philosophy*. New York: Macmillan, 1916.

Judah Halevi. *The Kuzari (kitab al khazari): An Argument for the Faith of Israel*. New York: Schocken Books, 1964.

Loewe, Raphael. *Ibn Gabirol*. London: Grove, 1989.

Malter, Henry. *Saadia Gaon: His Life and Works*. New York: Hermon Press, 1969.

Morewedge, P. *Islamic Philosophical Theology*. Albany: State University of New York Press, 1979.

Neugebauer, O. *A History of Ancient Mathematical Astronomy*. Berlin/New York: Springer Verlag, 1975.

Peters, Francis E. *Aristotle and the Arabs: The Aristotelian Tradition in Islam*. New York and London: New York University Press, 1968.

Plessner, M. "The Natural Sciences and Medicine," in J. Schacht and C. E. Bosworth (eds.), *The Legacy of Islam*. New York and Oxford: Oxford University Press, 1979, pp. 425–61.

Rabinovitch, Nachum L. *Probability and Statistical Inference in Ancient and Medieval Jewish Literature*. Toronto: University of Toronto Press, 1973.

Rosenberg, Shalom. *Good and Evil in Jewish Thought*. Tel Aviv: MOD Books, 1989.

Rudavsky, T. M. "Medieval Jewish Neoplatonism," in Daniel H. Frank and Oliver Leaman (eds.), *History of Jewish Philosophy*. Vol. II of *Routledge History of World Philosophies*. London and New York: Routledge, 1997, pp. 149–87.

Saadia Gaon. *The Book of Beliefs and Opinions*. English translation by Samuel Rosenblatt. New Haven: Yale University Press, 1948.

Samuelson, Norbert M. "Medieval Jewish Aristotelianism: an introduction," in Daniel H. Frank and Oliver Leaman (eds.), *History of Jewish Philosophy*. Vol. II of *Routledge History of World Philosophies*. London and New York: Routledge, 1997, pp. 228–44.

Samuelson, Norbert M. "Medieval Jewish Philosophy," in Barry W. Holtz (ed.), *Back to the Sources: Reading the Classic Jewish Texts*. New York: Summit Books, 1984, pp. 261–304.

Saperstein, Marc. *Decoding the Rabbis*. Cambridge, MA: Harvard University Press, 1982.

Silman, Y. *Philosopher and Prophet: Judah Halevi, the Kuzari, and the Evolution of His Thought*. Albany: State University of New York Press, 1995.

Sorabji, Richard (ed.). *Philoponus and the Rejection of Aristotelian Science*. London: Duckworth, 1987.

Strauss, Leo. *Persecution and the Art of Writing*. New York: Free Press, 1952.

Key questions

1. Why does classical Jewish philosophy begin in the tenth century CE?
2. How do ninth-century Muslim studies in mathematics exemplify the place of Muslim philosophy in intellectual history?
3. What are the five Greek schools of philosophy that are the sources of Muslim and Jewish philosophy?
4. What are the three kinds of general philosophical world-views and life-views that the classical Jewish philosophers affirmed? Name the primary Muslim and Jewish philosophers who affirmed each view. What are their majors works in philosophy?
5. What was the apologetic purpose of Saadia's *Book of Beliefs and Opinions*? What are its two primary divisions? What are the topics in each division?
6. Explain Saadia's epistemology. What are the three ways to gain knowledge? Why will they in principle always be in agreement?
7. Explain Saadia's ethics. Why does the commitment to the Torah require a commitment to human choice? Does it require a belief in free will? What are the two main divisions of laws of the Torah, and what is the moral value of each?
8. According to Halevi, what is the central issue of contention between Muslim and Jewish theologians?
9. What is Halevi's epistemology? Why is philosophy in principle inadequate? What is the intellectual limit beyond which a philosopher, as a philosopher, cannot reach?
10. According to Halevi, what is the basis for a true religion? Why is Judaism the best religion?
11. What are the three books in Abraham Ibn Daud's *Exalted Faith*? What is the subject matter of each?

12. Summarize Ibn Daud's ontology. Why are physics and theology mutually dependent?
13. What are Ibn Daud's five fundamental principles of Judaism? How does his doctrine of divine attributes differ from Maimonides'?
14. Summarize Ibn Daud's astronomy. How is it dependent on mathematics? How are theology and angelology dependent on it?

The Philosophy of Maimonides

CHAPTER 16

The composition of *The Guide of the Perplexed*

Maimonides' life and influence

Moses, the son of Maimon, was born in the Almoravid city of Cordova in Andalusia in 1135. As we saw in the previous chapter, Cordova was possibly the greatest center of Muslim intellectual life in the world at that time or at any time. Certainly for Jews it was an ideal environment for all kinds of learning, from Jewish law to the most recent developments in the sciences, and it produced any number of important Jewish philosophers, not the least of whom were Judah Halevi and Abraham Ibn Daud.

Maimonides was born with the good fortune of having a wealthy father and a younger brother, and living in a culturally rich city. The rich father meant that Maimonides could hire the best teachers; the culturally rich city meant that there were great teachers to hire (for training both in Jewish law and general science); and the younger brother meant that Maimonides could spend his adulthood as well as his childhood in study (because the younger brother inherited the business responsibilities from the father).

Maimonides' good fortune came to an end when he was only 13 years old. At that time Andalusia in general and Cordova in particular were overrun by Almohads (spiritualist Muslim hordes from Morocco who believed that a Muslim state had no place for Jews, philosophers, or any other kinds of "foreign" influences). The family left in 1155 and wandered through Spain and North Africa, living for five years in the political center of the Almohads, Fez in Morocco, where Maimon's family had to hide its Jewish identity. By 1165, the family had sailed to Palestine, but they ended up settling in Egypt. By that time, Moses' brother David (David ben Maimon) had taken charge of the family jewel trade while Moses himself used his natural science studies to become a physician, a way to continue his studies while earning a living.

However, Maimonides' fortune took another turn for the worse when, in 1165, David drowned at sea on a business trip to India. Beyond the family tragedy, the death meant that Rambam himself had to compromise his studies, to which he desired to devote himself entirely, by taking over the management of a worldwide financial enterprise. Furthermore, at least in part (but only in part) connected to his position of wealth, Maimonides became the untitled head of the Jewish community of Egypt and one of the royal physicians in the court of Vizier Alfadhil in Cairo.

For many men these positions would have been the fulfillment of a life ambition, for, as royal physician, Maimonides could influence what was then the most powerful political state in the world. Similarly, the Jewish community that Maimonides led was the most influential Jewish community in the world at that time, precisely because of its location in the land of the world's leading military power. Consequently, Maimonides had enormous opportunity to influence Jewish law, an influence he would not have had otherwise, no matter how great his learning, his intelligence, and his character. However, for Maimonides, both honors were a burden, for they detracted from the one thing he wanted to do in life, which was to study the word of God as it is revealed in both nature and in the Torah, so that he might gain a reward far beyond anything that any nation could offer in this world (ha-ʿolam ha-zeh)—the success of receiving after his death a share in the world to come (ha-ʿolam ha-ba).

No other Jewish thinker was as influential in shaping what Jews as Jews believe since Judah I, as the Nasi of the Sanhedrin in Judea, published the Mishnah. In part Maimonides' importance as a rabbinic philosopher is as a consequence of his importance as a rabbinic legalist. In 1178 he published a fourteen-volume code of Jewish law entitled the Mishneh Torah or yah ha-chazakah (the strong hand).

As we saw in Chapter 15, the Mishneh Torah is one of the three works (the other two being the codes of al Fasi and Asheri) that served as the basis for Joseph Caro's shulchan arukh ("prepared table") that itself serves to this day as the single most influential guide for traditional Jewish religious practice. As such, Maimonides, the only notable philosopher of the three sources, had and continues to have an impact on the life of ordinary Jews unmatched by any other Jewish philosopher. Furthermore, his influence is not a mere accident. For Maimonides the law was an intrinsic part of his philosophy in general and his philosophy was an integral part of his understanding of Jewish law. Hence, to study his law was to learn his philosophy as to study his philosophy was to learn his law.

Maimonides' importance as a Jewish philosopher is also connected to his influence in general as a philosopher, because no other rabbinic thinker (including Judah I) has had as much impact on Christian European intellectual history as he has. When Thomas Aquinas (1225–74) wrote his *Summa Theologica*, his primary philosophical sources were two natives of Cordova—the Muslim Ibn Rushd or Averroes (1126–98) whom he called the "Commentator" and the Jew Maimonides whom he called the "rabbi." As the *Summa theologica* emerged as one of the (if not the) critical determiners of Roman Catholic beliefs at its most rigorous levels, the study of Aquinas' thought and sources became critical for any adequate understanding of western Christianity, and no understanding of his thought can be adequate without an understanding of Thomas' reading of the writings of Averroes and Maimonides. Consequently, both Averroes and Maimonides had significant historical influence on the development of Christian European history. This is especially true of Averroes' understanding of the proper relationship between science and religion, which Europeans call the "double truth theory," and Maimonides' understanding of the meaning of statements about God, which Europeans call "negative theology." (We will deal with the double truth theory in Chapter 20 and with negative theology in this chapter.) As such, Christians, and therefore Christian philosophers, have paid more attention to Maimonides' writings than to any other Jewish philosopher. In this case the work of Maimonides that they read was *The Guide of the Perplexed* (*moreh nevukhim*).

In general, Maimonides influenced Jews through the *Mishneh Torah*, which was and is largely unknown to Christians, and he influenced Christians through the *Guide*, which was and is largely unread by traditional rabbinic Jews. Still, in part at least, Maimonides' status among Jews is the unequaled level of prestige his writing has with non-Jews, for Jews, as perpetual members of a minority culture within a dominant culture, never cease to be influenced by Jews who influence non-Jews, whether or not the quality of the work of these influential Jews is worthy of the influence.

In Maimonides' case the influence is well deserved, judging from the quality of his work in and of itself. Maimonides is certainly one of the greatest philosophers to live, both in terms of the subtlety of his mind and his creativity as a thinker.

There are two ways to summarize Maimonides' thought. One way is as a legal judge (*posek*) who imposes a strong philosophical structure and system on his treatment and presentation of the law. Another way is as a philosopher for whom legal theory and practice play a deep and central role in his philosophy as a whole. If we were to take the former approach, then our emphasis in presentation would be on the *Mishneh Torah*. However, the second approach would be more coherent in general for an introductory book on Jewish philosophy. Hence, our emphasis in presentation here is on Maimonides' *Guide*.

There are some modern scholars of Maimonides' thought who believe that there is a radical separation between what he says in the *Mishneh Torah* and what he says in the *Guide*. This thesis has been debated by Maimonidean scholars since the first publication of the *Guide* in 1190, just twelve years after his publication of the *Mishneh Torah*. Clearly there is a different intended audience for the two works. The earlier product is directed to all committed Jews, while the later treatise is directed to a subset of committed Jews who have studied contemporary scientific philosophy. However, that does not mean that Maimonides said different things to these two different audiences and/or that what he said to one was incompatible with what he said to the other. Again, this is an issue that is still debated by Maimonidean scholars and will undoubtedly continue to be debated well into the future, for Maimonides' own works contribute significantly to the confusion. Still, it is my judgment, in agreement with almost all contemporary readers out of traditional Jewish communities, that the two bodies of work are coherent in content, and I will assume that the reading of Maimonides' philosophy that I present here by focusing exclusively on the *Guide* agrees with a proper reading of the *Mishneh Torah*.

The influence of Maimonides' philosophy on Jews is no less fitting than his influence on non-Jews. His philosophy is subtle, profound, and creative (in short, it is qualitatively superb philosophy) in ways that had no equal in philosophy before him and would have no equal in Jewish philosophy after him until the seventeenth-century thought of Baruch Spinoza (in Chapter 24).

The structure of the *Guide*

The *Guide* begins with a dedication to Maimonides' student, Rabbi Joseph ben Rabbi Judah. The dedication makes the purpose of the *Guide* clear. Joseph had professional training in and religious commitment to the central texts of rabbinic Judaism—the Hebrew Scriptures, the Mishnah, Midrash, the Babylonian Talmud, and the responsa (*teshuvot*) of the Gaonim. He also had interest (but not professional training) in the major texts in natural philosophy of his day—Arabic translations of Aristotle's work in physics, ethics, and astronomy as first interpreted by Alexander of Aphrodisias, Plato's *Timaeus*, and some knowledge of the physical and ethical theories of the Pythagoreans, the Epicureans, Galen, and Proclus, as well as the Muslim interpretations of this Hellenistic inheritance by al-Farabi, Ibn Sina, Ibn Bajja, and possibly Ibn Rushd, as well as the older Muslim philosophic writings of the Mutakallimun, especially Al-Razi.[1]

As a "rabbi," Joseph's primary commitment was to rabbinic Judaism; however, he also believed that truth is truth, philosophy makes truth claims as well as Judaism, and that the two systems of claims do not seem to be coherent with each other. This apparent incoherence had caused Rabbi Joseph confusion or perplexity (*nebukhim*), and the purpose of his studies with Rambam were to untie the knots that blocked the free flow of his thinking past these confusions. Now, for professional reasons, Rabbi Judah had to conclude his formal studies with Rambam before he could be completely cured of his mental ailments. Maimonides wrote the *Guide* primarily as a cure. Left on his own to continue his studies, the *Guide* would guide Joseph and those like him to good mental health, so that, relieved through his own efforts from his perplexities, he would free himself to pursue spiritual perfection for himself and for the members of his religious community.

In brief, what the opening epistle does is make the context of the work clear—it is in effect a responsum from a rabbi to a rabbi that deals with the proper way to attain true religious faith. As such, the work is subject to certain legal constraints that otherwise would not be an appropriate concern in a work of philosophy.

Maimonides believed that the Torah taught both what one ought to do as well as what one ought to believe, and that both oughts are obligations under Jewish law. However, teaching proper belief is more difficult than teaching right behavior. Not everyone can understand why some things that the Torah commands us to do are right, but everyone, despite capability for conceptual knowledge, is capable of performing those actions. They need to understand that God commands them, but they need not understand why God commands them. On the other hand, you cannot be commanded to believe something that you cannot understand. Such doctrines will be for us "mysterious" and/or simply "deep." It is not that they are inherently mysterious or deep. It is just that not everyone possesses the requisite ability and/or opportunity and/or leisure and/or training to be able to understand them. This is the case with beliefs whose adequate understanding requires knowledge of disciplines such as physics, astronomy, and theology. Such deep or mysterious matters include who or what God is, how God created the world, how he governs it, and how he revealed this knowledge through the prophets, especially through Moses.

Again, these are doctrines about which the law properly requires correct belief, for without correct belief the individual cannot attain redemption after death in the world to come. However, correct belief is not possible without adequate knowledge of the related sciences, and most people are not capable of attaining such knowledge. Maimonides called such perplexing items of dogma (in *Guide* Bk. I, Ch. 35) the "secrets" of the Torah.

Because of the inherent difficulty in understanding these "secrets" concerning which proper belief is a necessary condition for a life of spiritual virtue, Maimonides understood the law to prohibit such teaching in public. What readers can understand of any of these dogmas depends on their level of understanding. Simply to tell them the truth as it is would only confuse them and, as such, not lead them to a true and proper faith. On the contrary, it could be religiously destructive, for it could produce a misunderstanding, in which case you, the teacher, would have led your student to error, not truth. Or, even worse, it could lead the student to attribute to you false beliefs, which would misdirect other students from true belief and might even lead to your own punishment for false belief. (Some scholars think that what Maimonides has in mind here is the fate of Socrates, whose sin, on this interpretation, is that he taught truths to students before they were ready to understand them, and he did his teaching in public where he could not control who was hearing and absorbing what he was saying.)

How then do you teach those who are not capable of understanding? Maimonides' answer is that you follow God's example in the Torah. You teach using parables and equivocal expressions which different students will understand at different levels depending on the level of excellence they have achieved in ability to understand the deep matters of God and the universe.

Understanding this way of teaching is critical to solving the perplexities or confusions in affirming belief in the truth claims of Judaism in the comparative light of the truth claims of contemporary science. No important statement in the Torah is univocal, i.e., has only one ("uni-"), simple clear meaning (or voice, "vocal"). What the Torah says is not ambiguous or equivocal (i.e., having many ["equi-"] meanings or voices), because it is unclear. On the contrary, it is very precisely unclear, intending to speak to each reader at the appropriate level of his knowledge.

Notes

1 What Maimonides himself knew, let alone Rabbi Joseph, of earlier works of Jewish philosophy is a matter of speculation. Maimonides himself mentioned none by name, but it is difficult to imagine that he did not have some familiarity with the work of Saadia, let alone his fellow Cordovan, Judah Halevi, or even of his fellow Cordovan Aristotelian, Abraham Ibn Daud.

Suggestions for further study

Broadie, Alexander. "Maimonides and Aquinas," in Daniel H. Frank and Oliver Leaman (eds.), *History of Jewish Philosophy*. Vol. II of *Routledge History of World Philosophies*. London and New York: Routledge, 1997, pp. 281–94.

Heschel, Abraham Joshua. *Maimonides*. English translation by Joachim Neugroschel. New York: Farrar, Straus & Giroux, 1982.

Kreisel, Howard. "Moses Maimonides," in Daniel H. Frank and Oliver Leaman (eds.), *History of Jewish Philosophy*. Vol. II of *Routledge History of World Philosophies*. London and New York: Routledge, 1997, pp. 245–80.

Leaman, Oliver. *Moses Maimonides*. London: Routledge, 1990.

Maimonides, Moses. *The Guide of the Perplexed*. English translation by Shlomo Pines. Chicago: University of Chicago Press, 1963.

Maimonides, Moses. *Mishneh Torah*. English translation by Eliyahu Touger. 25 volumes. New York/Jerusalem: Moznaim, 1989.

Pines, Shlomo and Yovel, Yermiyahu (eds.). *Maimonides and Philosophy*. Dordrecht: Martinus Nijhoff, 1986.

Strauss, Leo. "How to begin to study *The Guide of the Perplexed*," in the Sholomo Pines' English translation of Maimonides' *Guide of the Perplexed*. Chicago: University of Chicago Press, 1963, pp. xi–lvi.

Strauss, Leo. *Philosophy and Law: Contributions to the Understanding of Maimonides and His Predecessors*. Translated into English by E. Adler. Albany: State University of New York Press, 1995.

Twersky, Isadore. *Introduction to the Code of Maimonides (Mishneh Torah)*. New Haven: Yale University Press, 1980.

Key questions

1. Why is Maimonides important as a philosopher and as a Jewish thinker?
2. Why did Maimonides write *The Guide of the Perplexed*?

CHAPTER 17

God and the Bible

Maimonides' *Guide of the Perplexed* is divided into three books, each containing a number of chapters on different topics. (See the chapter topic headings at the end of this chapter.) This chapter and the next two will each present a summary of the distinct topics in each book. We begin in this chapter with the main topics of the first book Maimonides' method of interpreting the meaning of key biblical terms (what I call his "biblical criticism"), his interpretation of the meaning of statements about whom God is (what I call "divine attributes and names"), and his presentation of a number of distinct philosophical demonstrations of the existence, unity, and incorporeality of God.

Biblical criticism

It is the task of the student of the Bible to unpack as many possible different layers of meaning to the words of the Scriptures, and then, armed with his or her own rational abilities and knowledge of other parts of Torah (oral and written), as well as of the natural world, to determine which possible meaning of the text is the right meaning. The rule (as Maimonides explains in *Guide* I:26–35) is, always take the simplest meaning of a text (its *peshat*) as what the text means unless the simplest meaning does not make sense—either because it is unintelligible or nonsense in itself, or because it is incoherent or inconsistent with other parts of the text—or it is simply not true. In that case, some other meaning is the text's true meaning.

Most of the chapters in the first part of the *Guide* are examples of Maimonides' way to read the Bible. Every instance deals with terms affirmed of God whose literal meaning cannot be affirmed to be true of God. For example, the human is said in Gen 1:26 to have been made in "the image of God" and after God's "likeness." The question is, what do "image" (*tselem*) and "likeness" (*demut*) mean here? The question is important. The end or goal of human existence is to imitate God. Just what it means to imitate him depends on what it means to be in God's image/likeness.

Maimonides tells us that the simple meaning (*peshat*) of an "image" is a material likeness, but he gives examples where "image" means the intelligible form, in the Aristotelian sense of the expression, of a thing. Similarly, while a "likeness" is a physical similarity, so it can also mean a conceptual likeness, in which case the likeness of a thing is the same as its image, viz., an intelligible form. Hence, what it means to say that God and the human are alike or similar is that both can be said (in ways that Maimonides will explain later) to have an intelligible form. Consequently, human perfection consists in developing the excellence of the human rational intellect, which is both its form and the way the human is like the divine.

Maimonides follows the same approach with every term discussed. (See the topic headings at the end of this chapter.) The general conclusion of his close reading and analysis of the words of the Hebrew Scriptures, which he begins to discuss in Part I, Chapter 46, is that God is absolutely incorporeal. This claim was made by Jewish philosophers before Maimonides, and it clearly reflects the influence of Muslim philosophy on Jewish philosophy, since before that influence Jewish thought was far more open to admitting some positive sense to material ascription to deity. However, no one before Maimonides expressed this new dogma (viz., that God is in the most radical sense possible incorporeal) with the rigor and clarity of Maimonides. Maimonides' understanding of divine incorporeality was to become a foundation for all subsequent discussions of God's nature in both Jewish and in Christian theology, and Kabbalah's affirmation of material images for God should be understood to be primarily a reaction against the extreme character of Maimonides' negation of the value of the physical.

Divine attributes and names

Maimonides' extreme interpretation of the standard Kalam dogma that God is incorporeal is no less extreme than his discussion of God being one and God existing. This argument is presented in Chapters 47 to 60 of Part I. The argument can be summarized as follows:

The standard form of a sentence that claims to tell you what something is has the form "S is P." "S" is the subject term, which is a substance; "P" is the predicate term, which is an attribute; and "is" is the connection affirmed between the substance and attribute. A substance is the kind of thing that exists in the world. In general it is a concrete particular (such as a stone or a tree or a dog) that occupies a single space at any single time. An attribute is a universal quality (like a color or a shape or a texture) that can be in many things at many places at a single time. (So, for example, my shirt can only be in one place at any one time, but its red can be many places at that same time, for the same red can be in the shirt that I am now wearing and in the roses in the garden outside my study.) "S is P" says that that quality or characteristic is now in a specified subject. The attribute can be in substance in one of two ways—it will be either an accidental property or an essential property. It is an accident if it may or may not be true of its subject substance without the substance ceasing to be what it is; on the other hand, if the absence of the property from its host makes its host to be something other than it is, then the property is either the "essence" of the thing or at least part of the essence of the thing. So, for example, a raven can be fat or thin or large or small and still be a raven. Hence, when it loses and gains weight it remains the same raven. However, should it cease to be a black bird (which is its essence) or it ceases to be "black" or a "bird" (which are parts of its essence), then it is no longer the same thing.[1]

Furthermore, the statement of a substance's essence involves the affirmation of at least two attributes. One expresses the genus, which is that property or set of properties shared in common by all things so designated; and the other expresses the specific difference, which is that property or set of properties that differentiates the thing named from all the other members of the genus. For example, in the case of a raven the genus is bird and the specific difference is black, for a raven (if the definition is correct) shares in common everything else that makes a bird a bird, but it differs from all birds that are not ravens in being black.

All of the above is presupposed and not explicitly stated in Maimonides' explanation of divine attribution to his student Joseph and those like him, which is to say that readers of the *Guide* will have at least this much background in Aristotelian studies in language, logic, and physics. Maimonides goes on to argue that, if two things share in common a genus but not a species, i.e., they are defined by different specific differences, then they cannot be compared. (For example, you cannot compare apples and oranges even though both are fruit.) How much the more so is it the case that there is no comparison between things that do not even share a common genus, which is the case when we talk about God and anything else, for God created everything else. God and God alone exists as a creator while everything else exists as a creature of the creator. Hence, not even existence is the same when we talk about God and anything else.

The radical non-relationality between God and everything else is also a consequence of God's radical oneness. Because God is the creator of everything, he can in no sense whatsoever be composite, for if he were composite then his being would ultimately be dependent on the simpler elements or features from which he is composed, in which case they would be the creators of God and he would be their creature. Now, if God has a definition, then there are some attributes, at least two, that define him, and, as such exist in him, in which case he would not be simple, for he would contain within himself two attributes that, while they define him, would not be identical with him, in which case they would be more the creature than he is.

This radical non-relationality between the creator God and his creatures entails that there is no literal way to make positive affirmations of God (sentences of the form "God is f," where f is an attribute of God), and any attempt to do so would constitute, albeit unintentionally, an affirmation of idolatry, since it entails the worship of a deity of whom it is not true that he is one and that he is the creator of everything. In general, all that can be said literally of God is what he is not, and the only reason we admit any positive statements about God at all is that many such statements occur in the Hebrew Scriptures.

The result is that we can make positive affirmations about God, since the Scriptures do so, but we cannot say anything more than what they say, and whatever we think those affirmations mean they cannot be taken literally.

Maimonides tells us what he believes they properly mean in Part I, Ch. 57. For any attribute f, there is a contrary attribute g; what it means to say that God is f is that God is not g. In other words, all affirmations of God are to be understood instead as negations. In general, given anything of which you as a human being can think, that is not true of God, and this situation uniquely defines God, for God and God alone is such that in principle no affirmative and every negative claim is true.

This general conclusion has the apparent consequence that language about God is meaningless. If, for example, you can say that God is good and mean by that that he is not bad, you can also say that God is bad and mean by that that he is not good, because both negations are true of God. Hence, God-talk, so understood on Maimonides' semantics, should admit the claims "God is good" and "God is bad," as well as every other set of complements. However, in such a language there can be no distinction between true and false claims, so that the language, admitting contradictions, in the end breaks down as no language at all, i.e., as something meaningless.

Maimonides himself was aware of this objection. He raised it and solved it as follows: On the principle of the imitation of God as the moral ideal for human existence, you may only affirm of God a moral virtue, not a moral vice. Hence, to say that God is f not only means that God is not g but also means that f is a human virtue and g is a human vice. Hence, "God is good" means that human beings ought to be good and ought not to be bad. Similarly, for human beings existing is better than not existing, incorporeality is better than corporeality, and unity is better than diversity. In other words, God-talk turns out in the end to consist of statements about human morality, i.e., about *halakhah*, in the guise of statements about who or what God is.

To say the same thing differently, religion or theology must be discussed in the language of ethics. This is a profound point, viz., that theology is reducible to ethics, that had major consequences in the development of twentieth-century Jewish philosophy in Germany and America (see Chapter 26).

Proofs of God's existence

Saadia, following the example of Kalam philosophy, began the constructive part of his Jewish philosophy by discussing the tripart claim that God exists and is one and is incorporeal. We have seen that Maimonides does the same in writing his *Guide*. The discussion of God's existence begins in Part I, Chs. 71 to 76, and it is concluded in the introduction and first chapter of Part II. It can be summarized as follows:

There were in the science of Maimonides' time two dominant theories of the physical world, and there was no way to prove which was correct. The old view was that of the atomists that the Mutakallimun adopted. It argued that the universe is ultimately constituted of "atoms," i.e., indivisible units of extended matter that are in every respect identical except for their spatial–temporal location, that occupy indivisibly small spaces in indivisibly small time periods called "moments." There is a vast plurality of atoms, but in terms of what each is, they are identical. Hence nothing has qualities. The same can be said of time and space. Therefore, the only laws that govern things are quantitative laws of constant conjunction. Different numbers of things randomly come together and again separate. Hence, there is no real knowledge in the sense of certainty, since everything happens by chance. "Chance," that is, except for the will of God. God is a pure will who imposes his order on the randomness of the universe. Hence, there is order in the universe, but the order is exclusively an expression of the will of God.

The new view was that of the Aristotelians. In this view the universe ultimately consists of substances that are composed of forms that express what they are, and matter that accounts for the fact that some forms actually exist. Put differently, substances can be understood to be either informed matter or materialized forms, and both expressions describe the same reality. Forms express ideals towards which the substances strive. Hence, what any substance is is something in movement towards an end, where the thing's reality is its motion whose primary cause is the end it seeks to become. In general, nothing in the universe is random. Everything is moved by and towards an end that defines it. This is true "in general," but not entirely, because the end expresses the form of the thing, but only insofar as something is materialized does it actually exist, and matter is itself a principle of randomness. Hence, while everything is knowable and determined, it is not entirely knowable and not entirely determinable because nothing is real without matter of some sort. Nothing, that is, except God, who is solely form and as pure form is the cause of all that is.

There is no way to know, Maimonides argues, which of these views of the universe in general is true, because there is no vantage point from which a human being, who is within the universe, can stand, see, and reach intelligent judgments about the universe as such.

Since we cannot know which of these two overviews of everything is true, we cannot merely assume one of them to prove that the deity of everything exists, is one, and is incorporeal. If the argument is based, for example, on the assumption of a random material universe, then our conclusion at best can only be—if atomism is true, then God exists, etc. However, it cannot be that necessarily God exists, is one, and is incorporeal, because we as humans cannot know if atomism is or is not true. The same is the case if we assume an Aristotelian position on physical cosmology.

How then is it possible to provide proofs that God exists, is one, and is incorporeal? Maimonides does have an answer. His approach is to use what is called in Aristotelian logic a "modus tollens" form of argument. The structure of such an argument reads as follows: Let P, Q, and R be propositions. P or Q; if P then R; if Q then R; therefore, R. In this way you can know that R is true even though you do not know which is true, P or Q. At the end of Part I (Chs. 73–76), Maimonides argues that, if the atomist view of the universe is correct (P), then God exists, is one, and is incorporeal (R). Next, in the introduction and first chapter of Part II, Maimonides argues that, if the Aristotelian view of the universe is correct (Q), then God exists, is one, and is incorporeal (R). Therefore, God exists, is one, and is incorporeal (R).

Note that in this way Maimonides proves three fundamental theological claims without claiming any knowledge of God. We know at the end *that* God exists, is one, and is incorporeal, but we do not know what these claims mean. If we could be certain that the Aristotelian view of the universe were true, then there would be a way of interpreting these three claims. The same would be true if we could know the truth of the Kalam view. In the end we know nothing about God for the same reason we know nothing about the universe as a whole; they both lie beyond the limits of human knowledge.

We may then ask, what does it mean to say God created the universe if creation lies beyond the limit of human comprehension? Furthermore, why does the Torah never seem to mean what it seems to say? How are we to understand prophecy, especially Mosaic prophecy? Furthermore, we know from the Torah that what God does is create the world and reveal the Torah. Given what we now know that we do not know about God, what do we know or not know about the creator of the world and the revealer of the Torah? These are the central questions of the second part of the *Guide*, which we will summarize in the next chapter.

Note

1 Another example of this Aristotelian view of language and the world would be the hero of Franz Kafka's short story, "Metamorphosis," who wakes up one morning to discover that he has become a cockroach. At first he thinks the change is only accidental. Yesterday he was a human and today he is a bug, but he is still the same him. However, he discovers in the course of the short story that he is no longer himself, because changing from a human to a bug is ceasing to be what you are and becoming something entirely different.

Suggestions for further study

Burrell, David. *Knowing the Unknowable God: Ibn Sina, Maimonides, and Aquinas*. Notre Dame, IN: University of Notre Dame Press, 1986.

Faur, José. *Homo Mysticus: A Guide to Maimonides's* Guide for the Perplexed. Syracuse: Syracuse University Press, 1999.

Seeskin, Kenneth. *Maimonides: A Guide for Today's Perplexed*. West Orange, NJ: Behrman House, 1991.

Seeskin, Kenneth. *Searching for a Distant God: The Legacy of Maimonides*. New York/Oxford: Oxford University Press, 2000.

Key questions

1. What is Maimonides' proposed method for reading and interpreting the Hebrew Scriptures?
2. What is at stake philosophically in interpreting what Genesis 1:26 means when it says that the human was created in God's image and likeness?
3. How, according to Maimonides, is it possible for human beings to talk about God? What does it mean to say that God exists, is one, and is incorporeal? Why does this understanding of God-talk reduce theology to ethics?
4. How does Maimonides prove that God exists, is one, and is incorporeal? What do those proofs tell us about God?

Chapter topic headings in *The Guide of the Perplexed*, Book I

Introduction Purpose of book, why it contains contradictions
Ch. 1   Meaning of *tselem* (image), *demut* (likeness), and *toar* (shape)
Ch. 2   On why men make errors
Ch. 3   Meaning of *temunah* (figure), and *tabnit* (shape)
Ch. 4   Meaning of *roah* (see), *habbit* (look at), and *chazah* (eye vision)
Ch. 5   Do not advance faster than you are able to advance
Ch. 6   Meaning of *ish* (man), and *ishah* (woman)
Ch. 7   Meaning of *yalad* (bear children)
Ch. 8   Meaning of *makom* (place)
Ch. 9   Meaning of *kisse* (throne or chair)
Ch. 10   Meaning of *yarod* (descending), and *aloh* (ascending)
Ch. 11   Meaning of *yeshivah* (sitting)
Ch. 12   Meaning of *kimah* (rising)
Ch. 13   Meaning of *adimah* (standing)

CHAPTER 18

Creation and revelation

Angels (*Guide* II: 2–12)

Maimonides' discussion of angels is an extension of his discussion of God. What he says about them is basically a repetition of what Abraham Ibn Daud said in the *Exalted Faith* (Ch. 15). However, there are important differences, most of which follow from the radical agnosticism of Maimonides' statement about human knowledge of God in Part I of the *Guide*.

In the Hebrew Scriptures there are no angels. Rather, what there are are "messengers" (*malakhim* [*malakh* in the singular]) whom God sends to earth from his sky (*shamayim*) to perform special tasks. The early rabbis of the Midrash are the ones who transform these divine messengers into "angels." In the Midrash they are creatures who, like God and humanity, have consciousness, speech, and reason. However, unlike humans, they have intimate association with God and reside in the heavens. It is in the writing of the rabbis that the "sky" (*shamayim*), i.e., the spatial region surrounding the globe of the earth where the stars are located, is transformed into the "heavens." They are a qualitatively different region that can only metaphorically be called spatial. There reside God and a host of other non-physical (i.e., "spiritual") beings that serve him.

It would be more accurate to say that the conceptual development of angels in Jewish thought is a continuous process. In early biblical texts, they play no role. There, all interaction between the divine and the human is between the deity and the nation; the deity has no specified suprahuman agents. However, it is also true that in this earlier material there are at least as many deities as there are nations. As the biblical literature tends to give a greater role to a class of entities intermediate between humans and deities called "angels," so this same literature tends to diminish the number of deities. By the end of the period of the composition of the Hebrew Scriptures there are many angels and only one God. In the imaginative biblical commentaries of the early rabbis, the number of these angels grows into a vast horde, possibly as numerous (no one counts them) as humanity itself.

A similar tendency can be seen in Hellenistic literature. The heavenly courts of the gods become increasingly less democratic (i.e., bodies made up of beings whose powers are more or less, if not equal, on a par) and increasingly more monarchic, as one of these divinities emerges within his court as *the* ruler and *the* most powerful deity. By the seventh century it would no longer be clear to any reflective person just what exactly was the difference between believing—as the pagans did—in a court of divinities, one of whom is supreme in every respect, and believing—as the Jews, Christians, and Muslims did—in a single deity who rules over a court of lesser deities, called "angels," who carry out his will in governing the world.

The Jewish and the Muslim philosophers interpreted the references to divine messengers in their holy texts (the Hebrew Scriptures and the Koran) to refer not to the creatures that resemble human beings, but to the created purely spiritual (i.e., non-physical, immaterial) and intelligent forces that impose (divine) order and structure on an otherwise materially chaotic universe. In the case of the Aristotelian Muslims and Jews, this interpretation is an identification of angels with the separate intellects of Aristotelian cosmology. This identification functions to bridge the gap between a humanity spatially located in the "sublunar world"—that most central sphere of space in the spatial globe of the universe in which the globe of the planet earth is situated—and an absolutely incomparable deity who has no spatial location whatsoever and hence can only be said to be beyond (not within) the space of the universe.

In Aristotelian philosophy, a "soul" is a principle of motion in bodies to the extent that those bodies are self-moved. As a principle of motion, these souls are rational, because the order they impose on their subject bodies is intelligible. By extension, as there are non-material souls that are the principle of the movements of bodies on the surface of the globe of the earth, so the space in which the earth is located also has a soul. It has a soul because it has a self-caused motion (viz., the vector of its rotation on its axis) as well as intelligible, natural laws. All of these self-originating motions and laws of nature were understood as manifestations upon space of the rational will of the sphere's soul, now called a "separate intellect."

Our souls that govern our bodies are subject to the intellect that governs the sphere of the planet earth. This particular intellect of the sphere below the sphere of the moon (i.e., the sublunar world) is called the "Active Intellect." That intellect in turn with the sphere it governs is part of a greater celestial sphere governed by a greater separate intellect. Ultimately, there is the sphere of the entire universe itself that is governed by the First Intellect.

Now, it would be natural for these Aristotelian Jewish philosophers to identify the Active Intellect with the *shechinah* (i.e., the form of divine presence to prophets) and the First Intellect with God as he is in himself (i.e., as the referent of the Tetragrammaton). However, given Maimonides' radical interpretation of God, the First Intellect cannot be God simply because it is to some extent intelligible in positive terms. For Maimonides even the First Intellect is one of God's creatures. Hence, there is communication between God and humanity, but that communication is only indirect. For Maimonides there is always a screen of ignorance separating even the wisest of human beings from God through which divine wisdom (Torah) is communicated. Hence, for all practical purposes, it is the knowledge derived from communication with the lowest of celestial intelligences or angels that constitutes in effect communication with God. In this communication there is knowledge of what God wills, but there is no knowledge of God himself.

Creation (*Guide* II: 13–28)

Maimonides moves from discussing angels to one of the two greatest mysteries revealed to the prophets in the Torah—the creation of the world. In this case Maimonides constructs the following argument: As we have already noted, the Hebrew Scriptures should always be taken literally unless what they literally say is known to be false. What the Hebrew Scriptures seem to say literally is that the universe and everything in it was created by God, and what Aristotelian science seems to say is that the universe is eternal and uncreated. Now, if we could know through science or philosophy (i.e., through physical cosmology) that the world is eternal and uncreated, then we could give the biblical texts that suggest otherwise a non-literal reading. However, in this case there is no necessity to do so. God's act of creating the universe is a special relationship between God as he is in himself and the universe as a whole. However, we have in principle knowledge neither of God as he is in himself nor of the universe as a whole. Hence, there is no way we can know anything about creation, which is the relationship between these two unknowns.

Furthermore, since there is no knowledge that what the Hebrew Scriptures say literally about creation is not true, we accept what it does literally say as true. Hence, a Jew ought to believe as a foundation-principle (*yesod*) of Torah-true Judaism that God created everything out of nothing rather than claiming, as the Aristotelians do, that the world is eternal.

The question should be asked just what is the difference between creation out of nothing (the Torah-true belief) and an eternal, uncreated universe (the Aristotelian belief)? From what Maimonides does tell us, an eternal uncreated universe operates by laws of necessity, i.e., laws that determine all that happens in the universe as necessarily happening, while in a created universe much that happens happens not by necessity but by chance or, far more important, by purposefully directed acts of human and/or divine intention. From this perspective clearly a Jew, in order to remain a Jew, needs to believe in a created universe. On these terms if the universe was not created, then there would be no room for human choice; if there were no room for human decision-making (i.e., for choice), then no one could be held morally culpable for disobeying God's laws and no one would deserve a reward for obeying them. Hence, in the case of Israel, if the Aristotelians are correct, then there is no reason to take the Torah seriously. The Torah is first and foremost a law code, but in a universe where there are no real choices, there is no moral responsibility for action. Hence, the Torah is superfluous, even foolish, because it commands people to do what they cannot help but do or not do. Furthermore, it is even unjust, because no one who does what he cannot help do deserves either reward for obedience or punishment for disobedience.

What is not clear in Maimonides' position is whether the difference between Aristotle and the Torah on cosmogony (the origin of the universe) has anything to do with time. The position attributed to the Aristotelians is that the universe is unending with respect to time and exists by necessity rather than by willful, purposeful intent. Clearly the Torah position is that the world exists by willful, purposeful intent. However, it is not clear that the Torah position requires the universe to have a finite, temporal origin. Maimonides tells us that creation involves the creation of absolutely everything, including time. But, if time is itself an object of creation, then creation cannot take place in time. Hence, creation itself is an eternal act in which the never-beginning and never-ending series of markings of events as before and after is in its entirety created.

To understand what it means to say that something that has within itself no beginning or end—i.e., a line (of time) that is infinite (i.e., is without limit, which is literally what "infinite" means in Hebrew [*beli tachlit*]) in both directions—is created in a time, i.e., has a finite origin, think about the persons, whoever they must have been, who first invented natural numbers. The list of natural numbers has neither a first nor a last number, because every number can be incremented by another natural number. However, there was a time when there were no natural numbers, because no one had yet conceived of them. Similarly, when God creates the universe he creates what occupies time and space as well as the time and space it occupies. As such, when created the universe exists spatially in endless times in both directions of what is before and what is after.

The philosopher who conceived of the universe as eternally created rather than merely created or eternal was Plato. He presents this view in detail in the *Timaeus*. Now, clearly Maimonides knew the *Timaeus*, because he says at least two different things about it in the *Guide*. First, there would be no difficulty reconciling the Torah view with this view of Plato's. Second, the literal meaning of at least some of the passages of the Hebrew Scriptures fits Plato's account more than the position that Maimonides calls that of the Torah, viz., that all of the universe and everything in it (including time) was created in time.

Readers should know that this interpretation of what Maimonides says here about creation is controversial. The recommendations for further reading at the end of this chapter direct your attention to books that offer significantly different views. Some say that Maimonides really agreed with Aristotle that the universe is eternal and uncreated, and others say that Maimonides really held what he presents as the view of the Torah that the universe is created and has a finite origin.

In any case, it is clear that creation is an act of God which lies in principle beyond anything that a human being can understand. This is so, primarily because "creation" defines the relationship between two terms, neither of which are in themselves in any way knowable—God as he is in himself and the world as it is in itself. This is the main point of Maimonides' presentation of creation. It is not to tell you, whatever he may have "really" believed, how the universe began.

The question we are now ready to ask is, why does the Torah say what it says in the way that it says it? All that can be understood and affirmed in the Scriptures is the system of law given in the heart of the Torah. That, too, of course cannot be taken literally, for it, too, in its literal sense is not what it truly means. However, in this case we have the guide of Judah's *Mishnah* (as well as Maimonides' *Mishneh Torah*) and centuries of continuously transmitted oral rabbinic commentaries to show us how to understand the law. Hence, prophecy as interpreted in rabbinic tradition is a clear guide to what we need to do in order to do the good on our way to human perfection. However, just what is it that we are supposed to learn from the words of the Scriptures about true belief, since the true meaning of the concepts of the Torah is even less literal than the right meaning of the precepts of the Torah? Furthermore, with concepts there is no clear and certain guide comparable to the path of *halakhah*.

The temptation might be to discount the philosophy of the Torah and affirm only its legal ethics. That certainly was the tendency of some rabbis, and, just before the dawn of modernity, that tendency became dominant in the lives of most European Jews. However, that is not what Maimonides himself encouraged. He believed that practice is not something engaged in for itself alone, but is to be understood as a discipline needing to be mastered before true belief can be acquired. As such, the precepts of the Torah are preconditions for the attainment of what really matters in the teachings of the Torah—correct belief about everything, especially about those things we know to lie beyond human capability, i.e., theology. How then does the Torah teach theology and why does it teach it in the way that it does? Maimonides' answer to this question is the concluding topic of Book II. Furthermore, being located in the middle of the treatise, it fits what we have already seen to be a dominant stylistic tendency in Jewish writing—what matters most is placed in the middle.

Prophecy (*Guide* II: 29–48)

Maimonides' Aristotelian universe has the physical shape of a spherical doll that contains within it multiple, increasingly smaller, spherical dolls, down to a centermost sphere. This centermost sphere is the globe of the planet earth. As such the earth is not what is most excellent and most valued. The opposite is the case.

Maimonides' Aristotelian universe can also be pictured as a moral array of numbers in which every item has an unique place that is defined by being located between one item (its immediate inferior) and another item (its immediate superior). In the substantial expression of this moral hierarchy, the lowest place is occupied by pure, formless prime matter, above which are the four elements (earth, water, air, and fire) composed from the conjunction of prime matter with the elemental forms. Above the elements, in ascending (causal) order and (moral) ranking are minerals, vegetables, animals, and heavenly objects. Within each of these broad genera there are further differentiations into species also organized in a hierarchy where every species has a unique location. At the borders of each species is a transitional subspecies that represents the best possible example of the genus below and the worst possible example of the genus above. At the border between animals and angels are humans; at the border between humans and angels are prophets. Hence, humans as a species are the most perfect animals, and prophets as a subspecies are the most perfect humans, the excellence towards which all human beings should tend.

What defines the excellence of the class prophets is the character of its knowledge. What these humans know is at the very horizon of the wisdom of the angels. However, just as there are all kinds of species, all uniquely rankable in an order of ascending excellence, so there are all kinds of prophets, also ranked in an order of ascending excellence. This order of prophets and what prophets know can be listed as follows:

The lowest ranking of human beings are the ignorant. Above them are politicians and fortune-tellers who compensate for the weakness of their intellects with highly developed imaginations. They can imagine what they cannot understand and so they can make wise practical judgments in concrete affairs of the world of the imagination—the world of time and space governed by opinions formed from the impressions of the five external senses (touching, tasting, smelling, hearing, and seeing). Beyond the politicians and soothsayers are the philosophers who, armed with their developed intellects, can understand a great deal of what happens in the universe, especially its most general laws and categories of nature. However, because of the relative weakness of their imaginations (by comparison with the politicians), they can rarely apply what they know in general to concrete cases. Hence, scholars tend to be failures in both politics and economics and in every other practical affair of the world. Beyond both philosophers and politicians in excellence are the prophets, who combine superior imagination with superior intellect. Hence they, like good politicians, can imagine the right concrete decision to be made in concrete situations, and, like good philosophers, they have the power to understand what it is that they are doing and seeing. It is prophets, more than politicians or philosophers, who write the texts to which we ordinary humans must turn to find a guide to human redemption.

Prophets themselves are distinguishable into a hierarchy of categories. Armed with their superior intellects they can understand what is happening, and combined with their superior imaginations, they can express the concepts they conceive in concrete instantiations as well as concrete images that they use to communicate what they know to the masses of people who lack their powers. The different types of prophetic visions determine the different ranks of prophecy. Maimonides lists eleven.

The first two are pre-prophetic levels of excellence. He calls them experiences of divine help by the biblical "wind (now thought of as "spirit") of God" (*ruach Elohim*). This is the rank of Israel's judges and kings, which is even more excellent when combined with a power of expressing divine communication in speech, which is the level of the patriarch Abraham.

Beyond this influence from the spirit of God comes prophecy proper. Maimonides lists nine ranks. The first five are subsets of prophetic image-forming that occurs in dreams. Beyond them are four levels of visions that occur while the prophet is awake.

Beyond this basic division (visions in sleep or while awake) the visions are distinguished by what literally appears. At the lowest level are parables without any sense references. Next is speech that is heard. Next there is the visual appearance of a man. Next there is the appearance (beyond sensation) of a spiritual angel. And finally there is the appearance, in some unexplained sense, of God himself.

On this fivefold division into two groups there are nine, not ten items. The visions of parables while awake is exemplified by Abraham and Joshua. Every other example given fits into the five subcategories of visions in dreams, and the one that is most frequent is the sixth of the eleventh-ranking (i.e., the middle location) of angels appearing in dreams. However, Maimonides gives no example, and does not even mention the category, of a vision while awake in which God himself appears as God.

My guess is that this unnamed rank would be the place to which Maimonides assigned the vision of the Torah to the prophet Moses, for Moses' rank as a prophet is as beyond human comprehension as is the nature of God beyond the nature of any creature and the nature of the act of divine creation of the world beyond any creaturely activity.

To say the same thing in different words, what God is, which is a single thing (a consequence of his oneness), is beyond anything that a human being can understand. Now the tradition of the Torah ascribes three acts to God—creating, revealing, and redeeming. All three are not acts that God does, for that would violate the radical simplicity that defines what it means to say that God is one. Rather what God does is who he is, and, because he is one, everything that God does, which is who he is, is a single thing. Hence to say that "God creates the world and reveals the Torah to Moses and redeems humanity" is identical with saying that "God is the creator is the revealer is the redeemer," and all three identities (creator, revealer, and redeemer) are a single thing that expresses God's nature, which is beyond human knowledge.

At the beginning of Part II we saw what it means to know that God is the creator. It is to know that the world exists eternally through a divine purposeful intention which is utterly beyond the limits of human knowledge in both how it works and what is its goal. Similarly, at the end of Book II we learn what it means to know that God is the revealer, viz., to know that prophecy is a form of human conjunction with the Active Intellect at the very horizon of human conceptual knowledge and imaginative application. Furthermore, at its highest level, viz., that of the prophet Moses in the theophany at Sinai, God revealing himself transcends anything that a human being can use language to express beyond the fact that it is more than a vision while awake of God himself as he is in himself. Presumably Moses and Moses alone of all human beings achieved this exalted state of perfection.

What remains to be explained is what it means to know that God is the redeemer. That is the primary theme in Part III, to which we turn in the next chapter.

Suggestions for further study

Bakan, David. *Maimonides on Prophecy: A Commentary on Selected Chapters of The Guide of the Perplexed.* Northvale, NJ, and London: Jason Aronson Inc., 1991.

Buijs, Joseph A. (ed.). *Maimonides: A Collection of Critical Essays.* Notre Dame, IN: University of Notre Dame Press, 1990.

Dobbs-Weinstein, Idit. *Maimonides and St. Thomas on the Limits of Reason.* Albany: State University of New York Press, 1995.

Goodman, Lenn Evan. *Rambam: Readings in the Philosophy of Maimonides.* New York: Viking Press, 1976.

Key questions

1. What are angels and what role do they play in Maimonides' philosophy?
2. Describe in general terms Maimonides' moral–conceptual map of the universe. How do prophets fit into this map?
3. Explain Maimonides' conception of creation. How important is it from the perspective of Jewish thought? How is it like his conception of God's nature?
4. Explain Maimonides' conception of revelation. How important is it from the perspective of Jewish thought? How is it like his conception of God's nature and creation?
5. Explain Maimonides' understanding of what it means to proclaim God's unity in the light of his conceptions of divine creation and divine revelation.

Chapter topic headings in *The Guide of the Perplexed*, Book II

Introduction	25 premises of the Aristotelians
Ch. 1	Four proofs that God exists. One proof that God is one. Two proofs that God is incorporeal
Ch. 2	Introduction to discussion of separate intelligences (Chs. 3–8)
Ch. 3	Aristotle's view on causes of sphere's motions
Ch. 4	Spheres endowed with souls or separate intellects
Ch. 5	View of Torah on separate intellects
Ch. 6	The meaning of *Elohim* and *malakh*
Ch. 7	Differences between *malakhim* as corporeal forces and intellects
Ch. 8	On whether or not heavenly bodies produce sound
Ch. 9	How astronomers disagree about number of the spheres (Intro to II:10)
Ch. 10	On the influence of spheres on elements
Ch. 11	Astronomy
Ch. 12	Emanation
Ch. 13	Different views about creation and eternity (Torah, philosophers, Aristotle)
Ch. 14	Aristotle's four arguments for eternity and his followers' five proofs
Ch. 15	Aristotle did not consider the matter proven
Ch. 16	Maimonides' belief about creation
Ch. 17	Reply to Aristotle's arguments
Ch. 18	Reply to proofs of Aristotle's followers
Ch. 19	Whereas Aristotle sees everything as necessary, Maimonides sees it

CHAPTER 19

Divine providence

The subject matter of the next two chapters is redemption. It is what Maimonides says in the third and concluding part of the *Guide*. I use the term "redemption" as a shorthand for a host of beliefs about the end of history, which includes traditional Jewish beliefs about the coming of the Messiah and the establishment of the kingdom of God. A cursory look at the topics (which are outlined below under "Chapter Topic Headings in the *Guide*") would suggest that what this chapter should really deal with is Maimonides' ethics. However, there is no discrepancy between these two claims. As we will see, Maimonides' statements about ethics and redemption are inseparably linked through the Aristotelian concept of human perfection (*shelemut* in Hebrew).

Since Part II of the *Guide* dealt with creation and revelation, you would expect redemption to come next. This is in fact the implicit way that Maimonides structured the statement of his thirteen foundational principles (*yesodot* [*yesod* in the singular]) in his commentary on the Mishnah (on Sanhedrin 10). There his first five principles deal with the attributes of God with reference to God as the creator of the universe, the next four deal with prophecy and Moses with reference to God as the revealer of the Torah, and the last four deal with questions of divine providence with reference to God as the redeemer. In fact, Maimonides' first five principles more or less correlate to the topics of the *Guide*, Part I, the middle four principles to the *Guide*, Part II, and the last four principles to the *Guide*, Part III.[1] Furthermore, the discussions in each part make significant references to biblical passages that the early rabbis considered especially difficult to understand. With creation it is the account of creation in the beginning of Genesis; with revelation it is the theophany at Sinai in the Book of Exodus; and here, with redemption, it is the account of the chariot, which is the opening chapter of the Book of Ezekiel.

The vision of the chariot

Maimonides, following in the tradition of his rabbinic predecessors, notes that the first chapter of the Book of Ezekiel, which is called "the Account of the Chariot," is an especially difficult text to understand, without an authentic tradition for interpreting it, which he, Maimonides, does not have. However, its interpretation is a critical part of Rabbi Joseph's cognitive perplexity, and so he must say what he can say about it. In its literal meaning, Ezekiel's vision is the most elaborate description given by any prophet of the experience of prophecy. However, in general the rabbis understood this text to be less of a "mystery" about revelation and more of a general picture of the cosmos that hints at the character of the end of days, when the Messiah will come and establish God's kingdom. This vision of the end rests on an interpretation of the foundational principle of divine providence.

Divine providence

"Divine providence" (*hashgachah*) is the theory that attempts to explain how God governs the world. What this theory must make intelligible are the biblical claims that God is the creator of the universe, the revealer of the Torah, and the redeemer of Israel who is more powerful and better than anything else in the world. The model underlying these judgments is that God is a ruler, the world is his domain, and as a ruler none is better. By the time of Maimonides, these biblical judgments had been interpreted to mean that God is not only the best that there is, but he is also absolutely the best or greatest in every respect. That means that God is not merely an extremely good governor; he is a perfect governor. That he must be so is a consequence of what the philosophers saw to be the consequences of claiming God to be the creator.

The classical Jewish philosophers interpreted "creator" to mean what the Aristotelians called "mover," and concluded that what it means to say that God created the universe is that God is the absolute first mover of the universe. They further deduced that to be an absolute first mover entails being absolutely perfect. If there is any respect that God is not perfect, then that missing perfection would not be part of what God is and it would function as an ideal or final cause towards which God would move. Hence, if God were in some respect imperfect, then that ideal would be a first cause for God, i.e., a final cause, i.e., an end toward which God is moved to become himself perfect. Therefore, the God who creates the universe must be in every respect perfect, including a perfect governor.

A governor who is a perfect ruler has the following characteristics: Whatever he wills to happen happens, which is to say he is perfectly powerful. Whatever he wills to happen is the absolutely best thing that could happen, which is to say that he is perfectly good. Finally, he must know everything about everything within his domain, for otherwise he would not control everything that happens and he could not will what is best for everyone. Hence, in addition to being perfectly powerful and perfectly good, he must have absolute knowledge. Furthermore, to claim that God is the absolutely perfect governor of the universe entails that everything that happens within it is good. However, based on human experience in the world, that does not seem to be the case. As good as the world is, it seems fairly clear that it could be better in a great many respects.

How then is it possible to reconcile all of these claims—God is absolutely good, he is absolutely powerful, and evil exists? Any proposed solution is what is called a "theodicy." Maimonides' theodicy is the heart of his theory of divine providence.

Theodicy

Everything in the universe is a composite of form with matter. Form is something positive, because it expresses what something is. In somewhat different words, a form of a subject is always the informational part of a positive declarative sentence. (It is the "f" in "S is f.") Conversely, matter is something negative, because while it says that something is it says nothing whatsoever about what it is. The ultimate expression of a form is as a moral ideal. To say that the subject "S" is f does not mean that it is actually f. Rather, it means that "f" expresses an ideal (not altogether different from what Plato called an "idea") of what S is striving to become. As such, a form is what is good. However, nothing is ever really its form.

What makes something actual not ideal is its matter. The matter makes the form concrete and actual, something with spatial and temporal-specific location. Without matter, as pure form, the thing is perfectly good but it is only an ideal; it is nothing that actually is. Matter makes something actually exist, but, in so doing, matter makes the ideal something cease to be an ideal. The real individual is more or less an approximation of the ideal (its formal definition); to the extent that it is not ideal it is imperfect, and to the extent that it is imperfect it is not good. Hence, as good is associated with the form, evil is associated with matter.

Now, nothing actual in the universe (past, present, or future) is totally bad, because nothing actual could be actual if it did not have a form. Hence, anything that exists, all factors being equal, is better than anything that does not exist. However, that does not mean that everything (or, anything) is good. Everything actual is to some extent evil, because in principle it must be imperfect. It is imperfect first because it is not God, and second because it is not even what it is, for what it is is an ideal towards which the concrete individual strives to become.

Armed with this conjunction of Platonic and Aristotelian physics and ethics, Maimonides could then construct his particular theodicy within the context of his general account of divine providence. Because God is absolutely (i.e., radically) one, there can be no distinction in God between who God is and what he does. Furthermore, what he does must be a single thing that cannot change. That it is a single thing is a consequence of God's radical oneness understood as radical simplicity. If God did two things then there would have to be a distinction within God of at least two aspects to account for them. Furthermore, this one thing that God does cannot change, because if it could something other than God would be needed to begin and/or end it. In such a case, God would be moved by something other than himself, which would entail that it, not he, is the first cause. Hence, God has a single action with which he is identical, and that action has neither beginning nor end.

If we ask just what is it that God does, then the answer would be what is most perfect. If we ask, what kind of act is most perfect, then the answer would be rational thought. If we ask just what is this thought like, then the answer would be perfect thought about a single, perfect object of thought. If we ask what is a single, perfect object of thought, then the answer would be God. Hence, what God is is eternal self-thought, and, because that thinking is perfect, the object of God's perfect thinking is actual. That object is the world.

God perpetually thinks the universe, which is the actualization of himself in the domain of space and time. Because he, what he thinks of, and the way he thinks of it is perfect, in principle the world must be good. What that means is that, insofar as the world is something that can be thought, it is formal, not material, and the world as form alone is perfect. Hence, God knows everything that is, for what it is ultimately in form is the perfect God. God does not know evil except for what it is, a lack of good, but the good, which is all that really is, is perfectly known to God.

This then is Maimonides' purely Aristotelian theodicy. God is perfect in every respect, which entails that there really is no evil, and in truth nothing that is is really evil. Why then does there seem to be evil? His answer is the inherent deficiency of human knowledge. In principle, the way that we know is inferior to the way that God knows, because what God as God does is perfect, whereas what we as humans do is inherently imperfect because we are material beings.[2]

Our knowing is inferior to God in any number of ways, of which two are for our purposes especially important. First, God knows everything from the perspective of their cause, which he knows as a single act of knowledge. Conversely, we know everything from the perspective of effects, which we know as multiple, disunified acts of knowledge. Second, God knows everything from the perspective of their true place in the universe as things whose end or purpose is part of a pyramid of ends/purposes whose penultimate end is the universe as a whole whose ultimate purpose is to serve the will of God. Conversely, we know everything from the perspective of our relatively low place in the universe.

All of our moral judgments about what is is from the perspective of what is good for human beings. However, humanity occupies a fairly low place in the hierarchy of the universe. We see everything below us as existing for us, but in fact they and we exist for the sake of the sublunar world, which itself exists for the sake of the higher universes of which it is an element, and we can have no inkling of this organic system. We know no more about the good of the universe than an atom in our body would know about what is good for us. Through the aid of prophecy from the Active Intellect we can have some weak level of knowledge about the good of our sublunar world, but no more than that.

Hence, there are many things to us that will seem to be evil, but we know in principle that they are really good, even though we cannot explain them. They appear to us to be evil for several reasons. First, we lack perfect knowledge of the way events are related to each other. It may be the case that something that seems to us to be only a possible effect of an earlier event is really a necessary effect. Similarly, events have consequences far beyond what we can see, so that a possible event that seems good in the short term could prove in the end to be bad and vice versa. Second, we tend to think that things that are bad for us are bad, but they may be good for humanity in general. Similarly, what is bad for humanity may be good for the sublunar world, and what is bad for the sublunar world may be good for the universe. Such knowledge lies totally beyond human, even prophetic, capability. Third, what is most valuable for our well-being (e.g., air and water) is most plentiful and therefore least valued, whereas what is least valuable for our well-being (e.g., precious metals) is more rare and therefore most valued by humanity. That humans tend to value most the rare over the plentiful is a consequence of human nature, that what should be most valued is most plentiful is a consequence of divine nature, and, in this case, the difference produces an apparent but unreal perplexity about divine providence.

The summary presented above is what Maimonides in fact says in Book III about providence. It is more the position of the Aristotelians than it is precisely what Maimonides says, because Maimonides' agnosticism about our knowledge of the divine is (as we have seen) far more radical than what this argument about theodicy claims. The argument as presented assumes that we have all kinds of knowledge about God and the world that Maimonides has already made clear we do not possess. Maimonides' radical doubt is what saves his theodicy from an obvious line of attack on Aristotelian theodicy that focuses on the character of divine knowledge.

God's knowledge of particulars

We said at the beginning of this discussion that to be a perfect ruler God must control everything that happens within his own domain and to control everything requires that God knows everything. A question that could be asked (and subsequently will be asked) about this claim is what it entails for a belief in freedom of choice. To the extent that God knows something it must be determined, and to the extent that it is determined there is no possibility of genuine human choice. This was a critical question that Ibn Daud discussed, and his answer was a position that some scholars call "soft determinism." It claims that, while everything really is determined, human ignorance gives the impression that some things are indeterminate, which gives room for humans to make choices. When they believe that what they choose really changes things, it does, because their act of choosing is part of the causal chain that brings about whatever was determined to occur. Still, everything that happens is really determined, including the belief that some things are indeterminate.

Maimonides' own answer is philosophically more radical than Ibn Daud's. We saw in the case of Maimonides' cosmology that he affirms a universe where everything happens by an act of (at least) divine will and not by any principles of mechanical necessity built into the physical world. That does not mean that all events are not determined. It means that if they are they are determined because God wills them to be so, but he could also will otherwise. That he does will otherwise is a consequence of the principle of matter. Insofar as something is formal, it is knowable, and therefore it is necessary, because to know something is true (rather than merely to have a true opinion about it) means that it is known to be necessarily true. However, insofar as it is material, it is unknowable in principle (to any one), and therefore it is contingent. Hence, we live in a universe where not everything is knowable and much that is unknowable is unknowable in principle. It is not that we do not know some things because our knowledge is inferior; on the contrary, to know that we do not know in these cases is a consequence of the perfection of the knowledge, for here we know all that there is to know, viz., that the things in question are the kind of things about which there can be no knowledge.

Principled unknowability is true of every concrete thing and event in the universe insofar as they are material. The question is, does this principle apply to God as well? If it does, then anything that is materially conditioned insofar as it is materially conditioned is not knowable by God and therefore not subject to divine governance. However, what falls into this category is every concrete thing and event in the universe, for all of them are concrete because of matter. The consequence is that, while God may rule the universe at its most general level, he cannot rule it at all in the concrete. Hence, everything that matters to us as human beings is in principle beyond God's influence.

It is Maimonides' theological agnosticism that enables him to escape this consequence. Insofar as we understand what it means to know something, it means to grasp conceptually a concept whose ontological referent is an attribute. However, attributes are universal, not concrete. Hence, in principle there is no knowledge of the concrete. All this is true, Maimonides argues, for the kind of knowledge we have, but it is not God's knowledge. Referring back to the discussion of negative theology, what it means to say that God is a knower is that God is not ignorant and knowledge is a human virtue, but it says nothing in any sense positive about what it means for God to know. God actually knows concrete particulars and that knowledge in no way entails that what he knows is determined. We also have no idea what these claims mean beyond the fact that they are true, truths that rest almost entirely on a literal reading of the Torah.

Notes

1 The thirteen principles are the following: [the grouping of them into three parts is my grouping and not what is stated explicitly in Maimonides' *Commentary on the Mishnah*]. (A. God) (1) God exists, (2) God is one, (3) God is incorporeal, (4) God is eternal (which, Rambam tells us later, entails that he is the creator), and (5) God is worthy of worship. (B. Torah) (6) There is prophecy, (7) Moses is the greatest prophet, (8) the Torah is true, and (9) the Torah does not change. (C. Divine providence) (10) God has perfect knowledge, (11) there is divine reward and punishment, (12) the Messiah will come, and (13) the dead will be resurrected.

2 Ibn Daud had discussed the question why in a perfectly good universe there need be anything imperfect. The answer was that, if everything were perfect, then there would be no universe. There would only be God. Hence, imperfection is a necessity of any universe, even a perfect one.

Suggestions for further study

Fox, Marvin. *Interpreting Maimonides: Studies in Methodology, Metaphysics, and Moral Philosophy.* Chicago/London: University of Chicago Press, 1990.

Kraemer, Joel L. (ed.). *Perspectives on Maimonides: Philosophical and Historical Studies.* Published for the Littman Library by Oxford University Press. Tel Aviv: Tel Aviv University, 1991.

Weiss, Raymond. *Maimonides' Ethics: The Encounter of Philosophic and Religious Morality.* Chicago: University of Chicago Press, 1991.

Key questions

1. How is the concept of redemption tied to the concept of ethics in Jewish philosophy? How do the rabbinic interpretations of Ezekiel's so-called account of the chariot enter into the discussion of this topic?

2. What is divine providence? How does it occur in the Bible? How is the biblical view explained in classical Jewish philosophy? What is problematic about this view, and how does Maimonides resolve that problem?

3. How is God's knowledge different from human knowledge according to the view of Jewish Aristotelians like Abraham Ibn Daud? How does Maimonides' differ in this respect from the Jewish Aristotelians?

Chapter topic headings in *The Guide of the Perplexed*, Book III

Introduction Account of the chariot has been lost, because it may be communicated only verbally, not in writing. Maimonides' interpretation of it is based on the biblical text and not on an authentic tradition about the text's meaning

Ch. 1 Description of the chariot vision in Ezekiel. Faces of lion, eagle, ox, and cherub and all the face of a man

Ch. 2 Explanation of the chariot vision: four creatures, their motion, *ruach*, wheels

Ch. 3 Explanation of Ezekiel's second vision as an interpretation of the first

Ch. 4 Jonathan ben Uziel's interpretation of the chariot vision considered

Ch. 5 Explanation of Mishnah in the Babylonian Talmud Hagigah 13a, where chariot "visions" discussed in terms of teaching prohibition

Ch. 6 Identity of prophetic visions of Isaiah and Ezekiel

Ch. 7 Further notes on interpretation of Ezekiel's vision. In vision God's cosmos (i.e., angels) appear but not God himself. This concludes the deepest mysteries of the *Guide*

Ch. 8 All corruption is due to matter. Tangential remarks on ethics: the mental is good and the physical bad. Miscellaneous remarks on the implications for ethics of the meaning of the commandments and the Hebrew language

Ch. 9 Appearance of God in clouds in the biblical text means that matter prevents human vision of God, even at Sinai, with the exception of those who are near to God (viz., Moses)

Ch. 10 The problem of theodicy is solved by the doctrine that evil is a privation

Ch. 11 All human moral evils are due to the privation of human knowledge

Ch. 12 What exists contains more good than evil, contrary to Abu Bakr

Ch. 13 There is no final end to the world. The world exists by divine will. The human species and the supralunar world exist as ends in themselves. The heavens are superior to the human, and thus they do not function for the sake of the human

Ch. 14 Use of astronomy to support the thesis that everything does not exist for the sake of the human. Rather, every sphere exists for the sake of the activity of its intellect

Ch. 15 God cannot affect the impossible, and this is no deficiency in God. However, there are issues over whether some things are possible or impossible, most notably, creation out of nothing

Ch. 16 Introduction of the question of divine knowledge as an instance of

CHAPTER 20

The reasons for the Commandments
(*ta'amei ha-mitsvot*)

An important consequence of Maimonides' discussion of divine providence is that there are matters concerning which human beings must have true belief even if they exceed what it is possible for a human being to know. This includes an adequate understanding of creation and revelation as well as redemption, for it is only from the perspective of the movement of the universe from its infinitely remote origin (creation) to its end in the kingdom of God that we can understand what in between is good and what is bad.

The difference is important, for choosing the good brings about the redemption of both the actor in the particular and the universe in general. This redemption goes by many names. Often it is called "the days of the messiah" and "the kingdom of God," and often Maimonides himself calls it "having a share in the world to come (*ha-'olam ha-ba*)." Within the context of the *Guide* it is called "perfection" (*shelemut*).

That humanity in general must realize in time its perfection is a necessity for the survival of the world. Human beings were created to govern the world and that governance requires a certain level of practical wisdom. However, the intellect that can reason practically can also reason theoretically. While humans are by nature designed for excellence in practical wisdom, they have no comparable excellence for theoretical wisdom. This is the point of Maimonides' story (or, more accurately, myth) of the Sabians in *Guide* III:30.

Myth of the Sabians

Based on human success in applying practical reason to problems such as growing food (agriculture), the Sabians extended through the use of analogy that practical reason to solving theoretical questions, and this time came up with disastrously false answers. They reasoned, for example, that as a farm has order and purpose that is imposed on nature by an intelligent farmer, so the world as a whole exhibits order and purpose that was imposed on it by some other intelligence, whom we call "God." So far the analogy was sufficiently appropriate to be justified. However, when they extended the reasoning to ask just who was this farmer of the universe, their answer was a disaster. They said it was the celestial stars that then became for them the objects of worship. The false worship led to equally reasonable but utterly false judgments about morality, which in turn led to the corruption of the world. That corruption was the flood at the time of Noah.

Maimonides does not tell us why God chose Noah to be the sole survivor of worldwide devastation by water, but, given his analysis of the causes of the flood, the answer was clear—Noah was not especially bright, which reduced the danger that humanity would again extend its natural gift for practical reasoning into the dangerous area of theoretical reasoning. However, even the descendants of Noah developed quickly to the advanced stage of idolatry. It is at this point that God determined it necessary to give the Torah.

The classification of the Torah's goals

The Torah, as Maimonides analyzes it, is first and foremost a system of commandments for the Jewish people whose purpose is to perfect the individuals, through whom the people will be perfected, through whom the world will be redeemed.

The laws fall into two general categories: commandments intended to guide the human mind to its perfection (which Maimonides calls "the welfare of the soul") and commandments intended to guide the human body to its perfection (which Maimonides calls "the welfare of the body"). "Body" here is both the individual human body and the body politic. The former are laws to govern the Jewish state which will maximize the opportunity for the citizens of the state to perfect their bodies and minds. The latter are regulations that will improve the physical health of the persons so that they could maximize their attention to the kind of mental improvement that would eventually transform humanity from the species whose success in reasoning was limited merely to practical reason to a species of theoretically wise human beings.

The reason why nothing said in the Torah means literally what it says is because it was written to initiate a process of learning. The literal meaning is directed to an extremely low (mentally) level of human beings. The literal meaning is something ignoramuses can understand which will improve their understanding, and with this improvement the readers will be better prepared to understand the Scriptures at a higher level. The sign of preparation for a higher level of learning is the emergence of perplexities (*nebukhim*) in understanding the sacred texts. These perplexities are realizations that the level at which the text was understood cannot be what the text really means, since what is understood is false, but the text, being the word of God, must be true. In this state of perplexity the readers carefully explore the text to find a better interpretation, which when found signals that the readers have reached a higher rung of human perfection, a rung at which they will remain without further perplexity until their understanding of and obedience to the Scriptures brings them to the next rung, which again will be signaled by new perplexities.

Just how many levels are there before perfection will be achieved, i.e., before humanity through the Jewish people achieves the redemption of the world in the establishment of the kingdom of God? No answer is given to this question because no answer can be given, since an adequate human understanding of the end of days is no more possible than an adequate understanding of the origin of the universe. As in speaking of the origin, it is necessary to present a myth (the "Account of Creation" in Gen 1), so in speaking of the end of the universe another myth is called for. In this case it is the "ruler–palace" parable in *Guide* III:51.

Political wisdom (*chochmah*) and the ruler–palace parable

The simple story of the palace can be summarized as follows: There is a city, within which there is a palace that consists of an antechamber encircling an inner court. Some people (h1) are outside of the city wandering about in all directions, primarily away from the city. Within the city proper but outside of the palace are other people. They fall into three groupings. Some of them (h2) are wandering away from the palace; others of them (h3) are simply walking around the palace; and still others of them (h4) are looking for a gate to get into the palace. Within the palace itself there are those (h5) in the antechamber, those (h6) in the inner court who nonetheless are not in the presence of the ruler, and finally those (h7) who are in the ruler's presence.

Scholars, both rabbinic and academic, debate just what this story is intended to symbolize. What is clear is that the story is about achieving human perfection, that perfection has something to do with wisdom, that the achievement of wisdom has something to do with studying natural philosophy and observing the Torah, and that the ruler is God. Beyond that, there is room for interpretation and what the interpretation is depends on what you think Maimonides means by wisdom as the ultimate end or happiness of human existence. My suggested interpretation is the following:

The city is not a place. It is the class of humanity that comprises intelligent animals. Those wandering around outside of the city (h1) are creatures who, while they are anatomically human, are (in Maimonides' judgment) not really human, since they have no real ability to reason.

The palace also is not a place. It is that subclass of humanity that has true opinions. Those humans outside the domain of the truth fall into three groupings. There are people (h2) who use their reason but use it poorly, so that they have beliefs based on reason that are false beliefs. (I take this category to include the pagans, especially the descendants of the Sabians.) There are other people (h3) who follow the Torah but have no idea whatsoever what it really means. (I take this category to include the greater mass of Jewish people, the so-called "masses" or "people of the earth" ['amei ha-arets]). There are yet other people (h4) who are rabbis (Maimonides here calls them "jurists") who know logic and math, which are the tools of reasoned thinking, but they have not yet applied these Jewish and philosophical tools to attain knowledge of the truth.

Within the domain of those who have true beliefs there are again three categories of people. There are those individuals (h5) whose knowledge is limited to what we would call the natural sciences. Beyond them there are those people (h6), like Joseph ben Judah, who are rabbis and natural scientists who study the metaphysical and theological foundations of both the law and the natural world. Finally, there are those (h7) who are in the presence of God, whom Maimonides says are, like the prophets, the wise men and scholars who ought to govern nations.

You would think that the philosopher-rabbis would represent the highest rung of human perfection. However, that is not what Maimonides says. As we have seen, to stand in God's presence, i.e., to know God, is beyond human capability. However, it seems not to be beyond the capability of prophets. It is they and only they—like Moses in the Hebrew

Scriptures and the philosopher-king in Plato's *Republic*—who should rule and direct the rest of mankind on its path towards perfection.

In this way, the letter of one rabbi (Moses Ben Maimon) to another rabbi (Joseph Ben Judah) ends with a judgment about politics. In the best possible world the nations of the earth would be governed by wise men such as Moses and Joseph, who devote their lives to the pursuit of theoretical wisdom through the sources of human reason under the guidance of prophetic revelation. The vision in the Hebrew Scriptures of a Utopian society of people governed by priests has been transformed in *The Guide of the Perplexed* into a vision of a Utopian society of people governed by philosopher-rabbis. How the mass of Jews, especially its rabbis, felt about this vision is our next subject.

Suggestions for further study

Benor, Ehud. *Worship of the Heart: A Study of Maimonides' Philosophy of Religion*. Albany: State University of New York Press, 1995.

Funkenstein, Amos. *Maimonides: Nature, History and Messianic Beliefs*. Tel Aviv: MOD Books, 1997.

Hartman, David. *Maimonides: Torah and Philosophic Quest*. Philadelphia: Jewish Publication Society of America, 1976.

Kellner, Menachem Marc. *Maimonides on Human Perfection*. Atlanta: Scholars Press, 1990.

Kellner, Menachem Marc. *Maimonides on Judaism and the Jewish People*. Albany: State University of New York Press, 1991.

Kreisel, Howard. *Maimonides' Political Thought: Studies in Ethics, Law, and the Human Ideal*. Albany: State University of New York Press, 1999.

Stern, Josef. *Problems and Parables of Law: Maimonides and Nahmanides on Reasons for the Commandments (ta'amei ha-mitzvot)*. Albany: State University of New York Press, 1998.

Key questions

1. Why, according to Maimonides, did God create the Torah when he did? What are its two primary goals and how are they related to each other? Why will readers of the Scriptures become perplexed, and why is this state of confusion something good?

2. Explain the parable of the ruler and the palace with which Maimonides concludes his *Guide*? What do you think it means?

Chapter topic headings in *The Guide of the Perplexed*, Book III

Ch. 26	Different views on whether or not the laws in the Torah have an end or cause or purpose. Maimonides' position is that they all do in general, even if we do not know all of them, but they do not have one in all of the particulars.
Ch. 27	Goals of the Torah: (I) The welfare of the soul, i.e., true opinions. (II) The welfare of the body: (a) Abolishing wrongdoing, and (b) acquiring human moral virtues. I is nobler than II, but II is prior to I
Ch. 28	Some laws appear not to fit as welfare of the soul or the body, but these will be explained. Kinds of true opinion: (A) Beliefs about God—that he exists and is one, and the account of his attributes. (B) Beliefs about political ends. (C) Beliefs in summary form about all areas of science
Ch. 29	The beliefs of the Sabians: the purpose of the Torah is to eradicate them
Ch. 30	Who the Sabians were and their appeal to agriculture
Ch. 31	Objection of those who say it glorifies God more if laws have no purpose or reason
Ch. 32	Sacrifices commanded in the Torah in order to lead Israel away from idolatry. Sacrifices are not part of God's concern in and of themselves
Ch. 33	Two purposes of the Torah are (1) to avoid and control the passions (food, drink, sex) and (2) to be clean in body
Ch. 34	Torah deals with general cases, not exceptions to the rules. Even though there are exceptions, the law must be universal and absolute in application, lest its authority be undermined
Ch. 35	A general statement of the 14 classes of laws (in relation to II:27 [I,II], 28 [A,B,C], and 33 [1,2]): (1) Fundamental opinions (IA); (2) Idolatry prohibition (IA); (3) Improvement of moral qualities (IIB); (4) Charity (IB); (5) Wrongdoing and aggression prohibited (IIA); (6) Punishments (IB); (7) Property laws (IB); (8) Days when work is forbidden, viz., the Sabbath and festivals (IA, IIA–B); (9) Worship, excluding circumcision (IA); (10) The Sanctuary (IA); (11) Sacrifices (IA); (12) Cleanliness (IIB, 2); (13) Food prohibitions, and Nazarite vows (IIB, 1); (14) Prohibited sexual unions (IIB, 1). [Note no example of Ch. 28, C.]
Chs. 36–49	With reference to Ch. 35, consecutive explanation of each of the 14 categories of laws of the Torah
Ch. 50	Account of certain mysteries of the Torah, viz., of stories that seem to have no purpose
Ch. 51	Ruler–palace parable: discussion of the highest state of man as that

of intellectual love of God in perpetual thought about God, fulfilled at "kiss of" death for Moses, Aaron, and (to a lesser extent) Miriam only

Ch. 52 True opinions in the Torah are intended to teach the love of God; moral actions in the Torah are intended to teach the fear of God.

Ch. 53 The meaning of *chesed* (loving-kindness), *mishpat* (judgment), *tsedakah* (righteousness) as divine virtues that operate in creating, judging, and governing this world by *chachmah* (wisdom)

Ch. 54 Meaning of *chochmah* (wisdom). Listing four human perfections (possessions, body, moral virtues, rational virtues). Conclusion: the ultimate end of man is to know that (1) God exists, is one, and is incorporeal; that (2) divine providence extends to individuals; and that (3) divine attributes are actions to be imitated by which man will act in general with loving-kindness, judgment, and righteousness

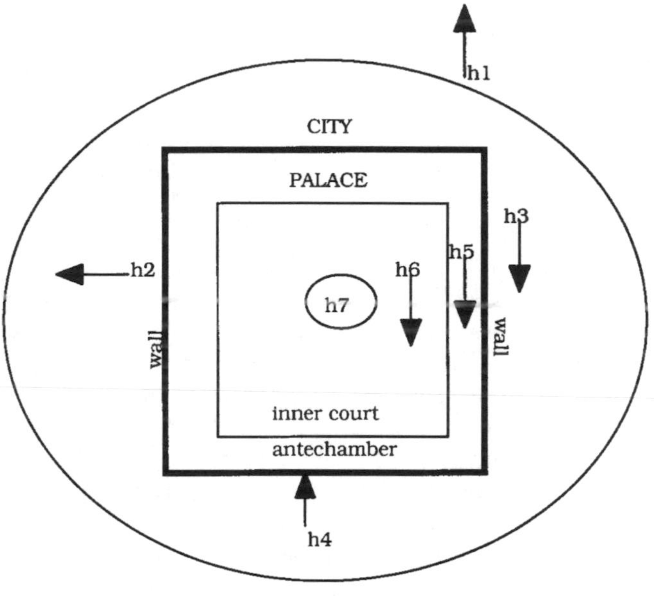

Diagram of Maimonides' ruler–palace parable (*Guide* III: 51)

Key: h1 those with no doctrinal beliefs; subhuman
h2 those who do speculation but hold false beliefs
h3 followers of law but ignorant
h4 jurists knowing logic/math
h5 individuals knowing natural science
h6 sages/scientists knowing metaphysics and theology
h7 sages/scientists who govern = prophets

Jewish Philosophy after Maimonides

CHAPTER 21

The rationalism of Gersonides

The ascendancy of Christian Europe

The period of Maimonides is a critical turning point in Jewish life in every respect. Its lowest point was the three military defeats by the Roman Empire which forced the Judeans to reconceptualize their understanding of the meaning of life, the universe, and how the Jewish people fit into both. The result was the birth of a new form of Judaism, rabbinic Judaism, that grew and developed out of the intellectual as well as physical ruins of the Jerusalem Temple. We have been tracing the development of the rabbinic philosophy that succeeded the biblical philosophy. So far all we have seen has been a development, most of which took place while the Jewish people lived as a minority culture within the politically and spiritually dominant Muslim empire.

Maimonides' life marks a high point for both Muslim and rabbinic Jewish civilization. What comes next is a decline for both as Christian Europe comes into its own as a dominant world civilization. Perhaps one of the most critical events leading to this change of direction is the Almohad conquest of Muslim Spain in the middle of the twelfth century. It is not so much the political victory itself that is important but that it symbolizes the intellectual decline of Islam, which could not but deeply affect all peoples within its cultural empire, including the Jews.

The immediate effect of Muslim decline and Christian ascendancy was economic. Jews had been primarily farmers in the biblical period. Many Jews moved to commerce in the Hellenistic period, but agriculture was still the dominant Jewish occupation. It was not until the period of Muslim control that the mass of Jews ceased to be connected with agriculture and entered instead into some form of occupation connected to commerce.

The heart of commerce is trade, and the major trade routes for Jews in the Muslim world ran across the Mediterranean Sea. This sea shipping was protected from theft by the Muslim fleet. As Muslim military and naval power declined and European power increased, commerce under the protection of the Muslims became less viable. Hence, because of new economic opportunities that followed European military success against the Muslims, Jews reluctantly but increasingly left Muslim lands for the more culturally primitive territories of the European Christians. The major consequence for our purposes is that Maimonides became the last major Jewish philosopher to write in Judeo-Arabic (which was largely [although not entirely] Arabic using the Hebrew alphabet) in a Muslim land. The subsequent generations of classical rabbinic Jewish philosophers wrote in Hebrew in Christian lands where the new dominant culture increasingly influenced, even altered, what the intellectual ancestors of these philosophers had thought before.

The philosophy of Gersonides

Solely from the perspective of philosophy, arguably the best of the post-Maimonidean classical Jewish philosophers was Levi ben Gershom, whom the Jews called "Ralbag" and the Christians called "Gersonides." We know very little about his personal life other than that he was born in 1288 into a prominent Provençal Jewish family, he excelled both in astronomy and biblical commentaries as well as in general philosophy, he occupied an academic position of importance in connection with the papal court in Avignon, and he died in 1344. We know about his proficiency as a Bible scholar from the many commentaries he wrote on different books of the Bible that remain as influential (as well as controversial) today in traditional Jewish rabbinic circles as they were in his own day. In general, what his commentaries do, following in the tradition of Maimonides and others from Maimonides' time period (notably Abraham Ibn Ezra [1089–1164, from Toledo in Muslim Spain]), is to present philosophical interpretations as the deeper meanings of biblical texts. The interpretations are rigorously Aristotelian, strongly influenced by the ways that both Maimonides and Averroes interpreted the so-called "philosopher." Of all those who used philosophy to interpret the Torah, Gersonides' was the most rigorous philosophy, and it is precisely that rigor that is what makes his writings so interesting as well as controversial, again, as much today as they were when he wrote them.

Gersonides' two most critical issues with Maimonides' philosophy both reflect his deeper or more passionate commitment to what we can call a "religion of reason." Under the influence of Aristotelian ethics, Maimonides affirmed the intellect as that function of human nature that was most divine, that the ideal of human life is a life in pursuit of intellectual wisdom, and that this philosophical standard of wisdom is also the standard for the good life from the perspective of the sacred, revealed texts of the Jewish people. However, Maimonides placed radical restrictions on the domain of possible human knowledge and believed that even God cannot communicate his deepest wisdom in a straightforward way to human beings. The limit beyond which human knowledge cannot ascend is knowledge of the universe as such. The closest we can come is astronomy, but even this knowledge is radically limited. Maimonides clearly considered the most fundamental claims of astronomy to be only opinion, and (what is less clear, but probably true) he believed this limitation was built into the subject matter itself.

The supralunar world is for him a very different world from the sublunar world. The two are governed by very different laws of nature. For example, natural motion in the sublunar world is finite and linear (up and down); whereas motion in the heavens is circular and unending. Both worlds are material in the sense that both worlds contain bodies, but the matter of the two is sufficiently different that while the celestial objects are created they do not perish, whereas everything in the sublunar world is subject to generation and corruption. Consequently it could be argued (and, again, Maimonides probably believed) that we can at best only have true opinions in astronomy, but not real knowledge. Furthermore, if we cannot even know astronomy, how much the more so can we not know cosmology (what the universe itself, in its entirely, is like, how it began, and how it will end). Furthermore, if we cannot know anything about the ultimate nature of the universe, its creation, or its end, how can we know anything about the creator deity who is himself beyond even the universe. However, Maimonides' Aristotelian moral rationalism claimed that wisdom (*hochmah*)—which is the goal of human life, whose attainment is the key to the redemption or salvation of having a share in the world-to-come—consists precisely in this knowledge that Maimonides claimed to be beyond human capability.

Gersonides converted Maimonides' timid rationalism into a rigorous one. Gersonides believed Maimonides' public agnosticism about creation, redemption and God's nature to have been intellectually dishonest. He thought that these were ruses that Maimonides feigned because he did not believe that he could reconcile the doctrine that God is a perfect creator with the perceived reality of evil in the world (i.e., the problem of theodicy). In this claim Maimonides could call for support on the weak status of astronomy, but he (or so Ralbag argued) no more understood correctly what he said about astronomy than what he said about Jewish theological ethics.

It must be remembered that Maimonides was not an astronomer and Gersonides was. In fact, he could arguably be considered the most important astronomer in Christian Europe before Galileo. His claim to fame in this respect is twofold. First, he developed a device, called the "Jacob's staff," that was the most valuable tool astronomers had before the telescope to measure relative distances between heavenly objects. Second, he modified the standard astronomical theory that had the earth at the center of the universe rotating on its axis by moving the earth slightly off the center so that it had an orbit around the center as well as a rotation on its axis. This spatial shift changed the vector geometry so that highly accurate predictions could be made about perceived stellar and planetary motions, or, in any case, at least as accurate as predictions that would later be made on the basis of an alternative heliocentric geometry that contributed so much to modern astronomers preferring a helio- over a geocentric picture of the universe.

Whatever the status of astronomy in Maimonides' age, by Gersonides' time it truly was a science, one in which scientists like Gersonides had deep faith. Maimonides' argument for the inadequacy of astronomy was that it affirmed as true, on the basis of empirical observation, certain contingent states of affairs about the heavens. For example, there is no inherent logical reason why the period of the sun's motion around the earth should be eccentric rather than an epicycle. Nor is there any inherent reason why the number of the spheres should be the number that they are. Nor is there any inherent reason why the distribution of planetary periods within spheres is what it is, so that some spheres have few if any bodies within them while other spheres have several bodies within them. In short, while we astronomers can deduce from the regular motions of celestial objects a number of spheres with different vector motions to be able to make intelligible what is observed, we cannot explain why the heavens exhibit the vector motions that they do exhibit and not different vectors (with different directions and rates of speed). These judgments seem to be contingent.

For Maimonides this conclusion—that what seems to be true of the motions of the heavens is contingently true—was unacceptable. It could not mean that the motions really are contingent, because if they were there could be no knowledge of them, not even by God. For Maimonides, to know that something is true is not only to know that it is true but to know why it is true, and to know why something is as it is is for that thing or event to be what it is necessarily. Hence, that the heavens seem to be contingent meant that we did not know their causes, because if they were in fact contingent, then God could not know them, and if God could not know them, then God would not be the perfect governor of the universe that he is.

Ralbag turns this argument on its head. The mathematical specifics of the movements of heavenly objects are contingent precisely because God created them. Maimonides had argued that the difference between believing in creation as opposed to Aristotelianism is that on the Torah's view the universe exists through God's will with purpose, whereas on the Aristotelian view it exists by necessity and therefore does not require any will or purpose to be since it could not be other than it is. Gersonides argues that, precisely because the universe is created, i.e., exists through an act of divine will for a divine purpose, what the universe is is contingent.

What God knows about the universe is precisely that. It is not that his knowledge is so radically different from ours that what seems to us to be contingent is to God necessary. Rather God knows what is precisely as what it is, and if it is contingent then he knows it as contingent.

For example, if the laws of meteorology were expressions of mathematical probability, so that these laws themselves require a 0.7 probability of rain tomorrow, and if we knew these laws, then we would know that there was a 0.7 probability of rain tomorrow, which means that while we know that rain is likely (likely enough to take an umbrella with us to work), we do not know whether or not it will in fact rain, and that ignorance is not really ignorance, because the ignorance itself is what is true. Now Gersonides does not talk the language of probability theory. (That mathematical language would not come into existence until several centuries after Gersonides.) However, what he does say is that sometimes not knowing is itself knowing perfectly and that is the case when the reality is a probability rather than an actuality or a certainty. God, Ralbag argues, has this kind of knowledge of the heavens in general, because while divine providence has determined them in general, i.e., insofar as they are subject to form alone irrespective of particularization in matter, they are knowable, but insofar as they are materialized and concretized, i.e., insofar as the forms have been materialized, they are contingent and can only be known, even by God, as what they are—possibilities and not necessities.

Maimonides, Gersonides argues, did not understand well enough the nature of what it means to know, and that ignorance forced him to assume absurd positions, such as his radical agnosticism about cosmogony, divine nature, and the end of days. Of course, what God is and what God knows is more perfect than, and therefore different from, what we know of God. However, the difference is not so great that we cannot grasp intelligibly just what the difference is. God knows as a cause of what exists and we know as an effect through perception of what exists. What God knows he knows through a single act of knowledge that is identical with himself. What we know is different from us and it is seen as a diversity of contingent events.

Gersonides believed that, insofar as the universe is in principle knowable, we human beings have the ability to know it. It is knowable to the extent that it is divine, because the forms that are in existing events materially are created by God as God is in himself. Furthermore, when we deduce from our sense experience the form of a thing, that form exists in our intellects mentally and is identical in form with the materialized form of the concrete particulars that we know. Hence there is an identity of form between what we know and what it is, for the form of both is the same thing. Physical things and our knowledge of physical things are both forms, and these forms differ only in the way they exist—mentally as true concepts of the intellect and materially as objects and events in the physical universe. Furthermore, the ultimate cause of the ideas we have is the mind of God as the revealer, the ultimate cause of the physical events of the universe that we seek to know is also the mind of God now as the creator, and these two divine mental acts—creating and revealing—are the same thing. There is a unity of knowledge because ultimately what exists physically and what is thought mentally are expressions of God existing absolutely, for the form that is absolute in the mind of God is material in the physical world and is mental in the intellect, but all three are the same, single form.

Again, the way that the human intellect grasps its intellectual products is different from the way God does, but the difference is not so great that we cannot understand it, for what is true of God absolutely and perfectly is true of us to a lesser extent in a derivative way. For example, what God knows causes what is and God knows all that he knows in a single act of uniform knowledge, whereas we know something as an empirical effect of its being and what we know we know as a set of discrete acts. Gersonides' theory of divine attributes differs radically from that of Maimonides. For Maimonides the attributes predicated of God are "absolutely equivocal" or "equivocal by chance," which means that there is no real relationship of meaning between what a word means when attributed to God and what that word means when attributed to anything else. For Gersonides these divine attributes stand in a relationship of "before" (*pros*) and "after" (*hen*, in Aristotle's Greek). "Before" means the meaning of the term has as its primary reference how it applies to God, and "after" means that the meaning of the term for subjects other than God is derivative from its use for God. As such there is a clear relationship (of *pros–hen* equivocation) between divine knowledge and human knowledge. In this way, Gersonides bridges the gap between the rationalism of the Judaism and ethics he shares in common with Maimonides and the clear recognition that humanity as a creature will always be distant from who God is. The question is just how distant. Maimonides, Gersonides argues, made the distance too great, for with his radical degree of separation there can be no intelligible Judaism or rationalist ethics.

Gersonides' life of reason in commitment to God provided a critical example for subsequent Jewish philosophers, including both Baruch Spinoza and Hermann Cohen, on how the life of worship of God was identical with the life of the rational pursuit of natural philosophy or science. By the twentieth century, this symbiosis of science and faith would serve as a model for the life of at least some Jewish scientists, notably Albert Einstein. However, the path from Maimonides to Spinoza to Cohen to Einstein is by no means direct. Gersonides was not alone in influencing future post-Maimonidean philosophy. On the flip side of Ralbag's rationalist faith were the equally skilled philosophical speculations of Hasdai Crescas.

Suggestions for further study

Baer, Yehuda. *A History of the Jews of Christian Spain*. Philadelphia: Jewish Publication Society of America, 1971.

Bleich, David. *Providence in the Philosophy of Gersonides*. New York: Yeshiva University Press, 1973.

Dobbs-Weinstein, Idit. "The Maimonidean controversy," in Daniel H. Frank and Oliver Leaman (eds.), *History of Jewish Philosophy*. Vol. II of *Routledge History of World Philosophies*. London and New York: Routledge, 1997, pp. 331–49.

Feldman, Seymour. "Levi ben Gershom (Gersonides)," in Daniel H. Frank and Oliver Leaman (eds.), *History of Jewish Philosophy*. Vol. II of *Routledge History of World Philosophies*. London and New York: Routledge, 1997, pp. 379–98.

Freudenthal, Gad (ed.). *Studies in Gersonides*. Leiden: Brill, 1992.

Goldstein, Bernard. *The Astronomy of Levi Ben Gershom, (1288–1344)*. New York: Springer, 1985.

Levi ben Gershom (Gersonides). *The Wars of the Lord*. English translation by Seymour Feldman. Philadelphia: Jewish Publication Society of America, 1984 and 1987.

Manekin, Charles. "Hebrew philosophy in the fourteenth and fifteenth centuries: an overview," in Daniel H. Frank and Oliver Leaman (eds.), *History of Jewish Philosophy*. Vol. II of *Routledge History of World Philosophies*. London and New York: Routledge, 1997, pp. 350–78.

Saperstein, Marc. "The social and cultural context: thirteenth to fifteenth centuries," in Daniel H. Frank and Oliver Leaman (eds.), *History of Jewish Philosophy*. Vol. II of *Routledge History of World Philosophies*. London and New York: Routledge, 1997, pp. 294–330.

Seltzer, Robert M. *Jewish People, Jewish Thought: The Jewish Experience in History*. New York: Macmillan, 1980. Part III. Chs. 9–10, pp. 373–505.

Smalley, B. *The Study of the Bible in the Middle Ages*. New York: Philosophical Library, 1952.

Sorabji. R. *Time, Creation, and the Continuum*. Ithaca, NY: Cornell University Press, 1983.

Key questions

1. What is most distinctive about Gersonides as a biblical commentator and philosopher? How did Gersonides differ from Maimonides?

2. Why was Gersonides an important astronomer? What role did his astronomy play in his Jewish philosophy?

3. How does Gersonides explain God's knowledge? How is God's knowledge related to and different from human knowledge?

4. What according to Gersonides is the relationship between mind, matter, and God?

5. How did Gersonides' thought influence later Jewish philosophers?

Key events in the life of Gersonides

1145–50	Almohads invade and conquer Muslim Spain
1147–49	Second Crusade
1189–92	Third Crusade
1240	Jewish–Christian disputation in Paris
1249–1517	Mamluk dynasty in Egypt
1258	Mongols capture Baghdad, ending caliphate
1263	Jewish–Christian disputation in Barcelona
c. 1286	Completion of the *Zohar* by Moses de Leon
1288–1344	Levi Gersonides
1304–78	Popes reign from Avignon
1325–45	Rise of Ottoman Turks

CHAPTER 22

The non-rationalism of Crescas

Hasdai Crescas (*c.* 1340–1410) is our last great Spanish Jewish philosopher. He is a fitting end to the era, for he was a brilliant philosopher in the technical sense of the term (whose only equal in the tradition is Gersonides) and the single most rigorous critic of this tradition in the entire history of Jewish philosophy. Jewish philosophy does not end with Crescas because he is unworthy as a philosopher. On the contrary, his critique was so devastating that for Jewish philosophy to continue it had to find a new path to follow.

This is not to say there were not Jewish philosophers after Crescas. In fact there were many of them. The decline in the immediate centuries following Crescas was not a decline in publication. On the contrary, in part because of the invention of the printing press, publications could flourish with a distribution previously unknown in Jewish history.[1] What did decline was quality. What seems to have become the medium during the next at least two hundred years for creative Jewish speculation about the meaning of life, the universe, and the place of the Jewish people in both was the diametrically different approach and form to this speculation in the Kabbalah, whose initiation into the realm of metaphysical speculation followed the completion and dissemination of the *Zohar* by Moses de Leon near the end of the thirteenth century.

We will say more in the next chapter about Kabbalah. Suffice it to say here that Kabbalah, too, is a form of Jewish philosophy, for it is an attempt to form an all-encompassing model for understanding everything in the universe out of the texts of traditional Judaism, especially the Hebrew Scriptures and the writings of the early rabbis. It is also philosophy in the sense that it is continuous with the tradition of classical Jewish philosophy out of Muslim civilization that has been our focus in this section of the book.

A story that remains for scholars to tell is how Kabbalah is indebted to European Christian civilization for both its form and its content.

Clearly, for better or for worse, it had significant influence on Christian European thinking in the late medieval, early modern period. Furthermore, I suspect—given that Jews are always a minority culture within a foreign dominant civilization—that the influence was not only in one direction. Again, just how Christian thought influenced the continuation of Jewish theoretical speculation in Kabbalah is a tale that remains to be told. However, one thing is clear. Kabbalah, no less than Christianity, exhibits the primacy of imagination and the use of visualization in modeling Jewish thinking in a way that was abhorrent to the entire tradition of classical Jewish philosophy, from Saadia through to at least Gersonides.

In part, the philosophy of Maimonides' *Guide* was about divorcing from authentic Judaism those speculative traditions within it, like the Midrash and books like *Shi'ur Qomah* (which reports the quantitative dimensions of every part of God's body). Because Kabbalah, especially the *Zohar*, not only reintroduces corporeal images of the divine, but flaunts them, it should be suspected that whatever else was going on in this literature, it is to be understood as a response to the perceived bankruptcy of the philosophical enterprise itself. Certainly, seeing Kabbalah in this context makes sense when Jewish theoretical speculation is seen together with the comparable directions of decline in the Muslim world at the same time.

Both Judaism and Islam presented three dominant paths to spiritual perfection—through rationalist/scientific study (philosophy), through legal study of and practice of the law (Torah for Jews, and Koran for the Muslims), and through mystical speculations and meditations rich in sensory (primarily visual) images. The legal traditions of both Judaism and Islam remain constant through this period of the ascendancy of Christianity as the dominant western world religion. However, in both Judaism and Islam, there is a qualitative decline in philosophy accompanied by a qualitative ascendancy of mysticism. In both cases the change is a response to failure. First and less important is the failure of philosophic Judaism or Islam to stand up in disputation to the challenges raised by Christian clerics who knew well the Jewish and Muslim interpretations of salvation. Second and more important is the failure of the rationalist faith to withstand its own self-criticism. In the case of Islam, the most important critique was that by the philosopher al-Ghazai (Baghdad, 1058–1111), especially in his book *The Incoherence of the Philosophers*. In the case of Judaism, the assassin's blow was delivered by Hasdai Crescas in his *Light of the Lord* (or *Adonai*).

In the introduction to the second book of the *Guide*, Maimonides listed twenty-six propositions that he would use as premises in his Aristotelian demonstration of the existence, unity, and incorporeality of God. In subsequent centuries those propositions came (erroneously) to be regarded as axioms of Aristotelianism, as if Aristotelian natural philosophy were a geometric system, à la Euclid, that stood or fell on the basis of the truth of each Maimonidean claim. Crescas opened his *Light of the Lord* with a detailed critique of each claim in order to defend his conservative conception, à la Judah Halevi's *Khuzari*, of a purely revealed Jewish faith in radical distinction to the rationalist Jewish faith of Gersonides. Crescas preserved much of Aristotelianism, but he rejected enough to place the entire system of naturalist science in serious doubt for subsequent generations. We shall not mention everything here, since that would be too detailed given the constraints of this volume. However, I will mention a couple of critical judgments.

First, the radical distinction between the supra- and the sublunar worlds collapses on Crescas' analysis no less than it does in the hands of Gersonides. Whatever is true of God's created universe, there is no physical difference between the heavens and earth, so that a physics that would be true of one would also be true of the other.

Second, whereas Gersonides affirmed a universe that is contingent in order to preserve human responsibility of choice while maximizing the domain of possible human knowledge, Crescas affirmed a universe that is necessary in order to maximize divine knowledge and goodness. In other words, the carefully sculptured Maimonidean dance between affirming human freedom and affirming divine governance collapses into two extreme positions in Gersonides and Crescas, with the rationalist Gersonides affirming choice and limiting God while the non-rationalist Crescas affirms determinism and limits humanity. A third position would emerge out of both in the seventeenth century—a rationalist (Spinoza) who affirmed determinism in order to maximize humanity's potential for perfection.

Third, and most important, Crescas, like al-Ghazali before him, demonstrated the fatal weakness of the Aristotelian epistemology (theory of knowledge). Non-materialized forms do not exist in the physical world; they exist only absolutely as the mind of God (where there they are a single unified idea that in principle is beyond human comprehension) and mentally in human intellects. At the same time, intellects (at least, human ones) can only grasp forms, not matter; hence an intellect can only understand something to the extent that it is immaterial. However, to say that any conception is true is to say that it corresponds to reality, where reality is understood to be physical reality. Hence, given this correspondence theory of knowledge, no concept of the intellect can be true because, in principle, the way it exists in the mind (without matter) is not how it exists in the physical world (inherently and inescapably with matter).

Gersonides offered no answer to Crescas because he lived before Crescas. However, there is an obvious one he could have given, which would in fact be the position of Spinoza three hundred years later. The object of human knowledge is not the physical world; it is God. And truth is not a matter of correspondence to anything in the physical world; it is a question of internal and general coherency and consistency, since the entire infinite domain of human conceptualization, when seen in its entirety with clarity and unity, is identical with the mind of God. Or, more appropriately, it is an infinite ideal which if it could be attained rather than just approximated would be the mind of God. However, this ideal is infinite, which means, in principle, that it is unattainable by finite beings.

When this critical judgment is applied to the inherent rationalist ethics of classical Jewish philosophy, it means that salvation (here understood as intellectual union with God) is in principle unattainable by any more than a very small number of people who acquire the requisite knowledge of everything.

In defense it could, and was, argued, that to live is enough of a reward of divine grace; no one needs or is entitled to anything more, including immortal life after death. But that is precisely what Christianity offered over and against both Islam and Judaism. Anyone, irrespective of natural born talents for reasoning or for anything else, can be saved, i.e., have eternal bliss after death, if they only accept Christ. No philosophically trained Jew or Muslim could make a comparable claim. No Jews who merely happened to affirm faith in the Torah would have a share in the world to come simply because they affirmed the Torah and obeyed its precepts; they also had to understand what they were affirming, and that was impossible if they had not attained a level of perfection in mathematics, physics, astronomy, and theology. Those Jews who disputed with the Christians knew this, as did those with whom they disputed, since many of these spokesmen for the Church were apostate Jews trained in Jewish philosophy. Even in the seventeenth century,

Spinoza could transcend this line of attack only by transcending both Christianity and Judaism for a new post-Christian and post-Jewish philosophy of secularist humanism. It is the philosophy of Spinoza that will be our bridge (in Chapters 23 and 24) from classical Jewish philosophy to its resurrection at the end of the nineteenth century in the renaissance of Jewish philosophy in a modernist form in Germany.

Note

1 Such a rapid quantitative growth in scholarship with corresponding decline in quality does not find its equal again until the twentieth century with the proliferation of mediocre publications made possible by the technical advances of the computer and the Internet.

Suggestions for further study

Chazan, Robert. *Barcelona and Beyond: The Disputation of 1263 and Its Aftermath*. Berkeley: University of California Press, 1992.

Gilson, Etienne. *History of Christian Philosophy in the Middle Ages*. New York: Random House, 1954.

Kellner, Menachem Marc. *Dogma in Medieval Jewish Thought: From Maimonides to Abravanel*. Oxford: Oxford University Press, 1986.

Lasker, Daniel J. "Chasdai Crescas," in Daniel H. Frank and Oliver Leaman (eds.), *History of Jewish Philosophy*. Vol. II of *Routledge History of World Philosophies*. London and New York: Routledge, 1997, pp. 399–414.

Lasker, Daniel J. *The Refutation of the Christian Principles by Hasdai Crescas*. Albany: State University of New York Press, 1992.

Silver, Daniel J. *Maimonidean Criticism and the Maimonidean Controversy, 1180–1240*. Leiden: Brill, 1965.

Southern, R. *Western Society and the Church in the Middle Ages*. Harmondsworth: Penguin, 1970.

Wolfson, Harry A. *Crescas' Critique of Aristotle*. Cambridge, MA: Harvard University Press, 1929.

Key questions

1. How did Jewish philosophy change in the first three centuries after Maimonides? What are the factors that led to its decline and the ascent of Kabbalah?
2. Why is Crescas an important Jewish philosopher?
3. How is Kabbalah like and different from classical Jewish philosophy?

4. How are the intellectual histories of Islam and Judaism comparable in the late Middle Ages? What are the three intellectual movements whose history has to be correlated in both of these world religions? How is the decline of philosophy in both related to disputations with Christians?

5. What is Crescas' critique of Aristotelianism? For what purpose does he make it? What were its consequences in subsequent Jewish philosophy?

6. Compare and contrast the philosophies of Gersonides and Crescas. What is Crescas' critique of Aristotelian epistemology? How could Gersonides respond?

Key events in the life of Crescas

1340–1414	Hasdai Crescas
1378–1417	The Great Schism (period of rival papacies in Avignon and Rome)
1456	The Gutenberg Bible, the first book printed with movable type
1479	Marriage of Ferdinand of Aragon and Isabella of Castille
1491	Fall of Muslim Granada to Ferdinand and Isabella
1492	Jews expelled from Spain
1497	Jews expelled from Portugal

III   MODERN JEWISH PHILOSOPHY

Jewish Philosophy before Rosenzweig

CHAPTER 23

Modern history: from Christian Spain to secular Israel

Eastward Jewish migrations through feudal Europe

We have identified the critical time of transition from the medieval world of Islam to the modern world of Christianity as 1492. This date was chosen because in that year the new Christian nation of Spain, united through the marriage of the ruling royalty of the Christian states of Castille and Aragon, asserted its Christianity by expelling the Jews. Many of the Jews expelled remained within the Muslim world, choosing to live in countries like Turkey which, since the middle of the fifteenth century, was at the heart of an eastern Islamic revival by the Ottomans. However, a great many more Jews moved closer to their Andalusian homes into the papal territory of France and the Germanic states of the western regions of what remained of the Holy Roman Empire.[1]

The migration of Jews from the Muslim world into Christian civilization was a marriage of economic convenience for both peoples. From the Jewish perspective, the Jews clearly saw themselves leaving "a civilized place" to live in a "primitive wilderness" where the worst wild animals they had to face were native Europeans.[2] From the Christian perspective, the Jews were aliens from a foreign universe. Even worse, they were from a universe with which Christendom was engaged in mortal combat, a war in which what was at stake was both the life of people in this world and their salvation in the world to come. What the Christians knew about the Jews was very little other than what the New Testament said about them. For these Christians, Jews were the people of Christ and the apostles, who refused to accept the salvation offered through Christ's death. Furthermore, they were people of education in all the mysteries of life from all the strange lands throughout the world. As such they were seen to be interesting and frightening, for who knew what "black" arts they practiced? The Jews preferred to live apart from Christians, and for that reason alone they were also suspected of being a nation of magicians, the proof of which was that they produced many physicians and seemed to be able to practice secret ways of escaping from the plagues that took so many Christian lives.

Jewish strangeness and separateness served the purposes of the leaders of Christendom—both nobility and clerics—who brought them in, because the primary service Jews were expected to perform was to advance money for the construction of cities and the establishment of new, international commercial markets. That the Jews of Europe tended to be exclusively in professions related to banking was not in itself an anti-Jewish move, since the general structure of feudal Europe was a fixed-class society with a fixed economy, which simply means that sons tended to go exclusively into the professions of their fathers (be they farmers like the peasants or professional warriors like the nobility), to marry exclusively daughters of fathers in the same professions, and to exclude both from the professions and from marriage any children whose fathers were not in that profession. As the ruling classes perpetuated their military place in the society by so restricting membership in its society, so did every other class. For Jews, that restricting class was banking (i.e., lending money to wealthy people, "wealthy," that is, because they could afford the necessary collateral to guarantee the loans) and all the occupations that were directly or indirectly connected to banking (which includes shipping—hence Jews were sailors to sail ships, carpenters to build ships, and even astronomers to make the maps to guide the ships at sea in the night-time—and wholesale trades—hence Jews were involved in the mining and sale of precious metals as well as other "special commodities").

The occupation of bankers and (in the case of selling money for money to the poor as well as the rich) moneylenders served to isolate the Jews further from their Christian neighbors. None of this seemed to matter during the city-building stages when the economy of the new commercial cities was expanding and the Christians could borrow money and make more money from the money than what they had to pay as interest on their loans. However, when the initial stages of city building ended, and the town's economic rates of growth leveled off or even declined, Jews found themselves owning the lands of the rich and powerful as well as the clothing of the poor and weak, i.e., owning the collateral that had been put up to guarantee the loans. When this happened, the Christian neighbors, who formerly took pride in the knowledge that the very figures of people they adored in the paintings on their church walls and in the stained glass of their sanctuaries were themselves all Jews (Aaron, David, Moses, and, especially, Jesus, Mary, and the apostles), suddenly remembered it was also the Jews who killed Christ. Then the Jews were driven from their communities (thereby negating the debts) and the Jews moved eastward into new pioneer cities that were only then beginning to develop and build themselves into commercial centers.

In this way, the Jews lived as pioneers at the ever eastward-expanding frontiers of European civilization, and, in their role as financiers, they provided invaluable service to Europe in its transition from a feudal agrarian civilization into a modern commercial civilization. However, these constant rounds of privilege to oppression followed by constant relocation deeply affected the soul of the Jewish people. They developed a negative collective identity that had been unknown to them as a people before the experience of Christian civilization. The Jewish people came to experience themselves for the first time not only as the chosen people but also as a people God had chosen to suffer, even to be martyred.

The sense of Jewish martyrdom was a consequence of everything structurally involved in their departure from the world of Islam and entrance into the world of Christianity. However, of those who oppressed them, the Church seemed to be the most benign, and in the long run Jews fared better in lands (such as papal Provence) where the Church was strong and the nobility weak, than they did in lands (such as England) where the nobility was strong and the Church was weak. The value from a Jewish perspective of the Church was consistency. The Church considered Jews to be tolerated second-class citizens, tolerated because of Christian mercy and second-class because the state was Christian and the Jews were not. It was not a desirable situation from a Jewish perspective, particularly since it put them at a significant commercial disadvantage with their first-class Christian competitors, but it was not an intolerable position, which was not altogether unlike the way the Jews had prospered as a people under Islam. In contrast, Jewish life in lands with strong nobility was a roller-coaster ride of excessive privilege in the early good times (which the Church opposed for Christian reasons) and excessive persecution in the late bad times (which again the Church tended to oppose for the same Christian reasons).

The age of Jewish mysticism and Christian science

The decline of the Jewish people was not limited to their physical and economic lives. It also fitted their intellectual and (possibly) their spiritual lives as well. In general, the intellectual situation of Jewish life under Islam was one of parity. As Islamic learning fared, so did Jewish learning in every respect—in law as well as in philosophy and science. The situation was radically different in Christendom. To simplify, the Jews entered Europe in (let us say) the thirteenth century with scientific and philosophical thirteenth-century minds, while their Christian neighbors were barely beyond the Stone Age. However, by the end of the nineteenth century, the Christians were fully in the nineteenth century, at the "cutting edge" of all developments in science and philosophy in the world. In contrast, the Jews were still in the thirteenth century. For the first time in Jewish history, Jews were the intellectual inferiors of their dominant host nations.

This disparity is certainly a major factor as to why the brightest and often the best of twentieth-century Jewry were at the forefront of a process of assimilation by which they readily abandoned Judaism in order to gain the advantages offered through citizenship in the new commerce-centered Christian nation states, and at the forefront of those advantages was education in Christian universities. There are two parts to this story. One is the decline of theoretical speculation in the *yeshivot* (*yeshiva* in the singular; the advanced schools of rabbinic study) and the other is the ascendancy of theoretical speculation in the Church-created universities of Christendom.

Kabbalah and the Maimonidean controversy

Maimonides and his followers radically restricted the use of imagination in Jewish theology and worship because of their epistemology. They made a radical distinction between what could be perceived through the use of imagination from the senses and what could be known through the use of pure intellect. Only intellect, whose content is pure of any particularity and any sensation, yields knowledge, and only the knowledge of the intellect serves humanity on its path to immortal happiness as a participant in the eternal kingdom of God. In contrast, imagination only yields opinions which may be useful for living in the shadow world of sensation but its indulgence moves one away in the wrong direction from salvation. As such, imagination serves no good purpose. As intellect saves, imagination damns; as intellect leads the human to union with God, the imagination leads the human into the evil power of idolatry ('*avodah zarah*, which literally means "strange service").

However, Crescas' critique of Maimonides' Aristotelianism made it clear that intellect could have none of the salvific power in which Aristotelians like Gersonides believed. Hence, given the inadequacy of intellect, there was no good reason to restrict the use of sensual images in grasping fundamental religious beliefs such as the nature of God, the meaning of the account of creation in Genesis, and the meaning of the account of the chariot in Ezekiel. It is Kabbalah, especially in its development after the publication of the *Zohar*, which carries out this immediate consequence of Crescas' critique of Aristotelianism. In this sense alone, post-*Zohar* Kabbalah can legitimately be understood as a philosophic response to the apparent bankruptcy of classical Jewish philosophy. As such it is an anti-philosophic (i.e., anti-rationalist) philosophy that divorces speculation about the general meaning of life and the world from rationalist, i.e., scientific, investigation. The result was that the best Jewish minds, "best" in the sense of most committed to the attainment of "theoretical wisdom," studied no science, and therefore, unlike Jews such as Maimonides and Gersonides, made no contribution to the development of science.

This intellectually isolationist trend in Jewish philosophy was reinforced at the level of Jewish political life by the results of the so-called Maimonidean controversy, which raged on and off among different rabbis in western Europe throughout the thirteenth century. On the surface the issue was whether or not Maimonides' *Guide* should be an acceptable part of the curriculum of Jewish education. It was not that the *Guide* itself said anything heretical. Maimonides was too well entrenched as the author of the *Mishneh Torah* for that claim to receive solid support in the European rabbinate. Rather, the issue was the beliefs of Jews who read the *Guide*. If they lacked Maimonides' knowledge of rabbinic sources and his intellectual talents, they could misunderstand what he said, adopt heretical views of their own based on his words, and lead others into the sins of their false but important beliefs.

The opposition to the *Guide* was more than an opposition to it. It was a dismissal from the Jewish curriculum of all that we would call "general" or "secular" studies, which is to say the dismissal of all speculation about the universe in every respect that is grounded in empirical observation (as it was in the works of Aristotle) and not in holy texts. The irony is that the opposition was not based on the anti-rationalism of the Kabbalists. On the contrary, these rabbis tended to agree with Saadia Gaon that everything can be known through reason, everything can be known through revelation, and knowledge is one, so that in principle the Scriptures properly interpreted would always agree with the proper use of reasoning. The dismissal of natural philosophy was, instead, solely based on pedagogy. It is very difficult to discover the truth through reasoning. It requires special talents, such as deductive abilities combined with good memory, and it requires a leisure that the Jewish people no longer had, given the conditions of their lives in Christian Europe. On the other hand, to discover the truth through the tradition of revelation was far safer, i.e., far less subject to the danger of error, and therefore far less likely to lead a Jew away from salvation. In this case all a Jew needed to do was to ask his rabbi, who could give a true answer, not because he was especially gifted at reasoning, but because he had a solid tradition of rabbinic commentaries and codes which he could consult in telling his congregation the truths that they ought to believe and the good that they ought to do.

These rabbis believed, like their predecessors, that the Torah properly understood contained all truth. However, they did not appreciate the creative effort it took to apply the truths of the tradition to new situations that daily arise in creation. They underestimated how difficult it was to apply what was already known to be in the Torah to what was yet to be discovered in the Torah. Hence, as Jews entered the emancipated world of Europe in the nineteenth century they found themselves as Jews still living intellectually in the thirteenth century.

The case was totally different in Christendom. While Christianity was far more comfortable than was Judaism with general ignorance in the mass of followers, Christendom, no less than Judaism, recognized that the life of intellect was no less of a way to serve God than was a life of prayer and charity. Hence, special orders were created, viz., the Dominicans and the Franciscans, where those who wanted to serve God in that way could spend their lives so doing. It was these monastic orders that laid the foundation for the modern university which, at least until the twentieth century, functioned primarily as a kind of retreat from the practical affairs of the world where incurably curious Christians spent their lives indulging their habit of asking why and seeking answers.

The European universities were created as institutions of Christian service through the Roman Catholic Church. However, this was only their origin. They significantly changed in the Protestant Christian modern world. In the political language of the seventeenth through the nineteenth centuries, liberalism ascended in Christian Europe over the opposition of conservatism, which means that Europe (at least in the West) tended to become Protestant rather than Roman Catholic in religion, commerce-centered rather than agrarian in economics, and republican democracies rather than monarchies in government. The ascendancy of the commerce-centered Protestant nation state moved the university out of the control of the Church and into the control of the state. With that change came important changes in the structure of the university, not the least being that it came increasingly to exist for the commercial and military needs of the state rather than for the intellectual and spiritual needs of the Church. Still, the university remained (as it continues to do today, more than any other government-sponsored institution) the center for the pursuit of theoretical wisdom. As such it offered an opportunity for a life of intellect that no other institution, especially in both Christendom and Judaism, could afford. By the twentieth century at the latest, the intellectually "best" Jewish minds were choosing to leave all that Judaism intellectually offered (both Kabbalah and *halakhah*) to study in the new secular-faith environment of the western, significantly "post-Christian" universities.

The response to this unprecedented flight of Jews from Judaism into secularized but nonetheless Christian society was to fight in the general society for full acceptance and admission while constructing new forms of Jewish identity to attempt (at least) to enable Jews to live integrated lives as both Jews and members of the general society. This reconstruction of Judaism took three forms—the development of a modern, scientific study of Judaism, the development of liberal forms of Jewish identity, and the development of a political model of Jewish identity based on the modern European nation state. As a shorthand, all three approaches can be called forms of Jewish modernity in the context of a secular humanism.

Secular humanism and modernity

The science of Judaism (Wissenschaft des Jüdentums)

The Maimonidean controversy drove a sharp wedge between the study of the sciences and the study of Jewish texts. At least in the world of intellectually curious Jews, this division seemed to be what was most at stake in the decision to embrace Jewish identity or to assimilate into the society of the majority. Because the line between the scientific and the Jewish had become so rigid, the choice of being Jewish or becoming a citizen of a European nation was also rigid. It seemed that one could be one or the other but not both. Of course this position was a distortion, because, as we have seen in this study, for most of the history of rabbinic Judaism the study of science and of rabbinic texts were intimately linked together. Hence, it seemed only reasonable that some Jews wanted to reintroduce science into the study of Judaica. The form that this bridging of worlds took came to be known as the scientific study of Judaism (*Wissenschaft des Jüdentums*). The pioneer in this respect was Heinrich Graetz, a Polish/Prussian Jew who at the University of Breslau was trained as a modern academic historian and used that training to write and publish in the middle of the nineteenth century a *History of the Jews*.

Graetz's work was history, but it functioned as philosophy. Both biblical and rabbinic philosophies were historical philosophies in the sense that they made sense out of life and the world not merely by using static concepts and principles, but by employing its schematic structure to tell the story of the evolution of everything in time as well as in space. The deepest difference between biblical and rabbinic philosophy is the way they tell this story, i.e., the way they use history, for that telling becomes the dominant mindset by which all of life and the world are rendered intelligible. As the rabbinic telling of Jewish history in the Midrash changed the way Jews had understood everything from the Jewish history of the biblical narratives, so Graetz's history restructured the way Jews would understand themselves in their world, a way that was significantly different from the way rabbinic philosophy told the same story. In both biblical and rabbinic philosophy, what happened occurred as a result of the interactions between humans with humans and humans with deities. In answering the question why are things the way they are, the Bible said look to what God said and how humans succeeded or failed in obeying God's will. Similarly, the rabbis said look to God's word and see how Israel obeyed or disobeyed. History was seen as a dialogue between two persons, the divine and the human. Graetz's history, however, primarily because it is a "modern" history that, as modern, wanted to make Jewish history something "scientific," is a story of human beings interacting with other human beings within a changing world context, and it is not a story about the gods. Neither God nor his angels play a role in Graetz's tale of how the Jewish people came to be who they are. In that sense, his history is modern and scientific, because it is radically secular. It thus became a paradigm for all subsequent developments in what would become known as the field of Jewish studies—a radically secularist, humanist philosophy presented in the form of an academic history.

Readers will undoubtedly be aware that the above portrayal of the development of the academic study of Judaism (of which this book is an example) is controversial. However, I do not think that its central thrust is controversial, namely, that the academic study of Judaism and the Jewish people developed in the middle of the nineteenth century in Germany as one major way that Jews sought to overcome the radical separation between the "general" and the "Jewish," in life as well as in study, that the late medieval rabbis had imposed on Jewish existence in response to the hostility of their European environment. As such, the academic study of Judaism became one of the three general ways that Jews sought to bridge Jewish identity with assimilation into the general society of Europe.

Settlement in America and liberal Jewish spirituality

At a mass level, far more important than the change in the way Jewish intellectuals studied were the changes in the way Jews lived and where they lived. The former had to do with the rise of liberal forms of Jewish religion, and the latter had to do with emigration to the New World of the United States.

Liberal Judaism began in Germany in the nineteenth century as a way for Jews to continue to be Jewish in terms of religion while they became fully integrated into the general society of Germany in every other respect. In part, liberal Judaism was about accepting a radical separation between the domain of religion and the domain of civil society. The former was what Christians called "the religious" and the latter was what they called "the secular." Jewish liberalism confined Judaism exclusively to the realm of the religious (or "spiritual"), and, in doing so, wrote out of Judaism most of the body of traditional Judaism.

The classical Jewish philosophers had argued that the Torah was about doing the good (which it understood in political terms) and believing the true (which it understood in dogmatic terms). The pursuit of the true was understood to be the privilege of the few who had sufficient mental talent and good fortune to pursue it. For the great majority of Jews, however, Judaism was not about the pursuit of truth, but about the attempt to do and be good, an ideal towards which they were guided by the bulk of

Jewish law (*halakhah*). What in effect the Jewish religious liberals did was to declare themselves and all modern, enlightened Jews to be just the elite for whom Maimonides' *Guide* was written. As such, they were committed to a Judaism that confined itself to the pursuit of the true. As for the political, communal dimensions of Jewish life, they abandoned them as a Jewish task and turned instead to the state. In effect, what they said was that the rabbinic Jewish state no longer deserved obedience because its rulers, like the royalty in Europe, had become too corrupt to survive. Instead they placed their political trust in the promise of wise leadership in the newly formed western democracies, the prime example of which was the United States.

Europe was too corrupt to become easily transformed from the "Old World" (an American expression that Jews heard as *ha-ʿolam ha-zeh* [this world]) into the "New World" (another American expression that Jews heard as *ha-ʿolam ha-ba* [the world to come]). The hope of the religious liberals was that the United States was truly a New World that, once redeemed from all trace of its European Old World legacy, would become a "light unto the nations." It is therefore not surprising that the form of Judaism that thrived in twentieth-century America was liberal Judaism— first as Reform Judaism, and then Conservative Judaism as a traditionalist break-off from Reform, and then Reconstructionism as a liberalist break-off from the Conservative.

What defined all three forms of American liberal Judaism as distinct from traditionalist Judaism (whose advocates developed into what is called "Orthodox [right-believing] Judaism,") was their embrace of modernist secular humanism while desiring to remain committed to Judaism. As such, liberal Judaism, like the academic study of Judaism, constitutes a reconstruction of rabbinic Jewish philosophy into a new modernist Jewish philosophy. The third form that this Jewish philosophical move took was Zionism.

Settlement in Palestine and secular Jewish nationalism

The idea of Zionism in itself is quite simple, far more simple than either *Wissenschaft des Jüdentums* or liberal Judaism. It said that, if the modern gentile nations of the world will not accept Jews as citizens of their nations, then Jews could form a nation of their own, modeled on the structure of the modern gentile nations, whose sole difference would be that it is a homeland for the Jewish people. In other words, if Jews could not successfully assimilate as individuals, then they could do so collectively as a nation. In this respect Zionism is the shadow copy of liberal Judaism.

Liberal Judaism accepted the modern Protestant European states' radical separation of the secular from the religious and opted to make being Jewish a matter of religion. It was thus an intentional distortion of classical rabbinic Jewish philosophy in which the religious and the secular are fused. Conversely, the Zionists[3] opted to make being Jewish a matter of secular national-ethnic identity, and in so abstracting out of the philosophy of Judaism any element of the religious, intentionally distorted what Judaism was no less than did the Reformers.

These judgments of distortion are not meant as criticisms of either liberal Judaism or Zionism. Both were enormously successful reconstructions of what it meant to be Jewish in the modern world—"successful" in the sense that they had great appeal to a great many Jews who were otherwise quite willing to abandon being Jewish in order to become modern. However, their success was also the source of their failure, for as the attraction of modernism (here meaning secular humanism) waned after the experience of the Holocaust[4] (as much as faith in biblical Judaism waned after the Jewish wars against the Romans), so postmodern (here meaning post-Holocaust) Jews no longer seem to be as enthusiastic as they once were about either institutionalized Jewish liberal religion or secularized Jewish nationalism. The source of the doubt in both cases was disillusionment with the ideals of liberalism—ideals whose philosophical source, for both Jews and non-Jews in European civilization, was the philosophy of Baruch Spinoza.

Notes

1   Just what the numbers were in these moves is obscure and a subject of current historical research. The problem is that there were no clear governmental structures for taking censuses. The issue is important. In any existing western European community at the end of the fifteenth century there were Jews who were descended from Roman Empire Jews who had left Judea either freely for business opportunities or as slaves who were subsequently freed by other free Jews. There were also Jews who, as early as the eleventh century, left Muslim civilization for the economic adventures opening up in the wilderness of Christian Europe. However, just what the numbers were is unknown, so it is not easy to determine if what European Jewry became by the modern period was a natural outgrowth of contact with the dominant culture (which would be the

case if the Jews from Muslim lands had minimal impact on changing the existing
culture) or if what European Jewry became (culturally at least) was a result of a
violent cultural change (which would be the case if the Jews from Muslim lands
had a maximal impact in changing the existing culture) resulting from this direct
three-way interaction of Muslim, Jewish, and Christian civilizations. (My
personal, significantly uninformed-by-historical-data opinion favors the latter
alternative.) Whatever the precise figures, the newcomers from Spain did disrupt
the normal course of Jewish life already established in Europe, that disruption
was not always welcome in the existing Jewish communities, and what emerged
ultimately as European Jewry would have been significantly different were it not
for the influence of these Jews from Muslim lands.

2 Besides the scientific and cultural differences between developed Islam and
newly developing Christendom, it must be remembered that most Christians
were illiterate, for literacy seemed to be a skill reserved primarily for clerics,
and even within this group, for clerics in certain "scholarly" orders, such as the
Franciscans and the Dominicans.

3 Or, at least the multiple versions of secular Zionism. There were also forms of
religious Zionism, most of which were rooted in one way or another in the
spiritualist political essays of Abraham Isaac Kook (1865–1935) who came to
Palestine from Russia as the Rabbi of Jaffa and later the Chief Ashkenazi
Rabbi of the entire Jewish settlement in Palestine (called the *yishuv*). Our focus
in this section is exclusively on secular Zionism, whose ideology was the
primary conceptual force in Jewish migration to Palestine, leading to the
creation of the modern State of Israel. We will turn in the conclusion of this
book to what has happened to the early Zionist ideology after the ideal of a
Jewish state became a reality, and there the kind of Zionism that Kook
proposed will come into view with greater prominence.

4 The name commonly applied to the systematic attempt of the Nazi
government under Adolf Hitler in Germany, from 1933 to 1945, to exterminate
all Jews.

Suggestions for further study

Baer, Yehuda. *A History of the Jews in Christian Spain*. English translation by
L. Levensohn, H. Halkin, S. Nardi, and H. Fishman. Philadelphia: Jewish
Publication Society of America, 1961.

Bonfil, Robert. *Jewish Life in Renaissance Italy*. English translation by A.
Oldcorn. Berkeley: University of California Press, 1994.

Chasan, Robert. *Medieval Jewry in Northern France: A Political and Social
History*. Baltimore: The Johns Hopkins University Press, 1973.

Copleston, Frederick C. *A History of Medieval Philosophy*. New York: Harper
and Row, 1972.

Dan, Joseph. *The Early Kabbalah*. New York: Paulist Press, 1986.

Dawidowicz, Lucy S. *The War Against the Jews, 1933–1945*. New York: Holt, Rinehart and Winston, 1975.

Ferguson, W. *Europe in Transition: 1300–1520*. Boston: Houghton Mifflin, 1962.

Finkelstein, Louis. *Jewish Self-government in the Middle Ages*. New York: Feldheim, 1964.

Gilson, Etienne. *History of Christian Philosophy in the Middle Ages*. New York: Random House, 1955.

Glazer, Nathan. *American Judaism*. Chicago: University of Chicago Press, 1972.

Grayzel, Solomon. *The Church and the Jews in the XIIIth Century*. New York: Hermon Press, 1966.

Herzberg, Arthur. *The Zionist Idea*. New York: Atheneum, 1969.

Hilberg, Raul. *The Destruction of the European Jews*. New York: Quadrangle, 1961.

Idel, Moshe. *Kabbalah: New Perspectives*. New Haven: Yale University Press, 1988.

Katz, Jacob. *Tradition and Crisis: Jewish Society at the End of the Middle Ages*. New York: The Free Press, 1961.

Kisch, Guido. *The Jews in Medieval Germany: A Study of Their Legal and Social Status*. Chicago: University of Chicago Press, 1949.

Laqueur, Walter. *A History of Zionism*. New York: Schocken Books, 1976.

Leibes, Yehuda. *Studies in Jewish Myth and Jewish Messianism*. Albany: State University of New York, 1993.

Lowenthal, Marvin. *The Jews of Germany: A Story of Sixteen Centuries*. Philadelphia: Jewish Publication Society of America, 1938.

Meyer, Michael. *The Origins of the Modern Jew: Jewish Identity and European Culture, 1749–1824*. Detroit: Wayne State University Press, 1967.

Parkes, James. *The Jew in the Medieval Community: A Study of His Political and Economic Situation*. New York: Hermon Press, 1976.

Sachar, Howard M. *A History of Israel*. New York: Alfred A. Knopf, 1976.

Scholem, Gershom. *Major Trends in Jewish Mysticism*. New York: Schocken, 1956.

Scholem, Gershom. *On the Kabbalah and Its Symbolism*. English translation by R. Manheim. New York: Schocken, 1969.

Scholem, Gershom. *Sabbatai Sevi: The Mystical Messiah, 1626–1676*. English translation by R. J. Zwiwerblowsky. Princeton: Princeton University Press, 1973.

Seltzer, Robert M. *Jewish People, Jewish Thought: The Jewish Experience in History*. New York: Macmillan, 1980, Chs. 10–11, 13–15, pp. 454–546, 580–766.

Tirosh-Rothschild, Hava. *Between Worlds: The Life and Thought of Rabbi David ben Judah Messer Leon*. Albany: State University of New York Press, 1991.

Tirosh-Rothschild, Hava. "Jewish philosophy on the eve of modernity," in Daniel H. Frank and Oliver Leaman (eds.), *History of Jewish Philosophy*. Vol. II of *Routledge History of World Philosophies*, London and New York: Routledge, 1997, pp. 499–573.

Trachtenberg, Joshua. *Jewish Magic and Superstition: A Study in Folk Religion*. New York: William Collins and World Publishing, 1961.

Wistrich, Robert. *The Jews of Vienna in the Age of Franz Joseph*. Portland, OR: Littman Library of Jewish Civilization, 1989.

Wolfson, Elliot R. "Jewish mysticism: a philosophical overview," in Daniel H. Frank and Oliver Leaman (eds.), *History of Jewish Philosophy*. Vol. II of *Routledge History of World Philosophies*, London and New York: Routledge, 1997, pp. 450–98.

Wolfson, Elliot R. *Through a Speculum That Shines: Vision and Imagination in Medieval Jewish Mysticism*. Princeton: Princeton University Press, 1994.

Yerushalmi, Yosef Hayim. *From Spanish Court to Italian Ghetto: Isaac Cardoso*. New York: Columbia University Press, 1971.

Key questions

1. Why did Jews leave Muslim lands to live in Christian lands? How did this movement change them as a people?

2. In general, how did Jews contribute to the eastward expansion of European civilization?

3. What changes occurred in early modern Christian and Jewish European societies that made assimilation attractive to Jews in the twentieth century? Why did Jewish study of natural philosophy decline while interest in Kabbalah increased?

4. What was the "Maimonidean controversy," and what impact did it have on the direction of change in Jewish intellectual history?

5. How did European universities evolve? What were they when they began and what did they become in modern times? How did they contribute to Jewish assimilation?

6. Why did assimilation become a problem for Jews? What are three primary ways that Jews fought it? How are these ways alike and different?

7. How are history and philosophy related as disciplines? What does it mean to understand the modern academic study of Judaism and the Jewish people to be a post-classical Jewish philosophy?

8. How are both liberal Judaism and Zionism inherently messianic movements?

Key events of modern history

1171	First Blood libel charge against Jews; in Blois, France
1182–98	First expulsion of Jews from France
1200–25	Establishment of the Franciscan and Dominican orders
1225–70	Thomas Aquinas
1347–9	Black Plague sweeps Europe
1453	Ottomans capture Constantinople, ending Byzantine Empire
1473–1543	Nicolaus Copernicus
1516–17	Ottoman conquest of Palestine
1517	Martin Luther's 95 Theses
1532	Establishment of Kabbalist school of Safed
1546–55	Lutheran–Catholic Wars in Germany
1559–60	Publication of the *Zohar*
1564–1642	Galileo Galilei
1567	Publication of Joseph Caro's *Shulchan Arukh*
1568	Beginning of the revolt of the Netherlands from Spain
1569–72	Isaac Luria resides in Safed, Palestine
1571–1630	Johannes Kepler
1595	Beginning of Jewish community of Amsterdam
1596–1650	René Descartes
1618–48	Thirty Years War
1626–76	Sabbatai Zevi
1630–54	Recife, Brazil, under Dutch
1632–77	Baruch Spinoza
1646–1716	Gottfried Wilhelm Leibniz
1649–60	England ruled by Oliver Cromwell
1654–1748	Jacques Bernoulli and his son, Jean Bernoulli
1654–1825	Sephardic Jewish emigration to North America
1656	Excommunication of Spinoza
1664	British capture New Amsterdam and rename it New York
1665	Cromwell readmits Jews to England; Sabbatai Zevi proclaimed messiah in Jerusalem
1666 (Sept 16)	Sabbatai Zevi converts to Islam
1670	Spinoza writes *Tractatus Theologico-Politicus*
1671	First Jewish settlement in Berlin
1687	Publication of Isaac Newton's *Principia Mathematica*
1700–60	The Baal Shem Tov (Besht, Israel ben Eliezer)
1707–83	Leonhard Euler
1711–76	David Hume
1724–1804	Immanuel Kant

1726–91	Jacob Frank
1727–86	Moses Mendelssohn
1743–1812	Mayer Amschel, first "great" Rothschild
1751–72	The *Encyclopedie*, edited by Denis Diderot and Jean le Rond d'Alembert, 1780.
1760	Establishment of Eastern European Hasidism of Israel Baal Shem Tov
1770–1831	Georg Wilhelm Friedrich Hegel
1771–5	Johann Wolfgang von Goethe writes *Der Ewige Jude*
1772–1881	Spread of Haskalah in Eastern Europe
1776	American Revolution
1783	Publication of Mendelssohn's *Jerusalem*
1789	French Revolution
1791	Emancipation of Jews in France; publication of *Tanya* by Shneur Zalman of Lyady
1804	Napoleon Bonaparte made Emperor of France
1807	Napoleon's "Great Sanhedrin" in Paris
1809–82	Charles Darwin
1814–15	Congress of Vienna
1818–81	Alexander II Tsar of Russia
1818–83	Karl Marx
1824	Reform movement established in Charleston, NC
1825–80	Central European Jewish immigration to North America
1838–1908	Lifetimes of major voices of modern pan-Islam: Muhammad Abduh (Egypt), Jamal al-Din al-afgani (Egypt), Muhammad Iqbal (India), Mirza Ghulam Ahmad (India)
1841	Publication of liberal prayer book of Hamburg Temple
1844–1900	Friedrich Wilhelm Nietzsche
1845–1910	Georg Cantor
1847	Reform synagogue opened in Berlin
1849	Beginning of Musar movement
1853–78	Publication of Heinrich Graetz's *History of the Jews*
1854	Opening of Breslau Reform seminary
1856–1939	Sigmund Freud
1861	Emancipation of serfs in Russia under Tsar Alexander II; Unification of Italy
1865–1935	Abraham Isaac Kook
1871	Unification of Germany
1872	Founding of Berlin Reform rabbinical seminary, the Hochschule
1873	Founding of Orthodox seminary in Berlin; founding of the Union of American Hebrew Congregations for American Reform synagogues

1875	Establishment of the Hebrew Union College, Reform rabbinical seminary in Cincinnati, Ohio
1878	Establishment of Jewish farming community in Petah Tikvah, Palestine
1880–1924	Eastern European immigration to North America
1881 (March 13)	Tsar Alexander II of Russia assassinated
1882	British occupy Egypt
1882	First Aliyah to Palestine begins; Leo Pinsker writes *Autoemancipation*
1885	Pittsburgh Platform of Reform movement
1889	First essays by Ahad Ha'Am
1894–9	Alfred Dreyfus Affair in France
1896	Herzl's *The Jewish State* published
1897 (Aug 29)	First Zionist Congress in Basel
1902	Establishment of the Jewish Theological Seminary, Conservative rabbinical seminary in New York City
1903	Kishinev pogrom; Sixth Zionist Congress passes Uganda proposal
1904	Second Aliyah to Palestine begins
1905	Russian Revolution; publication of the *Protocols of the Elders of Zion*
1907	Uganda scheme
1909	Tel Aviv founded
1910	Establishment of Deganyah, the first kibbutz
1914–18	First World War
1917 (Nov 2)	Balfour Declaration
1917 (Dec)	British under Allenby capture Palestine
1917	Communist revolution in Russia
1919	Publication of the *Religion of Reason out of the Sources of Judaism* by Hermann Cohen
1919	Third Aliyah to Palestine begins
1921	Jewish–Arab riots in Tel Aviv; establishment of Nahalal, the first moshav
1921	Publication of Franz Rosenzweig's *Star of Redemption*
1921, 1924	Johnson-Lodge U.S. restrictive immigration acts
1923	Publication of Martin Buber's *I and Thou*
1925	Establishment of the Hebrew University in Jerusalem
1930	*Mapai* party established
1933	Nazi Party comes to power in Germany
1936	*Haganah* established
1936–9	Spanish Civil War

1939–45   Second World War
1948   Establishment of the State of Israel
1950 (July) Law of Return passed in Israel

CHAPTER 24

The turning point—Baruch Spinoza

Spinoza as a bridge from the classical to the modern

The move from what Christians call the "medieval" period to "modernity" is a move from feudal states governed by nobility and Roman Catholic priests to nation states governed by popularly elected officials and influenced by Protestant clergymen. At a deeper level, the move is a transition from states whose economy is based primarily on agriculture to states whose economy is based primarily on commerce. The economics and the politics are at the heart of all of the conceptual changes associated with modernism.

In general, none of these changes affected the Jewish people until the nineteenth century because it was not until then that the Jews began to become full participants in European society. However, there was one notable exception to this judgment, and that is Baruch Spinoza.

Spinoza was a product of an ex-converso[1] Jewish community living in a most liberal state, Holland, whose liberalism was defined both by the commercial nature of its economy as well as by its Protestant opposition to Spanish Roman Catholicism. He also belonged to a society of freethinkers who were at the cutting edge of developments at the time in every field of natural philosophy, from optics (which was Spinoza's special interest as a scientist) and physics (which was the special interest of Spinoza's associate, Gottfried Wilhelm von Leibniz) to democratic political theory and humanist theology.

All of these factors combine to make Spinoza, as both a person and an intellectual, unique. In terms of Jewish philosophy, Spinoza is an heretical classical thinker and a most original and creative modern thinker. His heresy arises from his consistent and rigorous working out of the implications of the philosophy of people like Maimonides and Gersonides. His originality reflects the fact that his thinking about metaphysics, religion, and government points to every major new development in these areas in the next two hundred years of European civilization.

There is nothing paradoxical about this judgment. That Spinoza can be both, in a sense, the last of the classical medieval Jewish philosophers and the first of the modern Jewish philosophers means that there is no radical break between the two. Contrary to what many contemporary intellectuals believe, the move from the pre-modern to the modern is not a qualitative jump in thought. On the contrary, it is a continuous and natural transition where the new arises largely as a consequence of the impact of the old.

We will here limit the focus of our summary of Spinoza's philosophy to two topics. The first is what he says in a posthumous book called *The Ethics* (first published in 1677) about God and the world. The second is what he says about the structure of government and religion in one of the few works he published during his lifetime, the *Tractatus Theologico-Politicus* (first published in 1670).

Spinoza's philosophical theology and ontology

By the seventeenth century at the latest, European Christian natural philosophers had absorbed and moved beyond the medieval philosophies of the Muslims and Jews. Of critical importance were the developments in mathematics, which, for our purposes, involved better notation and notational interpretation to deal with concepts such as infinity. The importance of infinity is the critical role it plays in accounting for motion, which is the central issue of physics. Two of Spinoza's contemporaries, Isaac Newton (1642–1727) in England and Gottfried Wilhelm von Leibniz (1646–1716) in the Germanic lands, would develop calculus and, armed with this mathematical tool, would transform physics (in Newton's case) and logic (in Leibniz's case) into the modern disciplines that they are today. For our purposes, what is important about these developments is that they put science on a mathematical rather than a commonsensical empirical basis and had sufficient dramatic practical success to be able to claim that the new "science" had the power to present "truth."

No less important is René Descartes' demonstration that geometry and algebra are the same thing, for every algebraic equation has a geometric counterpart and every geometric shape has an algebraic expression. At stake here is the epistemic status of imagination and intellect, for it was the critique of the truth-value of the conclusions from reason (here associated exclusively with the intellect) that set the philosophical ground for the move in Jewish philosophy to the theological images of Kabbalah. The Kabbalists had thought that by modeling their thought through the imagination they had successfully moved beyond the propositional constructions of truth claims by the philosophers. In opposition to the claim, Descartes had demonstrated that there is no real difference between the two. The difference is only which tool—imagining shapes or conceiving concepts—is more flexible for grasping the way the human mind interprets what it experiences through its senses. Until the seventeenth century a case could be made reasonably for preferring imagination, but not after this date. The new math and the new physics gave the pursuit of the algebraic intellect a clear edge over the pursuit of geometric imagination in striving for salvation, i.e., for union with God.

It should be noted that the seventeenth century was also a time of great messianic expectation. It was the century that produced Sabbatai Zevi, the only Jew ever to believe that he was the messiah who succeeded in getting a large number of Jews to agree with him. Furthermore, messianism should not be overlooked as an important (at least) emotional factor in the political revolutions discussed in intellectual circles in the seventeenth century that became reality in North America and France in the eighteenth century. Behind these revolutions was an enormous confidence that human beings could do anything, even know God and the world.

The model that Spinoza used for "knowing everything" was Euclid's geometry. Euclid reduced all three-dimensional shapes (e.g., spheres and boxes) to two-dimensional shapes (i.e., planes) to single-dimensional shapes (i.e., lines), then defined what a line was and used that definition to construct every conceivable shape in the universe. In Euclid's geometry there is no information that you need to have, and all that you have to understand is what is a straight line. Everything else in the universe of physical shapes is an application of that single definition. Spinoza, like the other new rationalists of his time, wanted to apply Euclid's technique for geometry to all of natural philosophy. He hoped that he could find a single definition of a single entity from which everything in the universe could be deduced.

René Descartes before him had the same goal, and his starting point was the act of thinking. His first premise for a mathematical philosophy ("mathematical" in the sense that every truth claim in the philosophy was to be, at least in principle, a deduction from the initial premise) was the so-called "cogito," viz., the statement "Cogito ergo sum" (I think, therefore I am). From this claim Descartes argued that he could deduce his own substantial existence as an intellect, the existence of God (the perfect intellectual substance), the relative reliability of the senses, and the existence of the world of other intellects and physical objects.

Spinoza took Descartes' argument seriously but dismissed it. He argued that all that follows from the cogito is the existence of thinking, but not the existence of a thinker who thinks, for that judgment presupposes that there exist substances that perform actions like thinking, and that assumption does not follow from the act of thinking as such, for it is possible to conceive of thinking without thinkers.

In general, Spinoza found Descartes' deductions to be flawed, and none more so than his deduction of the existence of God. Descartes had argued as follows: I have the concept of a perfect being. Now I could not be the cause of this concept, because I am imperfect and an effect cannot be greater than its cause. Hence, the concept of something perfect can only be caused by something that itself is perfect, viz., God. There are a number of ways that this is a flawed argument, not the least of which is that an effect cannot be greater than its cause (e.g., can I not produce a child that is greater than me in any number of ways?). However, that is not what Spinoza emphasized. Rather, he pointed out that, even if the cause of something perfect must be perfect, our concept of a perfect being is not perfect. Quite the contrary (as Spinoza well knew from his study of Maimonides), our concept of God is anything but perfect, which entails that there is no reason why our imperfect minds could not themselves be the cause of our very imperfect idea of a perfect being.

Spinoza began instead with the definition of "substance" and from that definition deduced the basic kinds of entities and their relations that enable him (at least to his own satisfaction) to demonstrate absolutely everything. What is most interesting about Spinoza's philosophical speculations are the arguments for his very deductions, but to reproduce them here goes beyond the scope of this book. Instead, I will merely summarize his conclusions.[2]

Spinoza was a radical monist in the sense that he believed that in absolute terms there exists one and only one thing, which is called "God," whom he defined as the one and only absolutely infinite substance. He is a substance because he exists in and of himself and is conceived in and through himself. As such, God is not a "mode," which is the only other kind of thing that exists, even though it does not exist "absolutely." A mode is something that exists in and through something other than itself and is conceived in and through something other than itself. Now,

Spinoza suggested, at least initially, that there exist many substances as well as many modes of any single substance. However, this is something only granted initially, for, following his method of deduction, he went on to show that there can be one and only one substance, which entails that in absolute terms anything else that exists exists only as something that exists in and through the one substance and is conceived in and through the one substance. Briefly stated, only a substance that is infinite (i.e., without limit) in every respect would be absolutely a substance, for anything limited in any respect would be limited by what it is not, and that something other than it would (at least in part) define it, so that the substance in question could not be a substance for it would not be totally conceived in and through itself. Hence, there can be only one infinite substance and that substance would contain within itself everything else that exists or can be conceived.

"Contain" is a word that needs explanation. Its literal meaning is spatial and that is not what Spinoza intended because, as we shall see, at this level of discussion nothing occupies space. Rather, all "contain" means is that nothing other than an absolutely infinite substance can exist or be conceived whose cause for existence or reason for being thought is not ultimately God. To understand what Spinoza here said, think of a video game. When you look at its screen you see a world of objects in motion, but these objects and this world are not real, in the sense that what you see and hear exist only in the world of the video game, and that world is created by a mathematical program run in the hardware of the game box. In Spinoza's terms the world seen and heard in the video game is the universe of interrelated modes generated by the mathematical program. It is the mathematical program that is the closest analogue to what Spinoza meant by the absolute substance. The program does not exist in the way that the game exists, but it is what causes the game to exist.

For Spinoza there are two kinds of games—thinking games (the world of ideas) and extension games (the world of objects extended in space and time). Spinoza's term for these games is "attributes." There are as many attributes as there are ways to think of a substance. Hence, there are an infinite number of attributes of the one absolutely infinite substance, for if there were not it would not be absolutely infinite. However, of all of these ways, human beings can only know two. One attribute is the attribute of extension, which means the entire universe of objects in space and time, everywhere in the (for Spinoza, infinite) world of spatial extension at every time (infinitely into both the past and the future). This attribute of extension is what we normally call the physical or material universe. However, for Spinoza, it is not real, for it is only a way of "thinking" about substance; it is not the or a way that substance exists.

The other attribute by which human beings can think of God is the attribute of thought. Here the attribute is not the universe of physical objects, but the universe of all possible thoughts. When objects exist in the material world they have mechanical causes that are the motions of other physical objects in the material world. Similarly, thoughts are conceived in the mental world of the attribute of thought because they are logical deductions from other thoughts conceived in this same world. Nothing thought can be caused; it can only be deduced from other thoughts. Conversely nothing existent in space and time can be conceived; it can only be caused by some other spatial–temporal thing. Hence, these two modes are totally independent of each other. Only physical things cause physical things (which would make Spinoza a materialist and a behaviorist) and thoughts can only be deduced from thoughts (which would make Spinoza an idealist). However, the two worlds are related isomorphically, which means that there is a one-to-one relationship between every member of the world of thoughts and every member of the world of extended things, which creates the (inadequate) cognition that thoughts can cause physical events and physical events can be deduced from things.

The reason the worlds of thought and extension are isomorphically related is that they are both attributes of a single thing, i.e., ways of thinking about the one absolute deity who is all that absolutely exists. It is important not to forget that, from the point of view of God, i.e., from an absolute perspective, no attribute is real; only God is. For our purposes, what is most important to recognize about this judgment is that it is possible for a human being to see things from a divine perspective. In this epistemic optimism about humanity Spinoza is a most modern Jewish philosopher, which here means that he was in sharp opposition to all of the classical philosophers who went before him who, to relatively different degrees, agreed that knowledge of God as he is in himself lies beyond human comprehension.

Spinoza's political and religious ethics

Spinoza's messianic optimism about the unlimited power of human reason is the key to his politics, his religious thinking, and his understanding of the relationship between them. His messianic optimism was a consequence of his ontology. Ultimately there exists one entity (God) and that one entity is in every respect perfect, which includes his perceived activities as a governor of the world. Hence, the world must be perfect, and any perception of deficiency in it must be an error in thinking, caused by the imperfection of the thinker. Why then do we perceive evil if there is no evil? It is a consequence of our finitude, for we are incapable of knowing all the consequences of an act since the number of consequences is infinite. It is infinite because everything in the universe is determined; hence, everything is causally connected with everything else.

There is no room for freedom of choice, because there is no contingency. There is no contingency because everything that is follows from the will of a single perfect agent who can be influenced by nothing other than himself. Furthermore, there is no purpose in the universe, because the perfect being is not free to be anything else but perfect; hence, all that he does he does necessarily from his nature; he, no more nor less than anything else in the universe, has no freedom of choice.

This is not to say that God is not free. On the contrary, Spinoza's deity is perfectly free, but freedom here does not mean freedom to be wrong in any respect. Freedom means self-determinism, not options of choice. Because of God's perfect knowledge he knows what every option is and all the consequences of any option taken. Hence, God can know in every case what is the best possible choice, and, because of his essential perfection, God as God must always choose the best. Hence, there are no real options, so that nothing can really happen for a purpose since everything must happen as it happens. (In the words of Spinoza's contemporary Leibniz, since this is "the best of all possible worlds," it is a strictly determinist one.)

Government, therefore, is not about moral responsibility. Spinoza does speak about good and evil, but he uses the terms in purely pragmatic or utensil ways. Everything seeks by nature to be happy, which means to become fully what it is, so that it can maximize its ability to survive. All beings choose their own good ultimately by this criterion, viz., what will promote their survival and continuance. Wrong choices are choices that fail to promote this end; good choices are ones that do promote this end. In the case of the political governor, these choices are not so much about the good and bad of the individual (although they are that as well) as about the good and bad of the collective. A good ruler should do what both promotes the welfare of his state and his personal welfare as the ruler. To achieve this end a ruler is best served by either becoming himself a good philosopher or employing one. In short, all government should be guided by the light of reason, because reason and reason alone can guide the ruler to make wise choices, and the only ones who have this light are the good natural philosophers.

It is in this sense that Spinoza, like the classical philosophers before him, did not believe in any kind of democratic political structure. However, in another sense he actually was a democratic. That sense was messianic. There are, he argued, three kinds of government—rule by one (monarchy), rule by some (oligarchy), and rule by many (democracy). In absolute terms, democracy is the best system of government because it is better for a person to govern himself, i.e., to be free in the sense of self-determination. However, democracy is only good in a society of good, i.e., wise, people. In a less perfect society democracy would be disastrous, and in a truly base society, where you are lucky to find even a single wise person, the best government is the rule of one wise person who, hopefully, is the king, or, at least a king sufficiently wise to listen to and follow the advice of his philosophers.

Spinoza considered Moses and Jesus to be such wise men. It is Moses who created the system of the Torah as a political means to improve the fairly base children of Israel so that they might become wise and self-ruling. Jesus and Moses taught the same truths, only Jesus taught his lessons to people who had become, by means of Mosaic legislation, wise enough to be self-governing. Therefore Jesus had a universal humanist perspective rather than the particularist nationalist purpose of the Torah.

To teach these philosophical truths about life and the world in the context of politics, the wise philosophers, Moses and Jesus, both promoted religions of reason. However, the inheritors of their near perfect writings and sayings were mere politicians, who, as politicians were anything but wise. As Maimonides had argued, the skills of the politician are rhetorical skills that depend on talent to use the imagination, not reason. Spinoza said the same thing. Furthermore, Maimonides spoke of men who could combine in themselves the persuasion and governing imaginative talents of the ruler with the power to know what is really true through careful employment of the reason of the philosopher-scientist. He called these people "prophets." Spinoza, however, rejected this distinction. Prophets are simply politicians who lead religious communities. As such they are no different from other kinds of politicians, such as the priests of the Roman Catholic Church and the rabbis of rabbinic Judaism.

Spinoza was neither a believing Jew nor a believing Christian, although he was a religious man. He was religious in two senses. First, his philosophy was entirely centered on his theology, i.e., around his conception of God. Second, he advocated the religion of Moses (instead of Judaism) and the religion of Jesus (instead of Christianity) which he believed to be a single religion, a religion of reason.

A more difficult question is, was Spinoza a Jewish philosopher? Clearly his inclusion in this book says he was, but other scholars would say he was not. The reasons for excluding him are twofold. First, his primary community of identity was fellow freethinkers in Europe, most of whom were Christian. Second, his thought is deeply unJewish in its conscious rejection of many of the most fundamental beliefs of rabbinic Judaism, not the least of which are those who divine creation of the world and revelation of the Torah. The reply to both objections is an appeal to historical context. It is not that Spinoza was not Jewish; it is rather that he was a new kind of Jew, a "modern" Jew whose way of viewing the world and life was universalist rather than particularist and secular rather than religious. If Spinoza is not a Jew, then most contemporary secular Jews are not Jews, and if secularism cannot be Jewish, then most Jews are not Jews.

The reply to this reply is the question, was Spinoza a "good" Jew? For some, notably the liberal modernist, he was the best of Jews. It is interesting in this connection that the Hebrew Union College library in Cincinnati, Ohio, has a study room called the "Spinoza room" whose central artefact is a statue of the philosopher. No other Jew and no other philosopher has so prominent a place. However, most subsequent Jewish philosophers did not share this positive assessment of Spinoza's religion. Clearly the primary (but not exclusive) direction of Jewish philosophy in the twentieth century, despite the influence of Spinoza, was in opposition to him.

Spinoza's heterodoxy

Spinoza was excommunicated by the governing rabbinic court of Amsterdam in 1656. In the case of the Jewish community, excommunication meant social and economic ostracism from the Jewish community. Spinoza was 24 years old at the time. He was given an open invitation to repent of his heresy and return to the community, but it was an opportunity he never took. In fact it seemed not to matter to him. Spinoza never married. He lived in a small apartment, spent his day doing empirical studies in optics, and his evenings discussing religion and philosophy with friends. He had a small inheritance which freed him, given his modest lifestyle, from any need to earn a living. Instead he was free to spend every waking moment of his life in pursuit of his own philosophical ideal of happiness, an ideal which he called "the intellectual love of God." It is in this context somewhat ironic that what killed him was not his heresy but his free pursuit of scientific happiness, for he died of a consumption caused by breathing into his lungs small particles of glass from the lenses he polished for his experiments in optics.

The excommunication did more harm to the Jewish community than it did to Spinoza personally, for it marked a clear separation between the rabbinic leadership of modern Europe and the life of intellect that drove the most intellectually talented Jews of the nineteenth and twentieth centuries in their studies into the Christian-secular university rather than into the world of Jewish texts. For these incurably intellectual Jews, to be Jewish was an intolerable superstition to be transcended into the freethinking air of the modern gentile academy.

Was Spinoza really a heretic? Not if we go by what he was accused of, viz., being an atheist, for few thinkers in the history of western civilization have made God more central to all of their thinking than did Spinoza. However, clearly in other (not named) respects he was heretical. By advocating a strict determinism he denied creation and the rational grounds on which the study of Torah was grounded, for he knew enough Jewish philosophy to know that both Maimonides and Gersonides had made the contingency of the world a necessary condition for affirming creation, as well as their judgment that the moral justification and intelligibility of the precepts of the Torah rested on the conceptual foundation of the real possibility of human beings making real, i.e., undetermined-in-advance, choices. In keeping with this judgment, Spinoza believed the Torah had ceased to have authority over Jews once the Jewish state was destroyed. Hence Jews were morally free to become, not Jews, but human beings in general who governed themselves as citizens in new states like Holland by the universal dictates of reason.

However, this heretical picture of Spinoza is too simplistic, for practically every heretical idea he held was a reasonable deduction from the Jewish philosophical texts he studied. His heresy, in my judgment, was more political than conceptual. The bottom line behind all of Spinoza' heterodoxies (i.e., ways of varying from what is thought to be "right thinking") was his belief in the eminence of messianism. To be sure Spinoza's messianism was not the same as that of his contemporary, Sabbatai Zevi. Spinoza did not believe that he was literally what rabbinic tradition called the "messiah." However, he did believe that he had achieved a perfection that the tradition believed could only occur when the messiah comes. More accurately, Spinoza believed not in a personal messiah but in a messianic age, which he equated with the age of reasoned enlightenment. He saw himself, together with his fellow natural philosophers in western Europe (his real community), at the forefront of an age of reason that can best be explained in terms of traditional religious concepts, such as the "kingdom of God." That vision would dominate western civilization, Jewish and Christian, into the beginning of the twentieth century.

Notes

1 Conversos, or "Marranos" as they were derogatorily called, were Jews who openly professed Roman Catholicism but secretly practiced Judaism.
2 Readers should be aware that scholars propose many different interpretations of just what it is that Spinoza claimed to demonstrate. What I present here is a summary of what is my reading of Spinoza's world- and life-view, in the light (or lack of light, as the case may be) of the many academic commentators on his work. The "Suggestions for further study" lists a good spectrum of current interpretations, some of which (but not all of which) fit what I am saying. Readers are encouraged to read themselves what Spinoza says, then read what the commentators say, and make up their own minds.

Suggestions for further study

Bennett, Jonathan. *A Study of Spinoza's Ethics*. Indianapolis: Hackett Publishing Co., 1984.
Boyer, *A History of Mathematics*. Revised by Uta C. Merzbach. New York: John Wiley and Sons, 1968.
Carlebach, Elisheva. "The social and cultural context: seventeenth-century Europe," in Daniel H. Frank and Oliver Leaman (eds.), *History of Jewish Philosophy*. Vol. II of *Routledge History of World Philosophies*, London and New York: Routledge, 1997, pp. 589–99.
Curley, Edwin M. *Spinoza's Metaphysics: An Essay in Interpretation*. Cambridge, MA: Harvard University Press, 1969.

Curley, Edwin M. (ed.). *The Collected Works of Spinoza*. Princeton: Princeton University Press, 1985.

De Dijn, Herman. *Spinoza: The Way to Wisdom*. West Lafayette, IN: Purdue University Press, 1996.

Feldman, Seymour. "Spinoza," in Daniel H. Frank and Oliver Leaman (eds.), *History of Jewish Philosophy*. Vol. II. of *Routledge History of World Philosophies*, London and New York: Routledge, 1997, pp. 612–35.

Grene, Marjorie and Nails, Debra (eds.). *Spinoza and the Sciences*. Boston Studies in the Philosophy of Science, edited by S. Cohen and Marx W. Wartofsky, Vol. 91. Boston: D. Reidel Publishing Co., 1986.

Hart, Alan. *Spinoza's Ethics, Part I and II: A Platonic Commentary*. Leiden: E. J. Brill, 1983.

Kennington, Richard (ed.). *The Philosophy of Baruch Spinoza*. Washington, DC: Catholic University of America Press, 1980.

Levy, Ze'ev. *Jewish Aspects of Spinoza's Philosophy*. New York: Peter Lang, 1989.

MacNabb, D. G. C. *Emotion, Thought and Therapy: A Study of Hume and Spinoza and the Relationship of Philosophical Theories of the Emotions to Psychological Theories of Therapy*. Berkeley: University of California Press, 1977.

Marcorini, Edgardo (ed.). *The History of Science and Technology*. New York/ Oxford: Facts on File, 1988.

Mason, Richard. *The God of Spinoza*. Cambridge: Cambridge University Press, 1997.

Myers, Henry Alonzo. *The Spinoza–Hegel Paradox: A Study of the Choice Between Traditional Idealism and Systematic Pluralism*. Ithaca, NY: Cornell University Press, 1944.

Nadler, Steven. *Spinoza, A Life*. Cambridge: Cambridge University Press, 1999.

Pollock, Frederick. *Spinoza: His Life and Philosophy*. London: Kegan Paul, 1980.

Popkin, Richard H. "The Jewish community of Amsterdam," in Daniel H. Frank and Oliver Leaman (eds.), *History of Jewish Philosophy*. Vol. II. *Routledge History of World Philosophies*, London and New York: Routledge, 1997, pp. 600–11.

Rotensteich, Nathan. *Jewish Philosophy in Modern Times: From Mendelssohn to Rosenzweig*. New York: Holt, Rinehart and Winston, 1968.

Roth, Cecil. *A History of the Marranos*. Philadelphia: Jewish Publication Society of America, 1932.

Roth, Cecil. *The Jews in the Renaissance*. Philadelphia: Jewish Publication Society of America, 1950.

Roth, Leon. *Spinoza*. London: George Allen & Unwin Ltd., 1929.

Roth, Leon. *Spinoza, Descartes, and Maimonides*. New York: Russell and Russell, 1963.

Schorsch, Ismar. *Jewish Reactions to German Anti-Semitism, 1870–1914*. New York: Columbia University Press, 1972.

Spinoza, Baruch. *The Chief Works of Benedict De Spinoza*. English translation by R. H. M. Elwes. New York: Dover, 1955.

Spinoza, Baruch. *The Collected Works of Spinoza*. English translation by Edwin Curley. Princeton: Princeton University Press, 1985.

Spinoza, Baruch. *The Ethics and Selected Letters*. English translation by Samuel Shirley. Indianapolis: Hackett, 1982.

Spinoza, Baruch. *Opera*. Edited by Carl Gebhard. Heidelberg: Carl Winters, 1925; reprint 1972.

Spinoza, Baruch. *Tractatus Theologico-Politicus*. English translation by Samuel Shirley. Leiden: E. J. Brill, 1989.

Strauss, Leo. *Spinoza's Critique of Religion*. English translation by E. M. Sinclair. New York: Schocken Books, 1965.

Wetlesen, Jon. *The Sage and the Way: Spinoza's Ethics of Freedom*. Assen, the Netherlands: Von Gorcum, 1979.

Wirszubski, C. *Pico della Mirandola's Encounter with Jewish Mysticism*. Cambridge, MA: Harvard University Press, 1989.

Wolfson, Harry Austryn. *The Philosophy of Spinoza: Unfolding the Latent Processes of His Reasoning*. Cambridge, MA: Harvard University Press, 1934.

Yovel, Yirmiyahu. *Spinoza and Other Heretics*. Princeton: Princeton University Press, 1989.

Key questions

1. What are the three primary ways that the modern is to be distinguished from the pre-modern? How does Spinoza's philosophy bridge these differences?

2. What were the critical developments in modern European natural philosophy and mathematics that enabled Jewish philosophers to move so far beyond classical Jewish philosophy? How did these developments affect modern Jewish philosophy?

3. What are the important philosophical influences on Spinoza's philosophy? Your answer should include at least Euclid and Descartes.

4. What are substances, modes, and attributes in Spinoza's philosophy and how are they related?

5. How does Spinoza's messianism follow from his ontology? What consequences does it have for ethics, politics, and religion?

6. In what sense is God free? What are good and evil?

7. What are the three kinds of government? Which is the best? Why does a good governor seek the aid of a good philosopher? Why would a good philosopher want to aid a good governor?

8. Was Spinoza religious? Was he Jewish? Was he a Jewish philosopher?

CHAPTER 25

Cohen and Jewish idealism

From Spinoza to Cohen

The project that began with Spinoza—how to come to terms with being Jewish in the world (and faith) of modern Europe—continued in the nineteenth century as Jews were "emancipated" (i.e., granted citizenship with more or less social as well as political equality) in all of the newly formed nation states. Spinoza's solution as a Jew, viz., to transcend Jewish particularity and become simply a human, was accepted by a great many Jewish intellectuals—not the least of whom were Karl Marx and Sigmund Freud. However, many Jewish philosophers sought instead a symbiosis of their Jewish past with their modernity that did not require as negative a stance towards Judaism as Spinoza adopted (despite all of his "intoxication" with God). For some (and eventually many) the solution required a qualification of Spinoza's humanist optimism. Among them were Samson Raphael Hirsch (1808–89), Nahman Krochmal (1785–1840), and Samuel David Luzzatto (1800–75). However, most members of the small circle of committed European Jewish humanist philosophers shared Spinoza's faith in the Utopian expectations for a more secularist humanism. Of particular mention in this group were Moses Mendelssohn (1729–86) and a host of nineteenth-century Jewish intellectuals who were central to the formulation of Reform Judaism. Notable on this list were Israel Jacobson (1768–1828), Samuel Holdheim (1806–60), Solomon Formstecher (1808–89), Abraham Geiger (1810–74), and Samuel Hirsch (1815–89). However, of all of them, the best and most important (both in terms of the philosophic excellence of his thought and his influence on subsequent Jewish philosophy) was Hermann Cohen.

Cohen was born in Coswig in 1842, the son of a local cantor and Hebrew teacher. He acquired his Jewish education at home, his general education at the local state school, and continued to pursue both kinds of study throughout the rest of his life. His Jewish studies brought him to the

Jewish Theological Seminary of Breslau where he achieved prominence as a scholar of both Talmud and of classical Jewish philosophy. At the same time he studied mathematics and philosophy at the University of Berlin and earned his Ph.D. at the University of Halle, from which he went on to become a distinguished philosopher at the University of Marburg. There he became the founder of one of Germany's most important schools of philosophy, generally called "neo-Kantianism," which he continued to lead until 1915 when he retired to teach in the Liberal Jewish Seminary in Berlin. It is there, during the last three years of his life, that he had the greatest personal influence on the subsequent course of Jewish philosophy. Among the younger Jewish thinkers to learn from him in Berlin were Martin Buber (1878–1965), Joseph Soloveitchik (1903–93), Leo Baeck (1873–1956), and (last but not least) Franz Rosenzweig (1886–1929).

The philosophy of Cohen

Underlying all of Cohen's work as a philosopher was his childhood commitment to liberal Judaism. As he understood it, from his studies of both Talmud and philosophy, Judaism is a religion that is about the pursuit of a deity, who can best be understood as an absolutely infinite ideal of a life of reason. All of Judaism—both its emphasis on moral practice in law as well as its emphasis on proper thought in philosophy—is about this pursuit. The goal, God, is an ideal in principle, which means it is both inherently good in itself and it can never be attained. However, its principled non-attainability, at least in this world of finitude and sensation, in no sense diminishes its desirability as a guide to all of life. That life Cohen understood to be precisely the kind of life he led—a life of reason that involves the study of the meaning of life and the universe combined with a faith in the God of Israel who is at one and the same time the revealer of the Torah as well as the creator (in the infinite past) and the redeemer (in the infinite future) of the world.

Cohen takes Spinoza's unrestricted optimism about the inherent goodness and unlimited power of human rationality and combines it with Maimonides' rationalist interpretation and faith in the Torah and rabbinic Judaism. He renders this rational faith or faithful rationalism intelligible with what in his judgment was the best conceptual schema available, that of Kantianism. Hence, in Cohen's philosophy the philosophy of Maimonides, in opposition to Spinoza, is translated out of the naturalist philosophic world- and life-view of the Aristotelians into the rationalist philosophical world- and life-view of the Kantians, a world-view which he, as a philosopher, played a major role in developing.

At the core of Cohen's modern Jewish philosophy is his interpretation of the philosophical writings of Immanuel Kant (1724–1804), and at the core of Cohen's distinct way of constructively interpreting Kant is his work as a philosopher of science. We will talk in more detail about Kant (as interpreted by Cohen) later when we talk about the philosophy of Cohen's student, Franz Rosenzweig (in Chapter 27). For now I want to focus on a summary of his work as a philosopher with specific reference as to how it contributed to forming his new way of doing Jewish philosophy.

Philosophy, science, mathematics, and the infinitesimal

As a consequence of Spinoza's rigorous analysis of what it would mean, out of an Aristotelian conceptual language, to affirm the oneness of the incorporeal deity of Mosaic religion, Cohen inherited the faith that humanity through the study of science could know absolutely everything. Furthermore, the form that the knowledge would take would be mathematical. As Spinoza understood God, there was a single definition, expressible in mathematical language, through which absolutely every-thing could be understood so that, armed solely with an adequate knowledge of this definition, it would be possible to deduce any fact whatsoever about life and the world. The question was, just what is that definition. It is not, as Spinoza had thought, simply his Aristotelian definition of substance. Rather, it was more like Isaac Newton's three laws of motion. Now Newton's laws of motions, like almost every other statement of principles of physics, can only be stated clearly and precisely in the mathematical language of calculus, but a mathematical language in and of itself, i.e., without translation into a more "ordinary" language that prima facie refers to the universe as we sensually experience it, has no meaning other than a purely formal meaning. In other words, it would seem that there is a way (at least in principle) to understand life, the universe, and everything in it. It is the language of mathematics (and, in particular the language of calculus). Yet that language, in itself, has no interpretation. It tells us how to solve problems in the universe (such as building guns that can kill at long distances with considerable accuracy) and it can enable us to make reasonably accurate predictions about the universe (such as when it will end if left to its own resources without human assistance), but it cannot tell us what the universe means, i.e., what it is. To do that is to provide an "interpretation" of the mathematical expressions, and to do that is the function of the philosopher of science. At the end of the nineteenth century, Hermann Cohen was at the forefront of this profession.

The central problem Cohen and others faced was this: there is a difference between change (which is a continuous process) and alteration (which is a set of discrete acts or states). The most important kind of change for our purposes is motion, i.e., change of place. Consider a series of still pictures of different stages of a person running. None of these pictures captures what running is, because each is a still picture that does not itself change. If I make more pictures so that the time interval is much shorter, I still only have an alteration of pictures, and not really motion. Now, if the intervals are very short and they are shown to us in very rapid succession, we will have an illusion of motion. It is an illusion because our vision is not sufficiently refined to record the intervals. If we could see better than we do, we would see that these are still just more still pictures and not really motion. When then do we have motion? The answer is when the transition between pictures is continuous. And when is it continuous? When the time lapse between pictures is "infinitesimal."

Motion is a process of change over continuous segments, which means segments that are infinitesimally small. Another example of this process of thinking is thinking of a line as a series of points. In fact, if the points are discrete, there is no line; only the illusion of a line (which is what lines that we see on computer screens actually are, viz., series of points so small that our sight is not good enough to see the spaces between them). When again do the series of points become a line? Answer: when the distance between the points is infinitesimal.

What then is an infinitesimal? There are many ways to answer this question (the most influential having been given by Cohen's contemporary in the philosophy of science, Karl Weierstrass [1815–97]). An infinitesimal is a positive quantity (i.e., a number greater than 0) that is smaller than any other positive quantity. How then can such a number be calculated, since in principle there are an infinite number of possible numbers between any two numbers? (For example, between 0 and 1, there is 0.5, and between 0.5 and 1 there is 0.55, etc.) The answer is that the desired number can be calculated only as the limit of a process that is infinite.

Now, is it possible ever to calculate something infinite? Pre-modern philosophers thought that was impossible, but it is not. As we now know through the study of mathematical series, there are all kinds of infinities. Consider, for example, the series $(n+1)$ (i.e., any number with one added to it). If we begin with $(n=0)$, for example, then $n+1 = 1, 1+1 = 2, 2+1 = 3$, etc. Now, this is an infinite series that has no limit because, whatever n is, $n+1$ is a new and greater number. Consider, however, instead the series $1/(n+1)$. If $n=0$, then $1/(n+1) = 1/1 = 1, 1/(1+1) = 1/2, 1/(2+1) = 1/3$, etc. If this series were to go on forever, then each entry would bring us closer to the value 0. Hence this series, while infinite, has a finite limit, namely 0. Yet, 0 is not actually the number reached. No matter how great n becomes, we still have something positive, i.e., something greater than 0. Nonetheless, each calculation brings us closer to the infinitely remote limit of the calculation, which in this case is 0. In principle there can be many infinite series whose limits are all kinds of finite numbers.

What was of special interest to Cohen was that the language of calculus is ultimately a language about calculating limits or ends of infinite processes, and these ends/limits are what describe the world. So, for example, to calculate the volume of a three-dimensional space is to calculate an ideal end of a process that is actually infinite, and this stated ideal, the volume, is the real volume of the object in question. That means, for example, that the real volume of a body of water is something ideal rather than actual and it is the ideal that physics tells us is the reality.

We need not limit these applications of calculus to questions of physics. On the contrary, these calculations of ideals as reals are present in everything we do. The measurement that we read on something in our car called a speedometer gives us a velocity which is something ideal rather than actual, because it measures not an average change in speed over a certain amount of time (such as a year or a day or even a second); it measures our change of speed over an instant, which is an infinitesimal amount of time. Similarly, the interest our bank pays us on our savings is also a reality calculated from an ideal, for the interest rate is instantaneous.

Based on these kinds of experiential examples, on the assumption that science describes reality not as it appears to the senses but as it in fact is, and based on the assumption that the mathematics of post-Newtonian physics is the best possible expression of the physics of the universe, Cohen concluded that the ideal, which ultimately is God, is something moral, and this morally conceived entity is what is real, whereas the world that is actually experienced by human beings, that is expressed through declarative sentences (rather than moral imperatives), does not express what is real; it only expresses what is an approximation of the real whose value is to point us toward the infinitely remote ideal that ultimately is a single moral ideal, God. Furthermore, this understanding of reality as something morally ideal to which what is experienced merely points is what Kant meant to tell us, and, even more importantly, it is what Maimonides meant to tell us, which, even more importantly, is what Judaism tells us.

As such, actual rabbinic Judaism is, in the language of Spinoza, the language of reason. Spinoza projected a philosopher's model of a religion of reason whose purpose was to function as a paradigm by which all actual religions could be evaluated. Now Cohen argued that the very religion that Spinoza himself had abandoned in his youth, rabbinic Judaism, was in fact the ideal religion of reason that he pursued in his maturity.

Given that Cohen lived at a time when Judaism was considered anything but ideal, especially in European (and American) academic circles, Cohen's vision was indeed bold. While Germans were debating whether or not Jews were sufficiently civilized to be admitted to citizenship in Germany, Cohen argued that only the Jews are fully civilized. It was an intellectual move that discredited him in the eyes of his Christian fellow academics, but endeared him to the heart of all subsequent Jewish philosophers.

Cohen's philosophy is no less a critical link in the development of Jewish philosophy than is Maimonides'. No philosopher before Maimonides is as important as he is because after Maimonides it is inconceivable to do philosophy without arguing with him. Most who followed him cited him to disagree with him, but disagreement is itself an expression of taking someone seriously, and no Jewish philosopher has been taken more seriously than Maimonides. The same is true of Cohen. No Jewish philosopher after Cohen could do Jewish philosophy without arguing with Cohen, and only Cohen has that level of importance (not even Spinoza). Similarly, as Maimonides was cited primarily to refute Maimonides, so Cohen is cited primarily to refute Cohen. Similarly again, as the major charge against Maimonides was of an excessive rationalism that distorted both reality and the teachings of Judaism, so Cohen is accused by his students of the same excessive rationalism. We will look at two: Martin Buber (who was not Cohen's student) and Franz Rosenzweig

(Buber's friend who was Cohen's student and who loved Cohen as Cohen loved him).

Notes

1 Who was not literally a student of Cohen even though he was part of the group of young Jewish intellectuals in Berlin at this time who were Cohen's students.
2 Possibly the most important Orthodox Jewish theologian of the twentieth century.
3 Possibly the most important Reform Jewish theologian of the twentieth century.

Suggestions for further study

Brenner, Michael. *The Renaissance of Jewish Culture in Weimar Germany*. New Haven: Yale University Press, 1996.

Cohen, Hermann. *Religion of Reason out of the Sources of Judaism*. English translation by S. Kaplan. New York: Ungar, 1972.

Dietrich, Wendell S. *Cohen and Troeltsch: Ethical Monotheistic Religion and Theory of Culture*. Chico, CA: Scholars Press, 1986.

Kluback, William. *Hermann Cohen: The Challenge of a Religion of Reason*. Chico, CA: Brown Judaica/Scholars Press, 1984.

Kluback, William. *The Idea of Humanity: Hermann Cohen's Legacy of Philosophy and Theology*. Lanham, MD: University Press of America, 1987.

Mosse, George L. *Germans and Jews*. New York: Grosser & Dunlap, 1970.

Poma, Andrea. *The Critical Philosophy of Hermann Cohen*. Albany: State University of New York Press, 1997.

Rotenstreich, Nathan. *Jews and German Philosophy: The Polemics of Emancipation*. New York: Schocken, 1984.

Schwarzschild, Steven. *The Pursuit of the Ideal*. Albany: State University of New York Press, 1990.

Seeskin, Kenneth. "Jewish neo-Kantianism: Hermann Cohen," in Daniel H. Frank and Oliver Leaman (eds.), *History of Jewish Philosophy*. Vol. II of *Routledge History of World Philosophies*. London and New York: Routledge, 1997, pp. 786–98.

Tal, Uriel. *Christians and Jews in Germany: Religion, Politics, and Ideology in the Second Reich, 1870–1914*. English translation by Noah Jacobs. Ithaca, NY: Cornell University Press, 1975.

Zank, Michael. *The Idea of Atonement in the Philosophy of Hermann Cohen*. Providence, RI: Brown Judaic Studies, 2000.

Key questions

1. What problem did emancipation raise for Jews? How did Spinoza solve it? How did other Jewish philosophers solve it?
2. What did Cohen mean when he said that Judaism is a religion of reason?
3. In what sense is it true to say that Cohen was an "idealist"?
4. Compare and contrast Cohen and Maimonides as well as Cohen and Spinoza. In what sense could it be said that Cohen wrote as a defender of Maimonides against the objections of Spinoza?
5. What is the relationship between Cohen's religion, his philosophy, his understanding of physics, and his understanding of mathematics? How would Cohen interpret the prayer, "Hear O Israel the Lord God is one"?
6. Why is "change" a problem of special interest to a philosopher of science?

CHAPTER 26

Buber and Jewish existentialism

The life of Buber

Buber was born in Vienna (in 1878) but raised (by his grandparents) in Linow, Galicia. The disparity between where he was born and where he was raised says much about his philosophy. In the late nineteenth and early twentieth centuries, Vienna was the heart of European and Jewish modernist intellectual life in practically every academic and artistic occupation. Galicia in contrast was eastern and hasidic;[1] in short, it was the epitome of what Vienna was not. The contrast of civilizations was in Buber's early education as well. He was taught primarily by his grandfather, Solomon Buber, who was a well-respected modern academic scholar (in the tradition of *Wissenschaft des Jüdentums*) of Midrash. However, Buber also received an equally important education from observing the life of the hasidic communities that lived on his grandfather's estate.

At the age of 18 (in 1896), Buber entered the University of Vienna, and the focus of his studies became European. He primarily studied philosophy, specializing in Kant and Nietzsche. However, Buber continued to participate actively in Jewish life. Now its form was more secular and political and less religious and intellectual. He became one of the student leaders of the Jewish student union (*Die jüdischen Studentenvereinigung*) at the University of Leipzig as a Zionist. His Zionism was secular (rather than religious), and Utopian (rather than normalist). He believed in minimal government[2] and came to see the kibbutz as its most ideal expression. When he eventually settled in Israel he joined the President of the Hebrew University, Judah Magnes, in forming a political movement, called the "Ichud" (unity), that advocated a joint Arab–Jewish state in opposition to the prevailing opinion of both the international community and the Israeli Labor Party leadership that favored the establishment of two independent states in Palestine, one Jewish and the other Arab.

In general, Buber was politically an uncompromising moralist, who believed that being right and true to what is right is more important than being successful. Buber was for most of his life successful in just this way, as a spokesman for moral ideals irrespective of their short-run pragmatic costs. He gained few followers for his Ichud movement as he gained few supporters for his anarchist idealization of the kibbutz, an institution that never reflected more than a small minority of Jews within the Jewish state that, in the long run, failed to pass on commitment to the children of the founders. However, his influence has been profound as a moral and spiritual teacher in Israel, in world Jewry, and in the world, possibly more than any other Jewish intellectual in the twentieth century.

The story then of Buber's life is one of moral commitment with personal defeat in the short run that in many ways translates into long-term success as a Jewish teacher. Buber completed his Ph.D. in 1904 in Berlin where he met Hermann Cohen's student, Franz Rosenzweig, which changed the direction of Buber's life from what he might have otherwise anticipated. Buber probably contemplated (I cannot be sure) an academic career, not unlike that of his chief competitor as a scholar of Jewish mysticism, Gershom Scholem. However, whereas Scholem's central life focus continued to be academic studies of Jewish texts, Buber increasingly became committed to teaching Jews as Jews and used his deep knowledge of Jewish texts and philosophy to shape the practical life of the Jewish people. In 1916 he became the editor of the journal, *Der Jude* (the Jew), and in 1920 joined Franz Rosenzweig and Rabbi Nehemiah A. Nobel in Frankfurt to found a free Jewish school (*Die Freies Jüdisches Lehrhaus*) to offer Jewish students at the university the kind of Jewish education that they could receive nowhere else, neither in standard rabbinic Jewish community schools nor in the German (so-called secular) university, an education that combined deep knowledge of Jewish texts in the context of living in a Jewish spiritual community.

Buber was appointed as a professor at the University of Frankfurt in 1923, but the real focus of his life continued to be adult Jewish education. With the rise of the Nazis, Jews were at first barred from all university posts and eventually from public teaching of any kind. Most German Jewish academics left Germany as early as possible for positions abroad, many choosing to settle in Palestine and to teach at the Hebrew University in Jerusalem. Buber chose to remain in Germany as long as possible, in order to teach the greater number of German Jews who could not leave. He used his then international reputation (a reputation derived primarily from the popularity, with Christian as well as Jewish theologians and philosophers, of his 1923 philosophical publication, *Ich und Du* [*I and Thou*]) to pressure the German government into allowing him to publish and to teach in public. However, by 1938 all doors of opportunity to teach in public were closed. Finally, Buber left Germany and moved to Jerusalem where his friend, Judah Magnes, created a position for him as a chair of Social Philosophy.[3]

In Israel, despite his university appointment, the thrust of Buber's life continued to be political until his death in 1965. At first, his political thought was so embarrassing to the Jewish state that there was a virtual (although not official) ban on teaching it. In time the veil was lifted to allow his spiritualist ontology and theology to be taught, and eventually, after his death, the ban on his political Zionist thought was lifted as well. After the 1967 war between Israel and the Arab states, the nation felt sufficiently secure physically to allow, even to promote, Buber's political vision of a joint Jewish–Arab Israel, a religious political vision that grew directly out of his spiritualist philosophical vision. For the rest of the century that philosophy became the dominant influence in the development of the so-called "Israeli left." In this sense at least, Buber had more impact on Jewish life than any other twentieth-century Jewish philosopher.

The primary work out of which that influence arose was an early one. Although Buber wrote many books throughout his life on many subjects—including politics, psychology, sociology, intellectual history, ethics, and the Bible—none was more important and influential than *I and Thou*. Our summary here of Buber's philosophy will be limited solely to what Buber said in that work.

Buber's existentialism

Buber is generally known as an "existentialist." This classification includes twentieth-century Christian theologians such as Paul Tillich (1886–1965), secular (primarily French) philosophers such as Jean Paul Sartre (1905–80), and Jewish philosophers such as Abraham Heschel (1907–72).[4] What they all share in common is that they wrote philosophical works whose intended audience consisted more of general intellectuals than professional academics, their world-view was deeply influenced by Edmund Husserl's (1859–1958) phenomenology, and none of them believed that they were existentialists (including Sartre, who popularized the term). Rosenzweig, for example, who is also called an existentialist, instead referred to himself as an advocate of "the new philosophy," which was, as we will see in the next chapter, more of a "post-philosophy" (he used the term "meta-philosophy") than a philosophy of any kind.

There is no reason for us to debate here the appropriateness or inappropriateness of a term. I will concede that Buber can (maybe should) be called an existentialist, and take that designation to mean primarily that his philosophy in *I and Thou* presupposes Husserl's phenomenology. Let me then say a word here first about Husserl's thought to set the stage for Buber's *I and Thou*.

In *The Critique of Pure Reason*, Immanuel Kant (1724–1804) presented a defense of the claim that science is capable of discovering necessary truths (against the attack on this position by David Hume, 1711–76) with an ontology that divided the universe into three different domains that are the subject matter of three different disciplines. There is the world of the mind, that is to be studied through psychology as mental categories; there is the external world of what Kant called the "noumena," that is to be studied through ethics and theology as ideal objects of moral willing; and finally there are the phenomena. Phenomena are the world of trees, rocks, animals, and people that most of us call "the real world."

Kant argued, in keeping with modern physical science, that this world perceived through the senses, as it is perceived, is not in fact real at all. Rather it is a construct of the interaction of the way our mind is structured (by logical categories) with whatever it is that really is there. Kant argued that the domain of science is restricted solely to the realm of the phenomena. In this realm science can produce necessarily true claims, but the claims are not made about anything that is real. Reality, in the sense of what is external to the mind, can be also known, but not with certainty. In this case it is known, not as what is, but as what ought to be, i.e., as a dictate of moral reasoning rather than of discursive logic.[5]

Husserl argued from Kant's philosophy that we should suspend judgment about the external reality of what we experience and focus our attention as philosophers solely on phenomena itself. His hope was that, in providing rich descriptions of what we experience, i.e., in describing the world not as it is but as it is experienced, we may discover deep structures underlying the experience that are universal and that might facilitate ultimate judgments about the nature of reality itself.

Buber stood in this phenomenological tradition of doing philosophy. He suspended all judgments about the nature of reality and instead simply proposed structures to understand the world as it is experienced. These structures provide the basis for his analysis of absolutely everything, from metaphysics and theology to history and sociology.

The philosophy of Buber

Buber proposed two pairs of terms to describe how everything is experienced. They are "I–Thou" (Ich–Du) and "I–It" (Ich–Es). The I–It relationship is the kind of relationship that yields knowledge. There is a subject of consciousness (viz., the "I" of all statements of consciousness such as "I think," "I feel," "I see," "I doubt," "I hear," etc.) that has as the object of its consciousness (viz., the "It") some object, i.e., some thing that is not the subject that is aware of the thing. In contrast, there are other acts of consciousness not structured in this way. In this latter case there is no subject and object as such, but rather there is an awareness, functionally "subconscious," of togetherness with another in which no cognitive separation is made between a subject and an object. Buber talks about love as such a relationship, and, in general, he speaks of I–Thou relations as if they were moral relations while I–It relations are at least non-moral (if not immoral). Conversely, I–It relations exhaust all cognitive relations, and I–Thou are never cognitive, or, to be more accurate, almost non-cognitive. "Almost" rather than totally "non-cognitive," because it is possible to move from a non-reflective I–Thou relationship into a reflective I–It relation whose object of consciousness is an objectification from the I–Thou relationship.

It is in this way that we become consciously aware of ourselves as selves. Here the inseparable "I" of the I–Thou (as well as the "It" of I–It) becomes separate and identified conceptually as a "self." Similarly, from thoroughly (what Buber calls) "personal" relations where there is no separation of a self (I) and another (Thou), we can enter an I–It relationship in which the "Thou" (i.e., the intimate you as opposed to the "you" (Sie in German) that is impersonal or formal) becomes an it, a (as in pre-modern English) "you." That is why, for example, I can be so engrossed in doing something that while I am conscious of the object of my action I am not conscious of me so acting, but, based on this (what Sartre called) "pre-reflective consciousness" I am able (when asked what I was doing) to know and say that I (a separate self from the subject of my past action) was doing the action.

Buber used this phenomenological distinction to define consciousness of a self, an other, an other self (i.e., another person), an object, and all relations between persons, selves, and objects. These relations have a natural dynamic of movement from I–Thou (acts of pure consciousness such as are involved in being in love), to I–Thou/It (acts in which the loved one is associated with some object or sets of objects in order to preserve the remembered initial pure relationship), to I–It relations where the living "Thou" of the initial relationship has been reduced to and swallowed up by the dead, objective "It."

Buber uses this dialectic (viz., inherent progression in relationships between fundamental structural terms for ordering the phenomena) to explain everything, including religion and politics.

Relations are like marriage. They begin with a love between persons that has nothing to do with reason. They progress into series of more and more defined terms of relationship where being in relationship becomes more and more subject to rules or laws. In the end all that is left are the rules and the memory of the love with which the relationship began, but the loving foundation of the marriage is gone. What remains is death (lived or not lived) and/or divorce. In this way, social institutions or political states that are born as freely chosen cooperatives decay into systems of laws and norms that govern people whose association has become impersonal, dead, and generally immoral. The more a state or society becomes a state or society of law, the more the society decays in the direction of death, a death that results in conquest by another more vital society or nation, or in conversion into a new, reinvigorated form of association.

Similarly, religions begin with the pure loving I–Thou relationship between a prophet and God, progress into a relationship governed by rules of worship, and deteriorate into idolatry. The rules are doctrinal determinations of who or what God is and is not (theology), combined with set times, places, and ways to worship God properly (liturgy). All theology Buber told us is idolatry. If we can at all say who or what God is, God is the "eternal thou," i.e. that thou (i.e., that person) who in principle cannot be objectified (i.e., made into an it). In language that Rosenzweig's student, Emmanuel Levinas, will later introduce, God is "totally other," i.e., an other so other that nothing intelligible can be said about God.

Of course the source of this theology is Maimonides' negative theology whose affirmation here is clearly intended as a rejection of Spinoza's knowable deity, the one and only absolutely infinite substance. For Buber any deity so defined is in principle not the eternally thou God; hence, it is idolatry.

Buber claimed both that all religions tend to become idolatrous and that this tendency is unavoidable. We as human beings have a need to know. Knowing, or the attempt to know, satisfies our need for some security in lived life—at least the security that who we met and fell in love with today we can meet and recognize tomorrow. However, the one we know is not the one we encountered. It is an other.

Hence, religions always become idolatrous, and when they do they die. However, in the death of one religion is the birth of another. The new I–Thou of the new faith community arises as a separate religion (as Abraham's Judaism was a new religion out of the rejection of his Chaldean idol worship) or as a religious reform in the old, dead or dying religion (as rabbinic Judaism was a reformation of biblical Judaism, and Protestantism was a reformation of Roman Catholicism). An example of such a religious transformation of a new, living religion out of the dead remains of an older religion that had turned idolatrous was modern Hasidism.

A Jewish critique

It is not surprising that neither the academics nor the Orthodox Jews on the faculty of the Hebrew University in 1938 were particularly enthusiastic in welcoming Buber as a colleague, because his philosophy deeply undercut everything they stood for. For the Orthodox Jews, Buber's message was clearly that they were idolaters. Orthodox Jews are committed to the study of the Torah as the key form of worship of God, and many would go so far as to identify Torah with the body of God. It is what H. A. Wolfson called "enliberation," a term that applies equally to Islam's theology of the Koran and rabbinic Judaism's theology of Torah. It is a term which, in connection with Christianity's doctrine of divine incarnation in Christ, Buber associated with idolatry. Hence, for Buber, rabbinic Judaism (like most Islam and most Christianity) is idolatrous.

Similarly, Buber's phenomenology entails that what academics study in the university has little value. They can know what they know, but what they know is always a form of living death, for no matter how much life there is in what they study, when they study it it becomes dead. There can be no science of life, and because there is no science of life, there can be no philosophical ethics. Buber taught this at a time when Anglo-American philosophy was sufficiently intoxicated with the power of formal logic to believe that everything could be put on a scientific basis, including personal and political ethics. Clearly a philosophy department such as that at the Hebrew University would have no place for someone like Buber as a colleague.[6]

Hence, in Buber we find a modern Jewish philosophy that is itself the negation of both classical rabbinic Judaism in any modern form, especially that of Orthodoxy, but also of Reform and Conservative Judaism as well for similar reasons. Instead, Buber became the conceptual father of a new kind of non-institutional Judaism that developed in North America that goes by a number of names, from "*havurot*" (communes) to "spiritual" communities, where meditation and individual expression are emphasized in worship over all rule-centered, more traditional expressions of Jewish spirituality.

In summary, as Buber is the voice of a non-nationalist Jewish nationalism, so he is also the voice of a very non-institutionalized Jewish religion. The former is called "Utopian Zionism;" the latter is called "Jewish Spiritual Renewal." Their virtue is their moral purity and spiritual energy. They bring into Jewish life a vitality that was not present in the more established institutions of late-nineteenth- and twentieth-century Judaism. Their vices are the many ways in which they fail to reflect what is a critical part of Jewish life—the life of a unified people as a "we," as opposed to the life of a collection of idolatrous individual "I's" who never really become a "we." An alternative approach to Jewish philosophy, one where the philosophical emphasis is more on the "we" than on Buber's isolated "I," is the metaphilosophy of Buber's colleague and younger contemporary, Franz Rosenzweig.

Notes

1 Hasidism is a movement of Jewish spiritual renewal and popular mysticism that swept eastern Europe in the seventeenth century. While it has produced an extensive theological literature, the emphasis in its religious speculation is psychological rather than metaphysical, with a strong current of anti-rationalism (à la Crescas) in its thought.

2 What in the 1920s was called "Anarchism" or "Socialist Anarchism" and in the 1970s was called "direct democracy."

3 Jewish studies at the university were controlled primarily by Orthodox Jews who (rightly) considered Buber's religious thought to be heterodox and therefore (wrongly) used their political position to prevent him from receiving a chair in

Jewish Studies. The philosophy department, whose orientation was almost entirely "analytic," also excluded Buber, despite the fact that he had a better international reputation as a philosopher than any of them, because they considered Buber from the narrowness of their analytic definition of philosophy to be "too soft." Finally, Scholem made sure that Buber would not be appointed a professor of Jewish mysticism for obvious personal (and selfish) reasons. Were it not for his personal friendship with the President of the Hebrew University, Buber, Israel's most famous scholar, might have received no academic appointment at Israel's leading university. All of this, of course, only confirms Buber's central thesis of the great distance of the life of intellect from the moral and spiritual life, contrary to both Maimonides and Spinoza.

4   And even one Nazi philosopher—Martin Heidegger (1889–1976).

5   In the last chapter we examined Cohen's form of ethical idealism as an interpretation of Kant's ontological analysis of empirical science. Most contemporary philosophers of science would reject Cohen in favor of something that they often call "critical realism." Critical realism claims that the world is more or less the way that we sense it but not entirely. So, for example, when we see a stick slightly emersed in water, it is not really broken, although it appears to be, but the stick and the water nonetheless really exist external to our perception of them. However, at a deeper level these compound things perceived are really optical illusions of much smaller, simpler things such as subatomic particles. Now, if the very small particles are (in Kant's terms) the "thing-in-itself," i.e., what is really there in the world of noumena, just what is the ontological status of phenomenal things like sticks and water? The question need not concern us here. For our purposes all that need be said is that even modern scientific empiricism must assume that the things we experience in what Kant called phenomena are not what exists in Kant's noumena.

6   The university-level interest in Buber's philosophy in Anglo-American universities came in religion departments, not philosophy departments. However, the Hebrew University had no department other than departments of Judaica, which was taught as an expression of national history rather than as religion.

Suggestions for further study

Bergman, Shmuel Hugo. *Dialogical Philosophy from Kierkegaard to Buber*. English translation by Arnold A. Gerstein. Albany: State University of New York Press, 1991.

Buber, Martin. *Hasidism and Modern Man*. English translation by Maurice Friedman. New York: Horizon Press, 1958.

Buber, Martin. *I and Thou*. Translated into English by Walter Kauffman. New York: Scribner, 1970.

Buber, Martin. *A Land of Two Peoples: Martin Buber on Jews and Arabs.* Edited by Paul R. Mendes-Flohr. New York: Oxford University Press, 1983.

Buber, Martin. *Two Types of Faith.* Boston: Beacon, 1967.

Buber, Martin and Rosenzweig, Franz. *Scripture and Translation.* Bloomington: Indiana University Press, 1994.

Diamond, Malcolm. *Martin Buber.* New York: Harper and Row, 1968.

Friedman, Maurice. *Encounter on the Narrow Ridge: A Life of Martin Buber.* New York: Parago House, 1991.

Friedman, Maurice S. *Martin Buber and the Eternal.* New York: Human Sciences Press, 1986.

Friedman, Maurice S. *Martin Buber's Life and Work.* New York: Dutton, 1983.

Hodes, Aubrey. *Martin Buber: An Intimate Portrait.* New York: Viking Press, 1971.

Kepnes, Steven. *Buber's Hermeneutical Philosophy and Narrative Theology.* Bloomington: Indiana University Press, 1992.

Leaman, Oliver. "Jewish existentialism: Rosenzweig, Buber, and Soloveitchik," in Daniel H. Frank and Oliver Leaman (eds.), *History of Jewish Philosophy.* Vol. II of *Routledge History of World Philosophies.* London and New York: Routledge, 1997, pp. 799–819.

Mendes-Flohr, Paul R. (ed.). *A Land of Two Peoples: Martin Buber on Jews and Arabs.* New York: Oxford University Press, 1983.

Mendes-Flohr, Paul R. *From Mysticism to Dialogue: Martin Buber's Transformation of German Social Thought.* Detroit: Wayne State University Press, 1988.

Shapira, Avraham. *Hope for Our Time: Key Trends in the Thought of Martin Buber.* Albany: State University of New York Press, 1999.

Vermes, Pamela. *Buber on God and the Perfect Man.* Missoula, MT: Scholars Press, 1980.

Key questions

1. How would you generally describe Buber's life? Would you say he was successful? Give reasons for your answer.

2. Was Buber a religious Jew? Give reasons for your answer. How was he religious? How was he Jewish?

3. Was Buber a Zionist? Give reasons for your answer. What kind of Zionist was he?

4. Was Buber an existentialist? Give reasons for your answer.

5. What three realms of ontology did Kant isolate and how is each to be studied?

6. What are the limits that Kant places on science? How can reality beyond science be known?

7. What was Husserl's critique of Kant? How is phenomenology a solution to the criticism? How is Buber a phenomenologist?
8. How do the terms "I–Thou" and "I–It" function as foundation terms of Buber's philosophy? What do they mean? How do "I–Thou" and "I–It" function as foundation terms for Buber's ethics?
9. What is Buber's dialectic of I–Thou and I–It? Illustrate how it works in sociology and in religion. On Buber's terms what is the relationship between Judaism and Christianity as well as Roman Catholicism and Protestantism?
10. What does Buber say about God? From where does he draw this interpretation? Explain.
11. Why would Orthodox Jews object to Buber's philosophy and why would liberal Jews embrace it? Why would academic philosophers be more likely to be critical of Buber's philosophy than supportive?

The Philosophy of Rosenzweig

CHAPTER 27

The elements: God, world, and the human

Franz Rosenzweig's life

Rosenzweig was born on Christmas Day (December 25), 1886, into a prosperous middle-class, assimilated Jewish family in Cassel, Germany. It was a sufficiently liberal Germany that a Jew was acceptable as a citizen even if he did not convert to Christianity, provided he was not too Jewish. The Rosenzweigs were not very Jewish, but they were very German. Hence, their son was raised to be at home with the best of German culture in every area of the humanities, but with virtually no Jewish education whatsoever, despite the fact that there were notable Jewish scholars in the family only two generations removed.

While no one in the family denied or even hid being Jewish, it was not a point of pride. Certainly no one was religious—no one that is except two of Franz's cousins—Hans and Rudolph Ehrenberg (the grandchildren of the Judaica scholar, Meir Ehrenberg)—who were active and proselytizing Christians. The Ehrenbergs were Franz's closest friends in his college years, and they introduced him to the young Protestant theologian, Eugen Rosenstock-Heussey, and his wife, Margrit Gritli. In addition to these five there were also Gertrude Oppenhiem, Viktor von Weizsäcker, and Franz's mother Adele Rosenzweig. Together this group constituted Franz's "circle" of friends with whom he visited and corresponded constantly— constantly, that is, until he met his wife-to-be, Edith Hahn, whose Jewish identity was positive, strong, and religious. The circle did not especially care for her, and, as Franz turned more from his Germanic identity to develop (in both his life and his thought) his Jewish identity, he became increasingly alienated from them. Married to Edith, Franz left the world of German progressive intellectuals and moved fully into a life of religious service within the German Jewish community.

At one point in his life, under the influence of his university circle of friends, Rosenzweig seriously considered conversion to Christianity. He then decided, however, that to become a Christian he must first become a

Jew and not the "pagan" that he was. Hence, he decided to begin to study Judaism seriously in preparation for his possible conversion to Christianity. The result was that he became more deeply Jewish the more he studied and left his Christianity behind him—behind him that is in terms of his way of living life; Christianity never ceased to be an integral part of his thinking. In fact it is reasonable to say that no notable Jewish religious thinker has been so profoundly influenced by Christian life and thought as was Franz Rosenzweig.

The details of Franz Rosenzweig's life need not concern us here in a book dedicated to philosophy, although it is hard to resist telling the narrative. Some scholars claim that Rosenzweig attended a Yom Kippur service in Berlin on October 11, 1913, and there had a religious experience that convinced him that he must become Jewish and not Christian. He then turned his considerable intellectual and spiritual attention to the study of Jewish texts with Hermann Cohen. However, World War One intervened and, despite his fragile health, Rosenzweig used his family connections to join the military in an active combat role. Fortunately for us he was sent to the Eastern (rather than the Western) Front and lived (thanks to the Russian Revolution neutralizing the "second front" against the Germans). From 1915 on, Rosenzweig was stationed in the Balkans as an anti-aircraft gunner. There he was free to focus his mind on the book of Jewish philosophy he intended to write out of his personal religious journey, and in 1917 he composed its "Germ Cell" (*Urzelle*).

One year later, in 1918, he was sent to attend an officer's school in Warsaw, Poland, where, for the first time in his life, he actually met Polish Jews. For Rosenzweig this experience was no less transforming than anything that happened in a Berlin synagogue on Yom Kippur. Armed with the Germanic academic study of Judaism (the *Wissenschaft des Jüdentums*) to which Cohen had introduced him, as well as conventional German prejudices about eastern Europeans (including eastern European Jews), Rosenzweig believed that only a German Jewry could combine western culture with Jewish spirituality. However, here in Poland, sitting around the Shabbat table of families he met while in officers' school, Rosenzweig encountered Jews whose knowledge of western culture was as broad and as rich as anyone he had met or read in Germany, who with ease combined that knowledge with an equally sophisticated knowledge of rabbinic texts, including works on the Bible, the Midrash, the Talmuds, and the corpus of literary products of classical Jewish philosophy. Furthermore, these Polish Jews were able to combine all this knowledge with an equally rich life of commitment to Jewish law (*halakhah*). What Rosenzweig experienced on these Sabbaths in Poland became a model for what he would try to create for himself and others in Germany for the rest of his life.

The period of 1918–21 was the best and the worst of times in Franz Rosenzweig's life. It was the height of his realization of all he had previously contemplated and it was the beginning of his end as well. He wrote *The Star of Redemption* (*Der Stern der Erlösung*)[1] while still at the front, and began discussions of the work with his "circle" on his return home. In 1920, he married Edith Hahn and, in 1921, he accepted the invitation of Rabbi Nehemiah Nobel (the modern Orthodox rabbi of Frankfurt) to become the director of the *Freies Jüdisches Lehrhaus*. In that same year he wrote an introduction to his Ph.D. dissertation, "Hegel and the State," two short books—*On Education* and *Understanding the Sick and the Healthy*, and finally published his philosophic magnum opus, the *Star*. However, that was also the year that he contracted amyotrophic lateral sclerosis (ALS). The disease progressed over the course of three years, leaving him unable to perform any motor functions whatsoever except to move his eyebrows. In the end, it was through eyebrow movement, interpreted by his nurse and his wife, that Rosenzweig continued his active life of studying, writing, teaching, and leading the Lehrhaus. He lived this truly spiritual life until his death in 1929.

The structure of *The Star of Redemption*

The *Star* is Rosenzweig's ultimate response as a Jewish philosopher to his circle, especially to the Christian philosopher Eugen Rosenstock-Heussey, as to why he would and should become a religious Jew. At a deeper level it is a response to the Germanic, liberal, Christian triumphalism of Georg Wilhelm Friedrich Hegel (1770–1831), whose philosophy lurks behind Rosenzweig's dialogues with Rosenstock-Heussey. Let us first say a brief word about Hegel.

The publication of Hegel's *Encyclopedia of the Philosophical Sciences* in 1817 was the culmination of the project of rationalist philosophy that Spinoza began in the seventeenth century. Spinoza's thesis was that there must be a logical formula, comparable to Euclid's definition of a line in geometry, which, when understood, would make it possible to know everything—past, present, and future. While Spinoza thought this "first principle" would be a definition, it turns out to be a form of logical progression that Hegel called a "dialectic." In its simplest terms, a Hegelian dialectic begins with a "thesis" for thought and action which is thought and acted upon. The thinking shows the inherent logical problems of the thesis and the actions show its practical difficulties. These difficulties lead thinkers (philosophers and scientists) and actors (religious leaders and state politicians) to adopt the opposite of the thesis, called its "antithesis." The advantage, in thought and action, of the antithesis is that it is free of the problems associated with the thesis. However, careful attention to the antithesis reveals new and different problems of its own. There is continuous movement back and forth between the thesis and the antithesis, where what recommends the one (to thought and action) is that it is not the other, until, at long (or short) last, a new level of thesis is determined, what is called a "synthesis," an affirmation of thought and action that combines in itself all that is good about the thesis and antithesis and none of their problems. This synthesis then functions as a new level of thesis, from which will arise a new antithesis and ultimately a new higher-level thesis.

Hegel used his dialectic to explain absolutely everything that he could think of explaining, including the histories of nations, religions, sciences, and philosophies. His history of absolutely everything culminated in the liberal German state of the nineteenth century with its liberal Protestant religion and the total philosophy of Hegel.

Hegel scholars debate whether this culmination of Hegel's philosophy was intended to be messianic. Was it an end of history beyond which there is no further development, or just one more synthesis which will become a thesis for a new and higher synthesis? What is critical for our purposes is that Hegel and the Hegelians conceived each new thesis to be progress, both philosophically (in the case of thought) and morally (in the case of action), beyond all past theses. Hence, Hegel's account of history is not just a descriptive narrative intended to make the past intelligible; it is a cohortative narrative that intends to tell you what you ought to believe and do. For example, monarchy is intelligible in the context of its own time, but a liberal democracy is better, so an intelligent person will advocate liberal democracy. Similarly, an intelligent person will follow Newtonian physics over Aristotelian physics, Hegelian philosophy over British Empiricism (for example), liberal Protestant Christianity over Roman Catholicism, and (what is most important) Christianity over Judaism. Hence, any intelligent person will become a liberal Protestant because that religion is religion at its best, as the dialectic demonstrates.

How is a Hegelian claim to be refuted? Ultimately by showing historical developments that do not fit the schema and proposing an alternative schema that renders intelligible what Hegel renders intelligible as well as what falsifies Hegel's dialectic. In general, this is how early-twentieth-century philosophers responded to Hegel. Bertrand Russell, for example, began as a Hegelian and rejected him ultimately because he knew that Hegel's account of the history of mathematics was not correct, and he proposed instead a metaphysics of material atomism. Rosenzweig does the same thing, only he detects the inadequacy of the dialectic in its history of religions rather than in mathematics. However, the strategy is the same. The dialectic succeeds only if every thought and action in the history of both is a necessary consequence of what occurred before, for this is a universe that admits no chance. Hence, if any claim in the presentation is wrong, then the entire system collapses, for if a consequence (b) of an antecedent (a) is false, then either (a) does not logically entail or necessarily cause (b) (in which case the universe is contingent and not necessary) or (a) is also false. In either case, anything wrong in the unfolding of the system entails that everything in the system as a system is wrong. This is the daring of Hegel's philosophy, but courage is not necessarily wisdom. Hegel (so both Russell, Rosenzweig, and others argued) is not just wrong; he is overwhelmingly wrong-headed. The universe and thought just are not the way he said they were, because (in Rosenzweig's case) Judaism is not a stage on the way to an Hegelian liberal Utopia. On the contrary, Judaism resides in the concrete lived faith of the Jewish people and that life is something eternal, i.e., unchanging in both being and truth.

The elements of reality

Rosenzweig's argument against Hegel took the form of an alternative dialectic to his *Encyclopedia*. The statement of that alternative philosophy is the *Star* itself. It consists of an introduction and three parts. The introduction is a history of philosophy, from Plato through Hegel. It reaches two sets of conclusions that determine the subsequent development of the *Star*. The first is that all philosophical issues tend to formulate around one of three topics—theology, physics, and psychology, or, in Rosenzweig's language, the elements God, the world, and the human. The three are related, for God ultimately is to be understood as the creator of the world and the person who reveals himself through Scriptures to human beings. Similarly, beyond the things that constitute the empirical (what Rosenzweig calls the "plastic") world there are their relationships with two non-things, viz., two types of conscious beings—God and humans. Similarly, humans have a body and a self by which they are situated in space and time, but they also have a will by which they stand over and against the world in relationship to other persons, both divine and human. Hence, psychology is primarily about how human beings will in these interpersonal relations, which we would call "ethics" but Rosenzweig tended to associate more with something he called "sociology."

The second conclusion of the introduction to the *Star* is that what philosophy discovers when it achieves all that it can achieve as philosophy is that it is inadequate. All that can be known through philosophy is all that can be known, but there is much more to reality (or, what Rosenzweig called "truth") than philosophy can know. The question is, what is it that transcends reality/knowledge, i.e. (à la Kant), what are the limits of rational knowledge beyond which there must be (à la Judah Halevi) faith (what Rosenzweig called "belief").

In the most general terms, Rosenzweig argued (à la Nietzsche) that in its origin philosophy is an attempt to escape death. Lived life occurs in the particulars of specific times and places with concrete persons and things. This world is perpetually changing, filled with things that, without interruption, begin at birth and progress on to the end at death. As such, lived life is unknowable. All that can be known is what is permanent and not subject to change. Now, if it were the case that reality is limited to this realm of the knowable, then we, too, as part of reality, are something that, insofar as we are real, are permanent and not subject to change, i.e., not subject to death. Rosenzweig argued that this illusion is the driving force behind the history of philosophy. It is a pursuit to know what is knowable in the hope that by knowing it everything else will be overcome, including death. The enterprise is an illusion because there is more to reality than what is and what can be known, and it is this "more" that is lived life in the particular. Aristotle called the knowable something "form" and the nothing of particularity in existence "matter." Rosenzweig called the form "something" (*Etwas*) and the matter "nothing" (*Nicht*).[2]

In general, philosophy begins with doubts and proceeds quickly (in what Rosenzweig called its "pagan" past, i.e., in the philosophy of ancient Greece and Rome) to believe that it knows something, only to come ultimately to the correct judgment that it was the original doubt that was correct. "Ultimately" is a logical ultimate and not temporal. The realization of philosophy's limitations occurs under three topics, which correspond to the three chapters of Book I of the *Star*. They are the elements "God," "World," and "Human" (*Mensch*).

God and metaphysics

Often philosophy reaches its wisest positions before it has run its full course. This is certainly the case in the history of the conception of God. Here the high point is Maimonides' negative theology. Philosophy begins with Plato wondering who and what God is, which it identifies with a permanent, unchanging Being from which everything that is has emanated. In time, it comes to recognize that what it means to say that God is the creator is not the same as saying he is an ideal Emanator, for creation and emanation are not the same thing. We know enough to know that the world was created by a creator, but in principle we have no idea what a creator is. Hence, we know by reason that there is a creator God, but we also know by that same reason that we know nothing whatsoever about the creator, and there is nothing else to know. Creation is at the very horizon of human knowledge. It lies beyond what can be known. All that is possible here is belief, but belief must come from a source other than our own intellect. Belief is something revealed by being open to hearing some person (not some thing) other than us. In brief, belief beyond knowledge requires revelation (*Offenbarung*).

Rosenzweig's theology ends with the move beyond the recognition of the limits of philosophy about God in negative theology to an openness to belief and revelation. He called this move from philosophy to theology "metaphysics." It is one of three types of what Rosenzweig called the "new philosophy." The other two kinds are "metalogic," which moves beyond philosophy's understanding of the world and the principles of logic by which it is made intelligible, and "metaethics," which moves beyond philosophy's understanding of human will and ethics.

In the case of metaphysics, the culmination of all that philosophy could say about God was Maimonides' negative theology. To be sure, theology continues after Maimonides, but nothing is learned. The subsequent history of theology is an attempt to resolve philosophy's doubts about God within philosophy, but these attempts all prove barren because there is no more that philosophy as philosophy can know than what Maimonides rightly showed it does not and cannot know.

The world and metalogic

As philosophical study of God as he is in himself achieves its most insightful moment in Maimonides' negative theology, so the philosophical study of the world as it is in itself reaches its high point in the epistemic doubt of René Descartes. Descartes argued that philosophy as philosophy cannot begin with God, who would be a transphilosophical source beyond human reason, but must begin with reason itself, i.e., with the human mind. Without an external source of information, i.e., without revelation, all the mind as a mind can know is itself. It cannot know anything else, including the external world. Yet, insofar as a human has a body and is defined by that body, humans cannot even know themselves without revelation from a source external to themselves.

The human and metaethics

In this case, the ultimate philosopher is Immanuel Kant. Kant had drawn radical separations between the realms of mind, noumena, and phenomena. Of the three, all that is knowable by discursive logic is the phenomenal product of two unknowns—mind and noumena. It is the noumena that is the world and it is the mind that is the human, for what is not mind is a part of the world. However, the mind is the subject of all consciousness, including consciousness of the many objects that constitute the world. What is distinctively human, therefore, is distinctively the will, but the will in itself is as unknowable as is the world.

Vectors and Asymptotes

What I have said above about Rosenzweig's metaphilosophy is in at least one sense misleading. It presents his philosophy as a set of conclusions. To be sure, the conclusions presented are what he said, but it is not as such any kind of "new philosophy" or "metaphilosophy." What is new that transcends the old is the way he philosophized and not the conclusions of the philosophizing. In different words, it is his distinct dialectic, as opposed to Hegel's dialectic of thesis–antithesis–synthesis and even Buber's simpler dialectic of I/thou–I/thou-and-it–I/it.

It is the way that Rosenzweig thought more than what he thought that was so deeply influenced by the philosophy of his teacher Hermann Cohen. Cohen's objection to Spinoza was not his modernism. Cohen was every bit as much a modernist, viz., a liberal religionist who affirmed without qualification the salvific power of reason. Rather, Cohen's objection to Spinoza was the latter's belief in the completeness of universal reason without religious revelation. Cohen saw this limit on reason to be what makes room for revealed faith in Maimonides' philosophy. Rosenzweig found his limit in Judah Halevi's philosophy. In one sense, Rosenzweig was first and foremost a disciple of Halevi, but he interpreted Halevi (much as Cohen interpreted Kant) with the use of Cohen's infinitesimal method for doing philosophy.

All of the elements of reality discussed above—God, world, and human—were presented by Rosenzweig not so much as substances or entities or things, but as movements, best characterized as processes that begin as nothing in their origin and that move in the direction of becoming something in their end, and the end is itself best understood as a limit to an infinite process (i.e., as an asymptote). In conceiving God, world, and the human in this way Rosenzweig is a close disciple of Cohen, whom Rosenzweig himself saw as a transitional figure from the old Platonic idealist philosophy to the kind of new philosophy that Rosenzweig represented, a kind of philosophy that other Jewish philosophers at the end of the twentieth century would call "post-modern." (See the conclusion of this book.)

Notes

1 Henceforth called the *Star*.
2 Except for the question of the proofs of the existence of God, which Rosenzweig attributed to medieval philosophers, Aristotle plays no role in his history of philosophy. As he presented it, the story of philosophy is the story of Idealism, and in that story there is no place for non-idealist philosophies such as Aristotle's (as well as Anglo-American philosophies such as Russell's Logical Atomism, Whitehead's Process Philosophy, or Peirce's Pragmatism).

Suggestions for further study

Anckaert, L. and Casper, B. *Franz Rosenzweig: A Primary and Secondary Bibliography*. Leuven: Bibliotheek Van de Faculteit der Godgeleerdheid Van de K. U. Leuven, 1990.

Cohen, Richard A. *Elevations: The Height of the Good in Rosenzweig and Levinas*. Chicago and London: University of Chicago Press, 1994.

Freund, Else Rahel. *Franz Rosenzweig's Philosophy of Existence: An Analysis of the Star of Redemption*. Hague: Martinus Nijhoff, 1979.

Galli, Barbara Ellen. *Franz Rosenzweig and Jehuda Halevi*. Montreal: McGill-Queen's University Press, 1995.

Gibbs, Robert. *Correlations in Rosenzweig and Levinas*. Princeton: Princeton University Press, 1992.

Glatzer, Nahum N. (ed.). *Franz Rosenzweig: His Life and Thought*.

Greenberg, Yudit Kornberg. *Better Than Wine: Love, Poetry, and Prayer in the Thought of Franz Rosenzweig*. Atlanta: Scholars Press, 1997.

Mosès, Stèphane. *System and Revelation: The Philosophy of Franz Rosenzweig*. English translation by Catherine Tihanyi. Detroit: Wayne State University Press, 1992.

Rosenzweig, Franz. *The Star of Redemption*. Translated into English by William Hallo. Notre Dame, IN: Notre Dame Press, 1985.

Samuelson, Norbert M. *A User's Guide to Franz Rosenzweig's Star of Redemption*. Richmond: Curzon Press, 1999.

Seltzer, Robert M. *Jewish People, Jewish Thought: The Jewish Experience in History*. New York: Macmillan, 1980, Ch. 16, pp. 720–66.

Vogel, Manfred. *Rosenzweig on Profane/Secular History*. Atlanta: Scholars Press, 1996.

Key questions

1. What are the events in Rosenzweig's life that brought him from his childhood as an assimilated Jew to his adulthood as a man devoted entirely to Judaism?

2. What were the philosophical and Jewish motives for Rosenzweig writing *The Star of Redemption*? What was Rosenzweig's strategy for refuting Hegel? How is Rosenzweig in this sense like Bertrand Russell?

3. According to Rosenzweig, what are the central three topics of philosophy? How are they conceptually related to each other? How are they conceptually inadequate?

4. What is the central goal of philosophy and why is its achievement impossible?

5. Why is the theology of Maimonides the limit of philosophical theology, the logic of Descartes the limit of philosophical cosmology, and the ethics of Kant the limit of philosophical psychology?

6. What is Rosenzweig's distinctive dialectic?

7. How is Rosenzweig's philosophy indebted to Hermann Cohen and Judah Halevi?

Key events in the life of Franz Rosenzweig

December 25, 1886	Birth in Cassel, Germany
October 11, 1913	Attends Yom Kippur service in Berlin
1915	Anti-aircraft gunner in the Balkans
1917	Writes the "Germ Cell" (*Urzelle*)
1918	Attends officers' school in Warsaw, Poland
1918–19	Writes *The Star of Redemption* (*Der Stern der Erlösung*) in the Balkans at the front
1920	Marries Edith Hahn
1921	Assumes the leadership of the *Freies Judisches Lehrhaus* in Frankfurt. Writes an introduction to "Hegel and the State," *On Education*, and *Understanding the Sick and the Healthy*. Publishes *The Star of Redemption*
1921–23	Becomes ill with amyotrophic lateral sclerosis
1922	Begins his translation of the poems of Yehuda Halevi
1929	Dies

CHAPTER 28

The course: creation, revelation, and redemption

Theology and belief

Rosenzweig's *Star* is a picture of reality that begins where philosophy ends—with three distinct but mutually dependent elements—God, the world, and the human. Each in itself is a vector from an infinitely remote origin in the direction of an infinitely remote end. Each begins as a distinct nothing that strives in itself to become something, something that each element can be only in relationship to the other elements, relationships that none can achieve in and of themselves.

Rosenzweig called these relations between the elements *Bahnen* (*Bahn* in the singular). In the standard English translation of the *Star* this term is translated as "courses." It is as good as any. What it means is a path (in the sense of the Hebrew term *derekh*) or a way (in the sense of the Hebrew term *halakhah*). I mention the Hebrew equivalents because each of these terms has deep theological meaning in early and classical rabbinic Jewish philosophy. In less theological language, I think the term can be translated as "vectors," i.e., end-directed movements from an origin.

The analysis of the relations between the elements lies beyond anything that either philosophy or metaphilosophy can grasp on its own. The logical thinking that characterizes the mind's rational activity can apply to the relations between the elements as it applies to the elements in isolation, but the data for analysis must come from a source other than the isolated mind. That source of data that is communicated, revealed, from another mind is called "revelation," and the written manifestation of that revelation is called "Scriptures."

Rosenzweig shifted attention in Part II of the *Star* from what the mind can use its senses to inform itself about to what the mind receives from some other mind. He called this shift a move from philosophy to theology. The texts for analysis in Part I are the human works that constitute the history of philosophy, from Plato to Hegel and beyond into the metaphilosophy of thinkers such as Søren Kierkegaard (1813–55), Arthur Schopenhauer (1788–1860), Friedrich Wilhelm Nietzsche (1844–1900), and (most important of all) Hermann Cohen. The texts for analysis in Part II are the purportedly divinely revealed Hebrew Scriptures.

The way of reasoning in all three parts of the *Star* is the same. Texts are introduced and Rosenzweig uses his ability to analyze rationally and logically the content of the texts to make claims about them. When the texts are philosophy, the discipline is called "philosophy" and the proper conclusions from the analysis are claimed to be "knowledge." Now, in Part II, where the texts are sacred Scriptures, the discipline is called "theology" and the proper conclusions from the analysis are claimed to be "belief" (*Glaube*). Note that the difference between philosophy and theology is not the way the texts are read.[1] It is rather the source of the claims and the epistemic claim about the inferences from the sources. In the case of philosophy the source is the independent human mind, and, because in this case the mind is dependent on nothing but itself, a valid claim of certainty (i.e., of knowledge) can be made. However, in the case of theology, the source is external to the mind, and this externality reduces the epistemic value of the claims, for insofar as the mind is dependent for its information on a source other than itself it can be less certain of what the source claims. Relying on external sources is always more problematic than relying on your own reasoning. Do I understand correctly what they are saying? Are they telling the truth? Why are they telling me that? None of these questions arises when you are only talking to yourself.

Hence, talking to yourself (philosophy) has a certain advantage over listening to a source other than yourself (theology), viz., you can certainly have less doubt about what you tell yourself than what someone else tells you. Listening to another requires more trust than listening to yourself does. On the other hand, listening has many rewards for the trust, viz., there is so much more that you can reasonably believe about reality than you can ever know. So, by risking being wrong, you open yourself to a richer and fuller view of what reality is. That information comes from studying sacred Scriptures within a community of other texts that have come before you in reading those original texts. In Rosenzweig's case all the texts discussed come from the Hebrew Scriptures (rather than from the New Testament), and he read the Hebrew Scriptures primarily (although not exclusively) in the light of what the rabbis have said about them in Midrash and in commentaries on the biblical texts.

Sacred Scriptures and relations

Theology (Part II of the *Star*) deals with relations between elements. The relations are all asymptotic vectors whose origins are in one of the elements and whose end is in another element. In general, God is the origin of two of the relations, the world is the end of two of the relations, and only the human both originates and ends a relationship. God creates and reveals. The world is what receives his creation, and the human is who receives his revelation. What the human does when he/she receives revelation is redeem the world. Hence, there are three relations between the elements—what God does to the world (creation), what God gives to the human (revelation), and what the human does to the world (redemption).

In each case the analysis grows primarily out of a single biblical text. In the case of creation the text is the first chapter of the Book of Genesis. With revelation the text is the Song of Songs. Finally, with redemption the text is Psalm 136.[2]

Creation and Genesis

The choice of Genesis for creation is obvious. Rosenzweig's analysis of the biblical narrative closely followed the line of interpretation given by the classical rabbinic philosophers, notably by Maimonides. Revelation is not something that happens at some moment in time in the past. Rather, it is something that happens all the time. It is what God does as God to the world, for he brings it life. On this view, what it means to say that the world was created out of nothing is not that there was a time that there was no world. Rather, it says that were it not for God's act of creation the world would be nothing; creation is what makes it something, namely, something living that serves God.

How then does creation serve God? The answer is a distinctly Rosenzweigian twist on Maimonides' negative theology. God is the only being of whom it can be said, whatever is is not God. Hence, everything that comes to be defines God by not being God. Now, there are an infinite number of things that in the course of endless time (both forward and backward) come to be and in coming to be define God by not being God. Hence, creation not only brings the world from nothing to something; everything that is generated also moves God from being a nothing, viz., nothing definite, to becoming something, viz., the unreachable end of everything that is.

Revelation and the Song of Songs

The choice of focusing on the Song of Songs for revelation is a less obvious choice if you are not familiar with classical rabbinic literature. It is not an obvious choice because , in the literal meaning of its words, the Song of Songs not only does not talk about revelation, it also has nothing to say about God. Literally, what it is is a story of a love triangle. It is a poem or set of poems about a shepherdess who is loved by and married to a king whom she does not love, because she loves a shepherd who does not love her. The rabbis, in accepting this book into the Bible, transformed this slightly bawdy tale into a theological drama. The shepherdess is the nation Israel, the shepherd is any foreign nation and/or foreign god, and the king is God. Hence, the story becomes a tale of God's unconditional love of Israel, a love that persists through eternity even though the people of Israel in itself does not deserve the love.

Rosenzweig used the Song of Songs as his primary text about revelation, because revelation is not understood to be a single event in time such as God giving the Torah to Moses at Sinai. First, in the rabbinic literature (both Midrash and philosophy) the giving of the Torah is no less a never-ending event than is creation. The Torah, we are told (based largely on the Book of Proverbs), existed prior to the creation of the world as the blueprint that God used in creating the world. Furthermore, the Torah is constantly being revealed every time the rabbis creatively interpret what it means.

As new, unique concrete situations that require new, creative interpretations of *halakhah*, the Torah is revealed anew, for every new interpretation is already contained in the Torah. In this sense a new application of the Torah in the concrete spells out just what the Torah has always meant in the way that each solution of a new, concrete problem in Euclidean geometry spells out just what the originating definition of a straight line means, for, in principle, nothing is new in geometry that is not already contained within an adequate understanding of the meaning of the definition.

More specifically, what God reveals to the prophet is not content but simply himself. That self-revelation to the other produces in the other a sense of guilt that calls for a concrete response. As it is normally played out in the ritual of the biblical text, God calls the prophet twice by name ("Samuel, Samuel" or "Moses, Moses"). The doubling of a word in Hebrew intensifies its meaning, but a proper name has no meaning, since it is totally individual. Hence the doubled statement of the name is not really a statement but an expression of the emphatic or total individuality of the meeting between God and his prophet. As such it cannot be expressed in language because, excluding the proper noun, words in language always have a general meaning. Here, however, language functions exclusively in the singular. It is a "face-to-face" (*panim El panim*), a total presence in the presence of a total presence. In short it is an expression of love between two persons.

The response of the prophet to being intensely called by name is a denial ("I can't do it, because ..."). The prophet gives reasons for not doing what he has called himself to do ("himself," because God hasn't said that he must do anything). In the end he does it because he knows his excuses are only excuses. What he is really saying is "I am guilty." What the prophet senses in the overwhelming presence of absolute divine love is his own inadequacy to love as God loves. That guilt or inadequacy is expressed by the prophet as if God had commanded him/her to do something, something so absolute that he/she knows that, though he/she must try, he/she will fail. Ultimately revelation is not revelation of content. It is the making bare through the other of one's own nakedness in the presence of unconditional love from the absolute divine other. The love produces shame and the shame translates into commandments. The commandments are the path that the loved one must follow in coming to terms with God's love.

Ultimately what everyone is commanded to do is two things whose meaning is the same—"Love God with all your heart and soul", and "Love your neighbor as yourself." These two expressions of what Rosenzweig calls "the love commandment" are the same, for, based on Maimonides' interpretation, every statement about God is really a statement about human morality.

In different words, the consequence of being loved by God is loving whoever is near to you (the neighbor), and through loving the neighbor you move the neighbor to love their neighbor, until, in the end of time, everyone loves everyone. It is this state of universal love that is redemption. It is what humans do to humans in the world. It is a state to be realized only in the infinitely remote end of days, that is known now only as an end-limit (asymptote) that makes human action meaningful in the now of this world.

Redemption and the Psalms

The text that Rosenzweig used to deduce this interpretation of redemption is Psalm 136, a psalm that plays a special role in the particular religious service that Jews recite before and after dinner in the special meal and service (the *seder*) that they conduct in their homes on the first two nights of the festival of Passover (*pesach*). It is a service that features a liturgical call for the coming of the messiah and the kingdom of God, a call that is symbolized by having a glass on the table for the prophet Elijah.

Elijah is the only Jew in the Hebrew Scriptures who does not die. We are told that he (like Enoch who lived on earth before there were Jews) "went to be with God" rather than "died." The rabbis understood this to mean that Elijah resides with God until God will send the messiah. At that time he will send Elijah to tell the people that the messiah is coming, and the time of this announcement will be on the first night of Passover. Hence, every Jew at the Passover *seder* opens the door to admit Elijah, which is a non-verbal liturgical act whose intent is to invoke Elijah's coming, i.e., to bring on the redemption of the world.

This understanding of the Psalms as more than a revealed text is picked up at the end of Part II in Rosenzweig's discussion of Psalm 115. Psalm 115 functions as a transition from the subject matter of Part II (revealed Scriptures and what is revealed in them) to the subject matter of Part III (liturgy and how people in worship invoke the end of days). Psalm 115 is a transition because it is both part of the Hebrew Scriptures (a psalm in the Book of Psalms) and a liturgical text, because it plays a central role in the special prayers (the Hallel) that are recited on each of the three pilgrim festivals—Passover (*pesach*), the feast of Weeks (*shavuot*), and Tabernacles (*sukkot*). As liturgy, the psalm is something that functions in a non-verbal way as a physical action in community whose intent is to invoke the redemption of the world at the "end of days" into something called the "kingdom of God." This invocation of the kingdom through non-spoken acts of a community united liturgically as a community is the subject matter of Part III of the *Star*.

Notes

1 Rosenzweig himself claimed that the way is different, because he called the reasoning of philosophy "logic" and "silent language" (as in the language of mathematics) and the reasoning of theology he called "grammar" or "spoken language" (as in dialogues between persons). However, I see no difference in

the use of logic or grammar in the two parts. The difference seems to me to be the source of the claims and not how the sources are analyzed.

2   Actually two psalms are discussed—first Ps 136 and then, at the end of the book, Ps 115. We will have more to say about this latter psalm below.

Key questions

1.   Explain the nature of the three relations (courses) between the elements. In each case, what is the origin, what is the end, and how are the two related.

2.   Compare and contrast philosophy and theology. Apply your answer to a comparison of Parts I and II of the *Star*. Why is the epistemic value of theological claims less than philosophical claims? Why can more be believed than known?

3.   What is the textual basis for belief about creation and what do we learn from it?

4.   What is the textual basis for belief about revelation and what do we learn from it? Why was this text chosen? How do commandments arise from revelation? How is revelation related to redemption?

5.   What is the textual basis for belief about redemption and what do we learn from it?

CHAPTER 29

The configuration: Jewish people, Christian way, and the Kingdom of God

The configuration of reality

The Star of Redemption is a construction of a picture of reality both to correct and move beyond the picture of everything that Hegel presented in his *Encyclopedia of the Philosophical Sciences*. Book I presents the elements of the picture that are connected into a course (*Bahn*) of movement from one element to another in Book II. The three elements (God, world, human) form three vectors (creation [from God to the world], revelation [from God to the human], and redemption [from the human to the world]). In Book III these vectors are combined to form a "configuration" that is the picture of reality itself.

The term "configuration" is the English translation of the German term "*Gestalt*" in William Hallo's translation of Rosenzweig's *Star*. Actually the term literally means "order" or "structure," which corresponds to the use in classical Jewish philosophy of the term *seder*. Gersonides in particular had argued that God imposes an order on creation that we humans discover through the study of science. For Gersonides everything is its order insofar as it is anything at all.

Spinoza transformed the concept that this term names into what he called the "conatus" of a thing, but conatus is not *seder*. It is the shadow of a *seder*. For the classical Jewish philosophers, what defined a thing is its purpose or end, for they conceived the universe and everything in it in terms of purpose. Hence, for them the universe is something inherently moral in quality. In contrast, Spinoza, our paradigmatic modernist, conceived the universe solely in terms of quantitative principles that admit neither purpose nor morality. Hence, conatus is *seder* in the sense that it is what defines a thing and what we can know of a thing. However, whereas *seder* expresses a final cause or purpose, conatus expresses mechanical, initiating-of-activity cause as what we can know of the thing. *seder* is an end towards which things move; conatus is a power or potentiality from which they move.

Rosenzweig returned the sense of what defines something to the purposeful end that it was for the classical Jewish philosophers. As everything is defined by the Gestalt which is its limit-end, so reality itself has a Gestalt, and the drawing of that Gestalt as a configured picture of reality is the goal in the third and final part of the *Star*.

In fact, identifying the final configuration as a picture of reality is my choice of terms. It is not literally what Rosenzweig said. Although he did sometimes use the word "reality" (*Wirklichkeit*), the term he most often used for his concluding structure or order was "truth" (*Wahrheit*). The choice of the term "truth" is interesting, because he did not use it to describe what he was doing until Part III, and that in itself suggests that he was using the term in a special way.

The movement from Part I to Part II to Part III is a movement from (1) the lessons of the silent speech (i.e., logical or algebraic language) of natural philosophy (i.e., what Rosenzweig and we call science and philosophy) from which we gain certain "knowledge," to (2) the inferences from the spoken speech (i.e., grammatical or dialogical language) of literary criticism and commentary (i.e., Midrash and theology) from which we gain trustworthy "belief," to (3) truth. From Part I we get all the knowledge that there is to know, and from Part II we get all the belief there is to believe, but neither knowledge nor belief give us truth. Truth is something that we can get only at the end of days. Until then the best we can do is anticipate it in our communal expressions of liturgy.

As the unfolding of Rosenzweig's textual readings in the *Star* has been a progression from philosophy to biblical commentary to liturgy, so have they been presented as a progression of religious insights. No Jewish philosopher since Judah Halevi and none before Halevi made religion as important as Rosenzweig. For most of the classical Jewish philosophers, religion and philosophy were essentially the same thing, viz., ways of discovering and expressing the truth, philosophy being the expression for the handful of individuals with leisure and developed intellect, and religion being the expression for the mass of Jews who rely on the pictures of the imagination. Spinoza made a radical separation between the two and agreed that, whereas philosophy is an expression of the intellect for an intellectual elite and religion is an expression of the imagination for the masses, only philosophy deals with truth. Now Rosenzweig accepts Spinoza's modernist separation and gives it (what would now be called) a "postmodern" twist. Truth resides not in the intellectual pursuit of the individual. It does not even reside in the textual-historical studies of the advocates of *Wissenschaft des Jüdentums* (the historical-critical study of Jewish texts). Rather it resides as a hope in the communal liturgy of the Christians and as anticipation in the communal worship of the Jews.

The *Star* is a dialectic of religions. The vision of reality in Part I as a universe of elements finds its expression in the pagan religions of ancient Greece and Asia. The vision of reality in Part II as a universe of distinct courses finds its expression in the religion of Islam. Islam speaks about revelation through Scripture no less than do Judaism and Christianity. However, on Rosenzweig's reading, Islam really is not a revealed religion. Rather it is just a philosophy, like the philosophies of the pagan Greeks and Romans, that pretends to be more. It pretends to have what Christianity and Judaism really do have—prophetic belief from divine revelation beyond anything that human beings as human beings can otherwise know. As such Islam is at best only a bridge between the pagan philosophies and the other two Abrahamic religions. At its worst it is philosophy disguised as revelation.[1]

As Part I was the study of a tradition of thinking whose roots were Hellenistic, and as Part II was a study of believed-to-be revealed texts whose analytic foundations were Islamic, so Part III is thinking about texts whose purpose is to invoke the end of days. For Rosenzweig this "work" of the redemption of the world can be performed only by human beings in community. It cannot be performed by God. And the only way that human beings can do this work is by praying together in religious communities, Jewish and Christian. It cannot be done by studying philosophy and science, and it cannot be done by political action programs. It is a power given solely to prayer. Hence, Part III is a book about the meaning of prayer, Jewish and Christian.

The sociology of Jewish life and the Christian way

Part III consists of three chapters. The first deals with the "life" of the Jews and the second with the "way" of the Christians. He calls Jewish life a "fire," and the Christian way "rays." The fire and the rays of Judaism and Christianity constitute together the origin of the vector that Rosenzweig's configuration of reality pictures. The origin, as Rosenzweig pictured it through words, looks something like the following diagram.

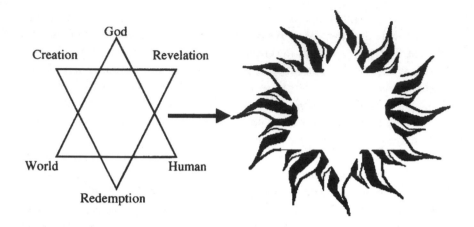

The elements—God, world, and human—form one triangle of vectors (not lines) from Part I upon which is imposed a second triangle of vectors (again not lines) from the courses of Part II. These vector-triangles come together at the end of Part II to form a six-pointed Jewish Star, the *magen david* (Shield of David), which also is a vector. Now, at the origin of the moving picture that will become the image of the truth of reality, this star is seen as a burning fire from which emanate rays.

The fire and the rays are both lights in the midst of darkness, but the lights are otherwise opposites. The light of the fire is an internal combustion feeding off itself that burns inward. In contrast, the light of the rays is a derivative light from the fire and it burns outward. At the origin there is only the fire from which the rays commence. At the end the rays will spread throughout the infinite darkness at which time the fire, the rays, and the light will all be indistinguishable, for without the dark there is no way for them to be differentiated.

On Rosenzweig's visual metaphor, the fire is the single life that the Jewish people live as a single people; the rays are the multiple ways or paths that Christians follow in fulfilling their mission as Christians to redeem the world; and the darkness is the world of pagans waiting to be redeemed into the light of the Christians. From Rosenzweig's Jewish–Christian liturgical perspective, this dynamic picture is the image of reality. The universe is populated by three groupings of persons—Jews existing as a single people, Christians illuminated by the light of the Scriptures of the Jewish people to transform the world of darkness by its light, and the individual pagans living in darkness awaiting the missionary light of the Christians. Now, only Jews are a people, because Jews and only Jews are enlightened by virtue of their birth. Christians are individuals yearning and striving through their Church to become a people, something they will only become when their mission is fulfilled at the end of days, when all the pagans will be transformed into Christians.

The way to the transformation, as we have already seen in Part II, is through love. From God's love we love our neighbor as God loves us, and our neighbors, so loved, go on to love their neighbors. This transmission of love requires participation in the world, which Christians do through the structures of their churches and the politics of their nation states.

Jews, however, are beyond the world of time and space. They live as Jews in a liturgical world that occupies all of their time. Every physical act requires a proper prayer. Three times each day they come together in community to pray. Furthermore, each week they set aside an entire day, the Sabbath, to do nothing but pray. They live in space, but the space is not theirs. They have no land of their own, for they live in lands that belong to other peoples (pagans and Christians), and the land that they own (the land of Israel) is something to which they never go, because it is something holy. Similarly the Jewish people have no language of their own, for the languages they speak are languages of pagans and Christians, and the language they own (the Hebrew language) is something they speak only in prayer, because it is something holy.

What they say in their holy language are prayers, and what the prayers (which Rosenzweig calls "gestures" rather than speech) do is invoke the end of days, the coming of the kingdom of God, when all distinctions will disappear into the unity of light that is truth. This work, that is for Rosenzweig the only Jewish work, is the invocation of the coming of the messianic age, which the Christians in the pagan lands of darkness bring into actuality, at least as long as they are guided on their way by the light of the Jewish people, the people of Torah.

The image of truth

This vision of the end of days is the final chapter and conclusion of Rosenzweig's *Star of Redemption*. Here all is light and truth, and no distinctions remain. Rosenzweig returns to Midrash, to biblical commentary, to create his final image of the end-limit of reality. In this picture (see next page) the fire and the rays have been transformed into a single luminous vision, a vision of a human face.

Rosenzweig labels this final picture—the end-limit of the configuration vector whose origin is the *magen david*—a configuration of truth (*Gestalt der Wahrheit*). Truth here is not a logical value of a proposition. It is the presence (*panim*, literally "face") of God, or, more accurately, it is how the face/presence of God will appear at the end of days. It is a presence that fills everything, allowing no space for difference of any kind, not even the differences betweens pagans, Christians, and Jews.

The face is constructed from two triangles that together form a *magen david* within the face. For one triangle the points of connection are the two ears to the one nose. The ears are for humans to hear the revealed commandments to perform sacrifices whose aroma is shared with God through his nose. The second triangle connects the two eyes to the one mouth. The eyes are how the humans see this final vision which follows from the kiss of God's mouth.

This final image of a kiss from God is an allusion to the Midrash's elaboration on the death of the perfect man, Moses, at the end of the perfect book, the Torah. We are told that Moses died in the land of Moab "by the mouth of the Lord" (Deut 34:5), which the Midrash tells us means that Moses uniquely dies (i.e., completes his perfect human life) by God's kiss. On Rosenzweig's Midrash on the Midrash, the world reaches perfection as Moses dies, namely, in a kiss of loving death/perfection from the mouth/revealed-words of the living God.

Note

1 I shall not try to defend Rosenzweig's presentation of Islam. It seems to me totally unfair. Islam is no more guilty of transforming religion into philosophy than is classical Judaism, as it is no more guilty than is early rabbinic Judaism of emphasizing revelation as a rule of law over and above revelation as a manifestation of divine love. All that can be said in Rosenzweig's defense are

three things. First, Rosenzweig's views of Islam express the best of the academic study of religion at the time Rosenzweig studied Islam in German universities. Second, Rosenzweig's estimation of the inferiority of Islam vis-à-vis Judaism is a good statement of the philosophy of his spiritual mentor, Judah Halevi. And finally, third, despite its negativity, no Jewish philosopher since Abraham Ibn Daud has dealt so extensively and seriously with the claims of Islam to be a revealed religion of faith. However, that does not change the fact that Rosenzweig's representation of Islam is not the strongest aspect of his (in most other respects) superb philosophical religious system.

Key questions

1. Compare and contrast what Rosenzweig means by configuration (*Gestalt*) with what Gersonides meant by order (*seder*) and Spinoza by conatus.
2. Explain how Rosenzweig understands the relations between knowledge, belief, and truth.
3. Compare and contrast Rosenzweig with Judah Halevi and Spinoza on the relationship between revealed religion and natural philosophy (or science).
4. Explain how Rosenzweig's vision of a *magen david* that transforms into a flaming human face is a picture of the relationship between Judaism, Christianity, and what both say about the end of days.
5. How, according to Rosenzweig, do the Jewish people and the Christians contribute to the realization of the redemption of the kingdom of God?
6. How does Rosenzweig describe the kingdom of God at the end of days? Why is the description a visual picture painted in words?

CONCLUSION

CHAPTER 30

Jewish philosophy after Rosenzweig

The futility of futurology

We now conclude a most general survey of the history of Jewish philosophy. The constraints on the project have been to produce as accurate a study as is possible in a text that (a) requires no background in either philosophy or Judaica so that any undergraduate students (be they in universities or not) can read this text with understanding, and (b) is sufficiently brief that it can be taught within an academic year (approximately 30 weeks of instruction) and is affordable for a textbook.

I have chosen in presenting this history to focus on single figures who I believe were the most important Jewish philosophers in the period presented (in terms of both their subsequent influence and in terms of their philosophical skills)—rather than to present generalizations that can apply to every Jewish philosopher in the period in a way that inevitably forfeits the precious uniqueness of each thinker—and I have focused on the single most important works (by the same two criteria) of these philosophers—rather than summarizing all their writings in a way that inevitably forfeits the uniqueness of each work. I believe that each choice I made is academically justifiable even though I readily grant that some other scholar doing this same project could present different thinkers and different works by these thinkers than those I presented. (I do believe, however, that with different choices, the picture of the course of Jewish philosophy would remain more or less the same as that which I have presented here.)

I concluded this book with the end of the first half of the twentieth century, i.e., more or less after the Holocaust and the creation of the third political state of the Jewish people. I end here because I think that, from the perspective of a half-century later, I can say with reasonable confidence that all of the philosophers studied and all of the directions in Jewish philosophy summarized here are integral to understanding the course of Jewish philosophy.

I did not end where I ended because Jewish philosophy has come to an end. On the contrary, there are probably published today more new works on Jewish philosophy by more Jewish philosophers than have ever been published before in Jewish history. However, quantity has no correlation with quality. For example, the seventeenth century was a seminal period in the history of Jewish philosophy because it was the century of Baruch Spinoza. I know of no other Jewish philosopher living in that century worth mentioning. Similarly, there were many Jewish philosophers between the times of Gersonides and Crescas at one end and Spinoza at the other end, but I know of none of them whose writings in philosophy are so important that they changed the direction of Jewish philosophy. These are judgments I can make from the perspective of the twentieth century. I could not have made them if I had lived during the lifetimes of the people mentioned. If I lived in a Jewish community in the lands of the Ashkenazim, I probably would not have heard of Spinoza, let alone singled him out for study. Conversely, if I had lived at the end of the fifteenth century, I might have reasonably thought that Jewish philosophers such as (for example) Shem Tov Ibn Shem Tov (c. 1380–1441) and Simeon ben Zemach Duran (1361–1444) were more important than they actually were, while philosophers such as Gersonides and Crescas were less important than I know them to be now. Perhaps scholarly studies will some day be published about Duran and Ibn Shem Tov that will lead me to revise this judgment. It is more likely, however, that the writings of other hitherto ignored Jewish philosophers will come to light that will be seen to have the philosophic importance of the work of Gersonides and Crescas. However, I cannot imagine any discoveries diminishing their importance. I would say the same with a similar degree of confidence about every philosopher and every philosophic work discussed in this text.

I cannot speak with the same confidence about constructive work in Jewish philosophy in the second half of the twentieth century. The problem is not that this is a lesser age than the past. Every age of philosophy tends to devalue what it has published in comparison with the past. In this respect, Jewish philosophy—being essentially backward-looking (and therefore essentially conservative) because of the emphasis that Judaism places on remembrance of the past—tends more to devalue its contemporary creative work than do other humanities.[1] However, I have seen too many futile predictions about the direction of the future in every academic area, including my own, to have any confidence based on valuing present work of what the future will be.

I cannot say what current works will endure. The problem with such predictions, of course, is that the past only resembles the present; no present is ever identical with any past. Hence, predictions from the present to the future based on similarities between the past and the present are at best only analogies, and, as any logician can tell you, argument by analogy is a form of rhetoric, not demonstrative logic. However, I think I am not completely irresponsible in making the following claims.

Jewish philosophy as a dialogue between Judaism and science

A constructive contemporary Jewish philosophy that is coherent with what Jewish philosophy was in the past ought to be a serious critical study of the interface of the general consequences for understanding the world, the human, and the divine (in Rosenzweig's terms) from contemporary empirical sciences with the tradition of Jewish texts, from the Hebrew Scriptures through modern Jewish thought (in Maimonides' terms). The goal is to formulate reasonable judgments about the viability of Judaism that are believable and have moral merit. This scholarly activity requires knowledge of relevant texts out of the religious history of the Jewish people as well as familiarity with the claims of contemporary sciences and the ways by which those claims are derived. In accord with this understanding of the discipline, an agenda for contemporary and future Jewish philosophy might look something like the following.

Ontology and creation

Classical Jewish philosophy interpreted Judaism's affirmation that the universe was created by God with the ontological categories of Platonic and Aristotelian natural philosophies. It posited a world in which existence was positive and divided into substances and their attributes. It also drew a sharp line of separation between what is material and spiritual, and the spiritual was judged to be inherently better than the material. In this model, space and time were nothing and what is nothing is not real. The presupposed ontological categories in contemporary physics are significantly different. It posits a universe of fields of space and time, occupied by very small particles, whose motions and interrelations are determined by sets of forces, also situated within the spatial–temporal fields. Substances are said to exist; they are the simple particles and their compounds. However, attributes as such do not exist, for what they express are reducible to quantitative judgments about the relationships among particles. No sharp line can be drawn between any positive things that exist, since, without real qualitative distinctions, all difference must be explained in quantitative terms. However, there are sharp distinctions drawn between fields and forces on one hand and particles and their compounds on the other. Only the latter are things; the former are not. This distinction is a distinction between substances and processes.

Some philosophers think the substances are real and the processes merely describe what the substances do; other philosophers think only the processes are real and the substances are only conceptual expressions of states of the processes. However, most physicists tend not to think in these terms. They instead discuss whether or not particles are discrete entities or continuous waves or both. The issue of the scientists is not unrelated to the philosophical question about substances and processes. In the light of quantum mechanics, I am more inclined to see the universe in terms of processes. In any case, few physicists find any ground in their science for dividing the universe into domains of the material and the spiritual, and for maintaining that moral values are exemplified in physical existence.

In the universe of physics there are forces, energy, mass, and motion, all translatable into each other, and none of them matches what has been called matter and spirit. Furthermore, the laws that govern these actions are quantitative, and, as such, are non-moral. Whatever are the grounds for moral judgments, they cannot be found in the physical universe.

On this model, our universe, which may be only one of many, began a finite number of years ago at a point of pure energy of infinite temperature and infinite density that has been consistently expanding ever since. Differentiation of this initial energy into different forms of being—from particles to constellations—is a consequence of this expansion. The laws that govern this differentiation are purely quantitative. They are instantiations of equations in calculus that express temporal rates of change in space, whose variables involve numerical expressions of density and temperature, whose only other relevant factor is a certain degree of sheer statistically expressed chance in every state of affairs that ever was, is, or will be. Contemporary physics describes a universe that was created only in one sense. Its origin is in time; but it is not created in any other, religiously interesting sense, for it is a picture of a universe devoid of any purpose or moral value. As such, contemporary physics posits a model for the general nature and origin of the universe that at least challenges what Jewish philosophers can reasonably mean by affirming that God created the world.

Psychology and revelation

Platonic and Aristotelian natural philosophies played no less a role in interpreting the foundational religious concept of revelation than they did with traditional Judaism's conception of creation. Revelation was understood to be the ongoing relationship between the nation Israel and God, and what defined that relationship was the system of law (halakhah) which was understood to have its foundation in a posited origin in Mosaic revelation at Sinai. No one in the worlds of the Jewish people seriously questioned that the Torah was a revelation from God to Israel through the prophet Moses. (In fact, this commonly held belief might be what most distinguishes modern from pre-modern Jewish intellectual history.) As revelation, the words of the Torah were universally accepted in these worlds of Jews and their neighbors to be true. Rather, the issues were (a) what is their correct meaning, because only the correct meaning is true, and (b) how authoritative is this text, for both Muslims and Christians affirmed other texts as revealed and as more authoritative. At least insofar as this debate involved Jews and Muslims, the critical issue was which nation had a greater prophet (the greater the prophet, the more authoritative his revelation), and that debate rested ultimately on mutually accepted criteria of human perfection (the more perfectly human the prophet, the greater his epistemic reliability). It was with an eye to the criteria for judging human perfection that the three Abrahamic faiths turned to the psychology of the natural philosophers of their day.

Platonism and Aristotelianism both assumed fixed, eternal species, but that assumption did not entail, as some religious thinkers claim, that there can be no evolution of the members of one species into another (since they all affirmed both the possibility and the reality of substantial change).

Hence, the species "human" is distinct and cannot become something other than what it is; however, the kinds of entities that now are human need not always have been so[2] and need not always remain so. Species were understood to be hierarchically ordered in a pyramid of moral values in which each species was uniquely located relative to others. Humans occupied the highest place in the order of all immediately below the level of the different kinds of entities that the science of the day called celestial "separate intellects" and religious thought called "angels." Members of species sought through their natures to become perfect instantiations of their species, which they could in fact realize, and, once realized, they were transformed into the lowest-level members of the next highest species. In the case of humanity, those entities who so perfected themselves as humans bordered on being angels. These transitional beings, i.e., beings at the very borders separating humans from angels, were said to be "prophets." Prophets then are the ideal of human perfection and that ideal is defined by what distinguishes humanity from all lesser kinds of beings but does not distinguish it from greater kinds of being except in excellence of realization. With few exceptions, all the philosophers—Jewish, Muslim, and Christian—agreed that the defining trait was rational thinking.

A significantly different conception of what constitutes human nature emerges in modern life and computational sciences. What is most important to our concerns is that, while most humans seem to think in ways that are not shared by the members of other species, the difference is not qualitative. First, the experimental evidence strongly suggests that other species, especially apes, reason, and whatever inferiority there may be in how they reason may have more to do with their anatomies (which limit their ability to develop a spoken language) and their environments than with any inherent intellectual inability. Second, man-made machines increasingly think better than humans by any of the criteria traditionally used to evaluate intelligence, and the possible convergence of current experiments in robotics and genomics suggests that in the not too remote future these machines may even be capable of self-replication and improvement. What makes human thinking distinctive is not any essential nature, contrary to the Aristotelians, but rather a set of accidents of being born in certain places at certain times. Other kinds of beings than humans had no less possibility of becoming rational and in different circumstances humans need not have been rational. What marks all species as being the kinds of things that they are is their history, not their nature.

The relevant history of humanity is the story of evolution told by paleoanthropologists and genetic psychologists. What kinds of issues are there when Jewish philosophers attempt to correlate the claims of the modern life sciences with the claims of traditional Judaism about revelation and human nature? They are not the same for Judaism and Christianity. So far Christian-oriented studies in science and religion have given primary attention to the apparent conflicts between so-called literal readings of Genesis and the claims of evolutionary psychology and genetic biologists. From the perspective of Jewish philosophy this issue is bogus. First, Jewish philosophy has never assumed that what the Hebrew Scriptures mean is what they literally say. Second, even read literally, these revered texts do not say what so-called Christian "creationists" say that they mean. Even the judgment that all life forms share a common genetic origin and shared procreational purpose is not in itself problematic. After all, Genesis does say that every life form on the earth is formed from the earth, including the human, and every one of these creations share in common God's first commandment—to be fruitful and multiply. Whatever it is that is distinctive about the human being, which enables them to claim to be created "in the image of God," it is not that they are beyond their shared purpose of creation out of their shared physical constitution as earth.

Rather, the real issues that arise from taking evolution and genetics seriously have to do with ethics. Let me now briefly list what some of them are:

1. Jewish philosophy has long associated the power of speech with intelligence[3] and has seen both as constituting human distinctiveness. Furthermore, it has associated excellence with respect to both as a human ideal that defines human virtue, human happiness, and the highest expressions of service to God. Both evolution and genetics call into question this kind of ethics. Reasoning is not unique to human beings. Furthermore, it is not even clear, at least from the perspective of evolution, how valuable it is. For example, if the good is to be judged by what best promotes species survival, the value of rational thinking is far from obvious. A virus, for example, seems far more adaptable to survival than is a human, and there is nothing about viral adaptation that suggests conscious thought is involved. Minimally, reasoning out solutions to life-threatening situations is far too cumbersome to be effective. When faced with danger there just is not sufficient time to

think out what is best to do. In at least this respect, viz., speed, the way man-made machines calculate and solve problems is vastly superior to what humans can do with their limited brains.

2. Are there any moral lessons that can be validly drawn from the conclusions that scientists base on their data? In principle the scientists themselves say no, but what happens in practice does not always agree with this principle. The different stories that evolutionary psychologists and biologists tell of human history suggest that there is a central purpose to the existence of every species, including the human, and that purpose is to propagate. In at least the human case, this primary goal requires differentiation in gender. Men and women are not created equal. Because of the size of the human brain, human children must be born too immature to survive on their own and require constant care, preferably by the female, for the first two years of their lives. That means that, for a period of close to three years, every female bearing a child must remain relatively sedentary. Differences in the size of humanoid genders have their source in this goal. Men hunt and women raise families, from which it follows that men are most suited to compete outside of the family unit for the survival of the unit, and women are most suited to remain within the family unit to spread collective information. Does this ancient gender differentiation still make moral sense in our age of technological advancement in which labor outside the family, including fighting wars against "predators," has more to do with sharing information (the natural talent of the female) than it does with physical aggression (the natural talent of the male)? Now there are all kinds of legitimate questions that can, and should, be asked about the soundness of this picture of human history, not the least of which is the legitimacy of characterizing humanoid genealogy in terms of purposeful direction. However, these are not the questions on which I want to focus here.

Let us assume, for the sake of the argument, that biological functions can be understood as determiners of goal-directed nature and those goals, because they define a life form's nature, entail moral judgments. If the primary natural directive to the human species is to perpetuate the species, and efficiency in this task requires gender differentiation, is it morally wrong to insist at the political level on gender equality?

It could be argued, even granting these debatable premises, that gender equality is morally correct on the following grounds: equality is not an absolute principle; whether or not it is applicable to any specific subset of humans depends on the nature of the functions that define the subset. Hence, for example, discrimination on the grounds of height is morally proper in the case of basketball players, but it is not proper in the case of accountants. In a less technologically advanced age, when warfare depended primarily on physical strength, speed, and agility, discrimination on grounds of gender made moral sense in the military, but today, when warfare is primarily a matter of using mechanized weapons guided by information systems, gender differentiation is immoral.

Similarly, it can be argued that given current advancements in the technology of conceiving and nurturing human offspring, gender differentiation no longer has the moral force that it once had. That women have loved women and men have loved men is not new in human history, and in most of at least the non-Abrahamic religious civilizations there has been no moral objection to same-sex love. However, there have been objections to same-sex marriage because marriage served the primary purpose of offering the most advantageous social institution for producing viable offspring, which required intercourse between a male and a female. Still, today the technology exists for children to be produced without heterosexual intercourse and this technology is constantly improving. Hence, while it made considerable sense in the past, it no longer makes moral sense to prohibit same-sex marriage. To enforce such a prohibition is "sexism" and sexism is no less morally wrong than is "racism," both of which are guilty of making social differentiation in societies where that differentiation is irrelevant.

Conclusion: philosophy and transcending categories

If I must find a single theme that runs through all of the issues raised above for future Jewish philosophy, it would be the breakdown of traditional categories for rendering intelligible the world and life within it. The God of biblical Jewish philosophy created distinctions (light and dark, earth and the sky, etc.) and called these separations "good." Classical Jewish philosophy hardened these separations and added others, notably the lines between the spiritual and the material, knowledge and opinion, and human beings and other life forms. Largely because of developments in twentieth-century technology, those classical divisions are breaking down, as well as others that were so taken for granted that they were barely discussed—notably between Jews and gentiles, and males and females. Can Judaism survive this transcendence of value-laden categories of understanding the world and life? I suppose that is the bottom-line question for Jewish philosophy, for, as the philosophy of science is committed to determining the rational grounds on which science is possible, so Jewish philosophy is committed to determining the rational grounds on which the survival and flourishing of the Jewish people is possible. So understood, the new questions for Jewish philosophy are not really new. The newness is only in the details of what is in general a continuous development of Jewish thinking about fundamental issues from the people's origins through and beyond the present.

Notes

1   In my opinion, secular philosophy seems to me to have the opposite tendency, viz., it underestimates the past in order to exaggerate the importance of contemporary contributions.
2   For the Midrash speaks of more kinds of descendants from Adam than just those who survived the flood. It would be more proper to call "humans" (i.e., the biological descendants of *Adam*) "Noahites" (i.e., the biological descendents of Noah).
3   For example, in Maimonides *Guide* II:41 and 45, especially with reference to the eleventh degree of prophecy, Maimonides identified vision as the highest sense activity associated with prophecy. Furthermore, in *Guide* I: 4 he identified "vision" as the sense generally associated metaphorically with intellection. There are some contemporary Jewish intellectual historians who share this judgment (for example, Lionel Kochen). However, other, more recent, scholars argue against assuming a general value primacy for hearing over seeing, notably Kalman Bland.

Suggestions for further study

Bland, Kalman P. *The Artless Jew: Medieval and Modern Affirmations and Denials of the Visual*. Princeton: Princeton University Press, 2000.
Cohen, Richard A. "Postmodern Jewish philosophy," in Daniel H. Frank and Oliver Leaman (eds.), *History of Jewish Philosophy*. Vol. II of *Routledge History of World Philosophies*. London and New York: Routledge, 1997, pp. 875–84.
Fackenheim, Emil L. *Encounters Between Judaism and Modern Philosophy*. New York: Basic Books, 1973.
Fackenheim, Emil L. *The Religious Dimension in Hegel's Thought*. Boston: Beacon, 1970.

Goodman, Lenn Evan. *God of Abraham*. New York: Oxford University Press, 1996.

Jonas, Hans. *Mortality and Morality: A Search for the Good after Auschwitz*. Edited by Lawrence Vogel. Evanston, IL: Northwestern University Press, 1996.

Kaplan, Edward K. *Holiness in Words: Abraham Joshua Heschel's Poetics of Piety*. Albany: State University Press of New York, 1996.

Katz, Steven T. "The Shoah," in Daniel H. Frank and Oliver Leaman (eds.), *History of Jewish Philosophy*. Vol. II of *Routledge History of World Philosophies*. London and New York: Routledge, 1997, pp. 854–74.

Kellner, Menachem Marc (ed.). *The Pursuit of the Ideal: Jewish Writings of Steven Schwarzschild*. Albany: State University Press of New York, 1990.

Kochan, Lionel. *Jews, Idols and Messiahs: The Challenge of History*. Oxford: Basil Blackwell, 1990.

Levinas, Emmanuel. *Nine Talmudic Readings*. English translation by Annette Aronowicz. Bloomington: Indiana University Press, 1990.

Novak, David. *The Election of Israel: The Idea of the Chosen People*. Cambridge: Cambridge University Press, 1995.

Plaskow, Judith. "Jewish feminist thought," in Daniel H. Frank and Oliver Leaman (eds.), *History of Jewish Philosophy*. Vol. II of *Routledge History of World Philosophies*. London and New York: Routledge, 1997, pp. 885–94.

Samuelson, Norbert M. *Judaism and the Doctrine of Creation*. Cambridge: Cambridge University Press, 1994.

Schneerson, Menachem Mendel. *Toward a Meaningful Life: The Wisdom of the Rebbe*. Adapted by Simon Jacobson. New York: William Morrow and Co., 1995.

Seeskin, Kenneth. *Jewish Philosophy in a Secular Age*. Albany: State University of New York Press, 1990.

Sherwin, Byron L. *Abraham Joshua Heschel: Makers of Contemporary Theology*. Atlanta: John Knox Press, 1979.

Soloveitchik, Joseph B. *Halakhic Man*. Philadelphia: Jewish Publication Society of America, 1983.

Wyschogrod, Edith. *Spirit in Ashes: Hegel, Heidegger and Man-made Mass Death*. New Haven: Yale University Press, 1985.

Wyschogrod, Michael. *The Body of Faith*. San Francisco: Harper and Row, 1989.

Key questions

1. What issues for future Jewish philosophy arise from comparing modern physics with classical rabbinic Judaism?
2. What issues for future Jewish philosophy arise from comparing the modern evolutionary psychology with classical rabbinic Judaism?

Key events after Rosenzweig

1882–1970	Max Born
1879–1955	Albert Einstein
1939–45	Second World War
1942 (Jan)	Wannsee Conference
1943 (Apr–May)	Warsaw ghetto uprising
1948	Establishment of the State of Israel
1950 (July)	Law of Return passed in Israel
1954–73	Vietnam War (US military involvement, 1961–72)
1956, 1967, 1973	Major Arab–Israeli wars
1964	Establishment of the Palestinian Liberation Organization
1977	Menahem Begin becomes Prime Minister of Israel
1979	Egyptian–Israeli peace treaty
1982 (June)	Israeli–Syrian War in Lebanon

Index